# Praise for *Standing Up*

"*Standing Up: Making the Best Out of Surviving the Worst is a* gripping, novel-like journey that slowly and powerfully reveals the truth about domestic violence and healing. Mary Devine's story is so relatable that you'll feel each struggle, each victory as if it were your own. Mary Devine is your new hero, and her strength and choices have changed so many lives. A must-read for those who seek both understanding and hope."

—**Tama Kieves, USA *Today* featured visionary career coach, author of *Thriving Through Uncertainty***

"Raw, real, and relatable, this book is the ideal read for fans of Tara Westover's *Educated* and *Wild* by Cheryl Strayed. *Standing Up: Making the Best Out of Surviving the Worst,* charts the author's harrowing, but inspiring journey from domestic abuse survivor to police detective, committed to helping women find the light in their own lives."

—**Elizabeth Ridley, author, *Searching for Celia***

"*Standing Up: Making the Best Out of Surviving the* Worst is a story of hope and resilience, that reminds us of our power to make a difference in another's life. Devine captures her lived experience and depicts the trauma that too many people experience in private. Mary's unvarnished style exposes pain and struggle and provides insight into the issues that trap so many."

—**Mariann Kenville-Moore, MSW DVS – Director of Advocacy & Policy Delaware Coalition against Domestic Violence**

*"Standing Up: Making the Best Out of Surviving the Worst,* invites the reader to join her on a personal journey through the crucible of domestic violence and her emergence of strength and enlightened perspective on one of law enforcement's most challenging issues.

—**John L. Cunningham, New Castle County**
**retired Chief of Police**

*"Standing Up* is an unforgettable roller coaster of emotions and unimaginable twists, pulling readers into a relentless, page-turning frenzy. Mary Devine, the hero of this true story, is a beacon of resilience and courage. As you journey alongside her, you will find yourself relating to her struggles, cheering for her victories, and ultimately celebrating her triumphs. This is more than a story—it is a testament to the strength of the human spirit and the power of standing tall when love so tragically descends into a dangerous prison. Mary's story inspires hope, proving that a brighter future awaits those brave enough to take the first step toward freedom."

—**Gina Graves, songwriter, teacher, and board-certified coach**

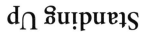

Standing Up

# Standing Up

## Making the Best Out of Surviving the Worst

Mary L. Devine

SHE WRITES PRESS

Published 2025
Printed in the United States of America
Print ISBN: 978-1-64742-885-3
E-ISBN: 978-1-64742-886-0
Library of Congress Control Number: 2025901781

For information, address:
She Writes Press
1569 Solano Ave #546
Berkeley, CA 94707

Interior Design by Kiran Spees

She Writes Press is a division of SparkPoint Studio, LLC.

Trigger Warning: This book contains subjects that might be troubling to some readers, including abuse and pregnancy loss. Please be mindful of these and other possible triggers.

Campbell, JC. (2004). Danger Assessment. Retrieved May 28, 2008, from http://www.dangerassessment.org .
Campbell JC, Webster DW, Glass N. (2009). The danger assessment: validation of a lethality risk assessment instrument for intimate partner femicide. Journal of Interpersonal Violence, 24(4):653-74

*Trauma creates change you don't choose.*
*Healing is about creating change you do choose.*

Michele Rosenthal

# Authors Note

THIS BOOK IS NOT INTENDED TO CRITICIZE OR HARM ANYONE involved. It represents my personal journey and perspective. While I have strived for accuracy, this memoir prioritizes emotional truth over exact detail. Conversations and events may be reconstructed from memory to capture their essence rather than precise wording.

To protect the privacy of certain individuals, some names, characteristics, and identifying details have been changed.

# Prologue

IT WAS SPRING, A FEW MONTHS AFTER OUR FIRST WEDDING ANNIVERsary and another of many nights when Vince had gone to the bar after work instead of coming home. This habit was so established that I didn't bother to call him anymore and instead waited until he got home to confront him.

I met him at the door at eleven o'clock. He looked surprised to see me, as if he had forgotten we lived together. His hazel eyes were bloodshot, and I smelled the stink of beer on him as he stumbled into the apartment, fiddling with his keys.

"Where were you? We were supposed to meet the accountant tonight."

"I had to meet a guy after work about a house," he said.

"What guy? You just started a new house."

"All right, whatever. I went to the bar, okay?"

"No. It's not okay," I shot back.

"Well, that's tough shit. You're going to have to get over it."

"What? Get over it? Maybe I need to get over you. I am so tired of this, Vince."

He rolled his eyes and shrugged, pointing at the still-open door. "Then get out."

I snatched my pocketbook off the sofa and strode to the door, but he beat me to it, blocking my path with his lean, muscular body, and grabbed my wrists. I tried to shake loose, but he held tight. "Let go of me."

"Where the hell do you think you're going?" he slurred.

"Don't worry about where I'm going!"

As I wrangled my wrists free, his facial expression changed from annoyance to fury, his filthy blond hair swinging recklessly across his contorted face. He pushed me, his palms thumping against my chest, propelling me across the room so hard I nearly fell. He slammed the door and closed the distance between us, whisking me away from the only exit.

"Stop, Vince, you're scaring me!"

"You're not going anywhere," he shouted and shoved me again, causing me to stumble backward and lose my balance. I screamed. His forward momentum bulldozed me onto the sofa, and he climbed on top, pinning me down with the weight of his body. Fear, anger, and confusion interfered with rational thought as my brain shifted into fight-or-flight mode. Gunshots blared from the TV in the corner of the living room, increasing my level of panic, while the weight of his body on mine suffocated me as I wrangled to break free.

"You're hurting me. Get off!"

"Stop fighting me. I'm not hurting you. You're hurting yourself."

I twisted beneath him, struggling to wrench free, but the more I resisted, the tighter he clenched. Sweat covered my body, slippery skin causing him to momentarily lose and regain control, and my body slapped against his chest with every near escape. I squirmed until my wrists ached, stinging from the salty wetness and his tightening grip. He drooled and slurred unintelligibly, grunting each time he regained control. His work boots scraped heavily against my bare legs, ripping the skin, the steel toes bouncing off my ankles and shins until I shrieked in pain. "Stop! Get off! I can't breathe!"

He pushed his body up and away from me, settling onto his knees, still holding my wrists. "Okay. If I let you up, you have to promise not to leave."

He outweighed me by eighty pounds, and I was exhausted. He was barely winded and wore a slight grin, which added to my hopelessness. I was trapped, and his offer to release me was a welcome truce. "I promise," I panted, fighting tears.

He stood up, swatting a wedding photo off the end table, and staggered into the kitchen. I sat up and rubbed my wrists, assessing the damage. He stood with his back to me as he ran water from the kitchen faucet, and options flashed through my mind. I considered running for the door, but fear that his reaction would be worse if I tried and failed convinced me to stay.

The injuries ended the fight, and Vince's mood flipped like a switch from rage to affection. He staggered from the kitchen with a glass of water, set it on the coffee table, and turned my trembling hands over in his, examining the red abrasions appearing on my skin.

He sat beside me and clung to my arm, drowning me in a deluge of apologies. "Damn, I'm so sorry, love. I never meant to hurt you. It's just that you're so thin and fragile. You know it was an accident. I love you more than anything in this world, but here, here are your keys."

I leaned away from him in disgust. He held the keys to my freedom in his outstretched hand, but I didn't trust him. What if I took the keys and started for the door? Would he let me go, or would the terror begin again? His stillness increased my anxiety, the uncertainty of his reaction governing my decisions.

"Go wherever you want. I don't know what I was thinking." His voice softened. "You would never leave me, and I promise it won't happen again. But if it ever does, I swear I will leave." I stared into my lap, and he leaned closer, kissing me gently on my forehead, continuing his pleas for forgiveness.

"I promise because you deserve better. You're so smart. I don't even know why you put up with me, but we'll get through this because we're a team, right? You forgive me, right?" He kissed my palms. "How can I make this up to you, love?"

I looked into his bloodshot eyes and worked up a smile of agreement, still terrified. "Yeah, I forgive you."

My struggles for freedom left abrasions and bruises on my ankles and wrists. It was the first time he had ever put his hands on me during an argument. Tears welled in his eyes as he caressed my hands and kissed my wrists. His pain seemed genuine, and his display of emotion was gripping, but two minutes earlier, he was a maniac.

I was so relieved that the fray was over that I didn't say anything more. I stared at the floor, watching him fade from consciousness. He passed out within ten minutes, snoring on the same sofa where he'd held me captive. He looked nothing like the man I'd married fifteen months previously—dirty, sweaty, and drooling all over himself. What happened to the hardworking, carefree, fun-loving musician who doted on me?

I picked up the picture he'd knocked off the table and placed it back in its place, face down. I walked the long hallway to the bedroom in darkness, thinking about the night the picture was taken. He would have done anything for me. He was my champion. He couldn't wait to get home to me. I slipped on a nightgown and picked up a cigarette by the bedside table, lit it, and took a deep draw, trying to make sense of things. How could he sleep after all that had just happened, and what should I do now? Something was very wrong. I was afraid. I had never been afraid of him before.

# Chapter One

I was not prepared to be swept off my feet at the tender age of twenty-three. He was handsome and sweet, and I was smitten from the moment I saw him. At twenty-five years old and six foot two, with shoulder-length blond hair and a bronze, tanned body, he was captivating. His cutoff jean shorts and tool belt made it clear that he worked a construction job, but I could just as easily envision him shirtless, playing beach volleyball. I was the manager of a Wawa convenience store. Every day he came into the store, I preened as much as someone in a chocolate-brown apron covering them from neck to knees could, acting less like a store manager and more like a schoolgirl.

It was always a madhouse at lunchtime, and that day was no exception. Crowds of people shuffled around the deli waiting for their turn to order, while others gathered cold beverages and ice for the hot summer day, squeezing past one another between the heavily stocked, too-close-together shelves. The aroma of Italian cold cuts and meatballs hung thick in the sultry summer air as customers made their way to the cash registers to pay. He had been ordering lunch in my store for months, but today when I spotted him, I heard one of his coworkers call him by name from across the store. My heart fluttered. *Vince.*

He sidled up to the counter, blushing.

"Hi, Vince. Can I get something for you?"

He averted his eyes and smiled at the use of his name. "Yeah, can I get a couple of sandwiches?"

"Sure. What would you like?"

"A ham and cheese sandwich with mayo and a bologna and cheese sandwich with mustard—no cheese."

I crinkled my eyebrows, reviewing the order in my mind. *Bologna and cheese sandwich with mustard. No cheese?*

"So, you'd like a bologna sandwich with mustard, then?"

He nervously shifted from one foot to the other, his face crimson. "Yeah, I guess so, but my boss told me to order that way because you guys keep getting it wrong. I'd appreciate it if you'd get it right today. He's already in a crappy mood." He was looking at his feet.

"Oh, jeez, I'm sorry. I promise it won't happen again. Which one is your boss? I want to apologize." I scoured the aisles for someone dressed like Vince.

"Oh, he never comes in. He always sends us, so don't worry about it. He's a good guy. Besides, it could be the guys messing with him." He smiled broadly, and my heart melted.

I handed his sandwiches across the counter, watching him walk away like every other day, willing him to come back and ask me for a date. That day, he paced awkwardly in circles, fake eyeing the Cheetos, waiting for just the right moment, and moseyed back to the counter like mall security conducting surveillance. Deciding the coast was clear, he smiled and whispered under his breath, "Mary, do you think I could call you sometime?"

I touched my name tag, grinning because he used my name too. "Okay, yeah, sure," I blurted before he had a chance to change his mind. "Let me give you my number."

It was the summer of 1984, so calling rather than texting was the norm, and forwarding digital contact information wasn't an option. I quickly jotted my number on a napkin and slid it across the counter to him. He winked and shoved it into his pocket, strutting out of the store triumphantly while I did a little happy dance, tickled that he had finally asked.

We talked on the phone for hours every day that week until the weekend when we had our first date. It was fun but casual, not the traditional dinner and a movie. I was glad, since those dates can be stressful, sharing lots of information instead of sharing experiences.

It was my first time at the Italian Festival in Wilmington, and it was thrilling. My impression that Vince was shy was dead wrong. He immediately took my hand in his, letting everyone know that I was taken, which, though presumptuous, made me smile. The festival was everything I had heard about and more. It was a carnival with a traditional spaghetti dinner sponsored by the St. Anthony of Padua Roman Catholic Church, but it wasn't just a carnival. Streets were cordoned off for blocks for live bands and bingo. Crowds milled about as the odor of marijuana and alcohol wafted through the air. Red, white, and green flags hung on every business, and strings of white lights kept patrons safe as they waited in line for beers or porta potties. The music was loud, and the atmosphere was festive as we made our way to the beer line and then to the bandstand to listen to music.

We couldn't hear each other so Vince leaned down and kissed my cheek, speaking into my ear. "I'm happy to be here with you tonight."

I took a drink of beer and smiled up at him with a beer mustache; he traced my lip with his finger, wiping the foam away, and licked his finger. I smiled and slipped under his arm, leaning against his body, his arm resting around my shoulder. "Me too."

It was a warm summer night, and Vince was wearing a black T-shirt with cutoff sleeves so I could see his biceps were ripped, but his boyish, clean-shaven face was a pleasant contradiction.

He knew everyone and introduced me to as many people as possible as they passed by us in the lines. We moved on to the games, where he tried and failed to win a plush dog.

"I'll buy you a real dog. What kind do you want?" Vince clasped my hand, accepting defeat but winning my heart.

I smiled. "A cocker spaniel."

"Of course. Cute and friendly, just like you."

The Ferris wheel seemed contrived until we stopped at the top and looked over the city of Wilmington, Delaware, which was more beautiful than I'd ever believed possible.

"Can I kiss you?" Vince asked.

I leaned in for my best-ever kiss.

After that night, Vince and I dated steadily. He was a gifted musician who could play anything he picked up. I was seduced by his talent and by him. He was the muscular carpenter-type combined with a sensitive musician, and I loved the balance. He played the drums in a local rock band, and I secretly loved that all the girls were jealous when they watched him sit with me after each set.

The chemistry between us was the stuff poets write about, with clouds parting and angels singing. We were exclusive, spending all our free time together, and I loved everything about him. He was my first serious boyfriend, sweet and attentive.

After a few months of dating, we lay sprawled out on the sofa in my apartment, snuggling in the afterglow of romance, when Vince shocked me with a story from his childhood.

"Dad drank," he said. "I mean, he really drank—like a lot—and when he did, he got mean. When he got mean, he took his frustration out on whoever was there, and usually, that was my mom, Janet. Most of the time, my brothers and I were in our bedrooms, but we could hear what was happening. We were afraid of him when he was drunk."

Vince sat up, reached for his wallet on the coffee table, and began flipping through pictures as he talked. I tickled his five o'clock shadow, unprepared for his disclosure.

"One night, he started knocking Mom around. We tried to stop him, but he was bigger than us. Later, when we were in our teens and towered over him, it was a different story."

Vince held out a picture, and I sat up so that I could see. It was a woman, expressionless, with two black eyes, a swollen face, and a split lip.

"Oh, no." I breathed out.

It was a heartbreaking picture, like a mug shot: a nonsmiling, hollow-looking woman. I pulled him closer as we gazed down at the photo between us, wincing.

"Yeah, I know," he said. "That's when we moved. I think maybe she left because she was afraid that we might kill him. She lives in Colorado now. Maybe it's weird that I carry this, but I never want to forget it. I never want to be that guy, the one who does something like this."

We sat in silence, staring at the shocking purple dishes under his mother's eyes and all over her pretty face. I wondered if she knew her son carried that photo. I loved him more for the fact that he did, not just for the compassion he had for his mom but also for the love and tolerance he showed for his father and his drinking habits. I didn't know how he balanced the two and wasn't sure I could have done that.

"Dad remarried, but he hasn't changed. He's doing the same stuff with his new wife, Ruby. She's a heavy drinker, but she's not like my mom. She's a timid woman. She tolerates his drinking, abuse, and cheating ass."

Vince leaned back, resting his head on my lap. I ran my fingers through his hair, brooding over how difficult living with his father must have been. He smiled up at me and drifted off to sleep, and I felt comfortable with his warm body across mine.

I lit a cigarette and watched the smoke drift in circles through the undisturbed air, listening to his rhythmic breathing. I looked at the picture of his mother again, wondering what made her stay with someone who would beat her, knowing I could never put up with it. I was raised in a dysfunctional environment too. My mother divorced my father when I was five, and she moved my brother, sister, and me from West Virginia to Pennsylvania, where she met my stepfather, Curtis. He loved her but didn't care much for kids. He dished out corporal punishment, whether it was warranted or not, but he also supported us, and it all seemed normal to me until I was about fifteen when she divorced him too. Years later, she married Jim Antonio, a man she had only known for two months. I gazed at the picture again, feeling sorry for Vince, for his mom, for my mom, and maybe a little for me. Vince and I were lucky to have found each other.

Vince had a place of his own but spent most nights with me in my one-bedroom apartment. We got along so well that he hardly ever left, but it was too small for both of us. After a few months, Vince found the perfect house for us to rent in Arden, Delaware, an artistic community that would allow him to play drums and had enough room for us to stalk off when we needed space.

Nothing I learned in school or at home prepared me for dating. I had no idea what a healthy, intimate relationship looked like, and Vince had no positive role models. I had been on my own for five years before Vince and I had a few short-term relationships, but nothing serious. From my perspective, things were great between us. We argued about stupid things, and sometimes they weren't so stupid. I was jealous of other girls he talked to, and he hated it. He wanted to spend every waking moment together, but I played on a Wawa volleyball team, and he hated that. We argued over our roles in the relationship and the fact that he wanted to play drums in the house until all hours, but I had to get up early for work. There was no shortage of conflict, and it was unnerving at first. Mom and Curtis had never argued in front of me and my siblings. I had never even seen them disagree, so I had no idea how to resolve conflict. No one in my house had yelled, but Vince hollered all the time, and when he got loud, it scared me.

"All couples argue," he said. "It doesn't mean we don't love each other. Everyone in my house yells. We're Italian!"

Thoughts of the abuse Vince had described crossed my mind and strengthened my argument. "I know, Vince, but it's upsetting. Can't we disagree without you yelling at me?"

"C'mon, honey. You know I love you. I can't change now. It's just my personality," he said. "You have to love me the way I am because this is what you get."

Those might have been the truest words he ever spoke to me, and if I had understood them to be guaranteed, my life might have been completely different.

Vince yelled, not necessarily at me but to me, about everything. He usually expressed himself with his hands flailing about, which seemed to fit the stereotypical Italian persona. I didn't like it, but I learned to deal with it, and the longer we were together, the more normal it felt.

We had been dating for six months, and the holidays were approaching. I was excited for Vince to meet my family at Christmas. He seemed calm and relaxed, but I was nervous. I wanted them to like him. Mom cooked one family meal per year, and she always went all out. We drove an hour to their house, a double-wide trailer near the beach, and Vince escorted me inside. The entry door led into the kitchen, which was poorly lit, so it took a moment for Mom's silhouette to appear. She was smiling, looking festive in her red Christmas sweater trimmed in white marabou, earrings shaped like tree ornaments dangling from her ears. The familiar fragrance of turkey and stuffing with too much sage took me back to Christmases past as I approached her for a hug. She hugged me with a pat on the back and went back to stirring the gravy.

"Mom, this is Vince." I stepped aside, making room.

"Merry Christmas, Mrs. Antonio. I can see where Mary's beauty comes from. You two could be sisters." Vince smiled and shook her hand. Mom beamed at the compliment, but he was right. Mom was in her midforties but could easily pass for thirty-five.

"Hi, Vince," she said with a thick southern drawl, leaning in for a hug. He slipped out of his leather jacket, and I took it to the spare bedroom and laid it on the bed, leaving Vince with Jim, who introduced him to my brother, Russ.

Jim was Sicilian, and he accepted Vince as family immediately. They spent the evening talking about the old country and where their families were from. Vince drank very little and made light conversation. My younger sister, Kena, had recently gotten married, and with a baby on the way, she didn't make it to dinner. Russ welcomed Vince like most brothers would, with a watchful eye.

Like most first-time visitors, Vince commented about the myriad of Elvis Presley pictures that were squeezed onto every open inch of wall space. Mom pointed out her favorites, describing where she had gotten them, which led to stories about seeing Elvis live in concert. Vince was at home discussing music, and his comments and questions were genuine.

The evening was casual and ended with gift-giving and dessert, like every Christmas before. Vince had been a big hit, and as we talked about the visit on the ride home, I knew he was a keeper.

Meeting Vince's father was a completely different experience. I knew what Tony had done to Vince's mom over the course of their marriage, and I couldn't unsee the image of her battered face. Knowing Vince had lived with the horrors of that abuse as a child caused me to dread meeting Tony, which hadn't been a problem because he was rarely around. Vince had forgiven him for the things he had done to his mom, but I hadn't.

I cringed inwardly a few days after Christmas when Vince told me that Tony and Ruby were coming over to exchange gifts, but Vince could not wait to see them. They told us that they wouldn't be staying long, so instead of dinner, I baked a cake for dessert. More than an hour before their anticipated arrival time, Vince was already walking in circles nervously, stomping around the hardwood floors in his cowboy boots, looking out the fogged-up windows, and wiping the glass with his hand repeatedly.

"Hey, quit stomping. You're going to make the cake fall."

Vince rubbed his hands together and shrugged. "I can't help it. I've never introduced my dad to anyone before. I'm just excited for him to meet you."

"Never? Are you serious?"

His exhilaration was heartwarming and even a little contagious. Maybe I was being too harsh, I thought. I smiled as he brushed past, kissing me on the lips.

"Nope. My dad is going to love you, and Ruby will too." He hurriedly swept his keys off the counter. "I'll be back in a half hour. I'm going to the liquor store to pick up a gift. Love you," he shouted over his shoulder, rushing out the door.

Tony came in two hours late like he owned the place, loudly proclaiming, "Ciao, Merry Christmas," grabbing Vince in a bear hug, and clapping him on the back. "There's my son. How are you? You look great. Apparently, this beautiful lady is good for you."

He walked toward me, his arms outstretched, and I smiled nervously. I hugged him back, but he clung to me a little longer than I was comfortable with, kissing me on both cheeks.

"Oh, you must be Ruby," I said, breaking free and exchanging hugs with her. She nodded but said nothing. I quickly learned it was because she was already half in the bag. Evidently, we weren't their first stop.

Tony was clean-cut with white hair and a mustache. He was stocky and about my height, which surprised me, considering Vince was so tall. He had rosy cheeks and he smiled a lot, like someone without a care in the world. I liked that about him, but when he talked, I got the sense that everything he said was exaggerated, like a used car salesman. Even still, I could see the attraction. Like Vince, he was charismatic.

Vince handed him the brown paper bag containing a bottle of Crown Royal, which he opened and offered to everyone as a Christmas toast. Ruby was barely hanging on to her dignity and, thankfully, passed the bottle to Tony without pouring any for herself.

"To my favorite son, on Christmas." Tony held the glass high in the air. "Salute!" He drank the shot and poured another. "You picked a winner, Son. Don't let this one get away." He winked at Vince, and they clinked glasses, sealing the agreement. The evening went well, and Vince seemed happy. I could see him relaxing as his father's approval became apparent.

Tony was gregarious and friendly, and I liked him more than I wanted to. Over the next five years, I would find Vince and Tony more alike than I imagined.

# Chapter Two

VINCE HAD A SOLID WORKING KNOWLEDGE OF THE CONSTRUCTION business because he worked for one of the best builders in the industry. He had been working for Roger for many years but was restless. He wanted to make more money and run his own crew. Roger saw talent in Vince but didn't think he was ready. Vince was stubborn, constantly pressuring Roger to let him run the crew until he finally gave in, leaving Vince in charge of the site for a week while he took a vacation. The crew respected Vince, and he was excited to be running the job on his own. I was excited for him too.

Vince came home from work that Tuesday dirty and sweaty. Monday had gone well, but I could tell by the silence that this day he was in a bad mood.

"Hey, sweetie, you want a glass of tea?" I asked. "I just made it."

"No."

He shuffled through a stack of bills, flipping them onto the floor, leaving them where they lay. I could tell by his furrowed brow and the discarded envelopes that he was angry about something.

"Are you okay?"

"It's those stupid fucking plumbers." He began pacing frantically through the hallway to the bathroom and back again like a charging bull, slamming doors and cursing. I wasn't sure whether I should encourage him to tell me what happened because sometimes he got himself so worked up that he couldn't settle back down. I washed my hands, watching him from the kitchen, waiting and hoping he would let it go, but his agitation only increased as he recalled the incident.

"They showed up a day early and put in the bathroom pipes before the carpenters finished framing it out, and now the carpenters are refusing to finish until the plumber comes back and rips it out. The plumber refuses to come back because the carpenter was an asshole to him, and all of this is costing money!"

He punched his fist on the counter, and I jumped. His face turned red, and he continued pacing the room clumsily, bumping the living room lamp so it clattered and wobbled in circles on the table. I trailed behind, settling the lamp back in place, waiting for an opportunity to interject, but then the odor of burning macaroni permeated the room. I rushed back to the kitchen, turned off the burner, and grabbed a dish towel, fanning the smoke detector just as it began blaring its warning to everyone in the neighborhood. The siren increased the feeling of panic, and tension filled the room as Vince stomped in, tore the unit from the wall, and tossed it across the room. It was the outlet he needed, and he began to breathe a little more slowly.

I held my head in my hands in disbelief. "Damn it, I'm sorry. I was distracted," I said, opening the windows. He strode past me and I reached for his hand, but he pulled away.

"Hey," I said and then hesitated. "Look, you're right. He was wrong. But you'll figure it out. Why are you letting it bother you so much?"

"Wait till Roger finds out. He'll be pissed." He shook his head in disgust. His words slowed at the mention of Roger's name, and I suddenly realized that he felt like he had let him down.

"Oh, honey, he'll understand. He's been in this business a long time. He knows what you're dealing with."

He relaxed at the word "honey," and his shoulders sagged. I crossed the room to where he perched against the arm of the sofa, his head down with his chin on his chest. I took his hand in mine, and he stood quietly and hugged me. I kissed him and brushed the hair out of his eyes.

"You didn't let him down," I said. "This is a blip on the screen. Don't let it get to you; just handle it."

"I'm sorry about the smoke detector," he said with a pout. "That was stupid."

"Well, if I'm going to keep doing the cooking, you'd better get another one quick."

We laughed, and the incident dissolved as though it had never happened. Sometimes, it felt like we were closer after a big fight when we'd made up, but it never seemed to last. Things would level off and get back to normal, then, slowly but surely, the bickering would start again.

Money was tight. The tougher things got, the more we argued, and the more we fought, the more volatile our arguments became. I was sure that things would get better when we weren't struggling financially. We had enough to get by, but Vince wanted to step out on his own, and we needed to have a nest egg for him to take that step. We couldn't build up the savings, but Vince decided to take the leap anyway. He left Roger and took two of his crew with him. I was shocked and so was Roger, who had become a father figure to Vince.

"What did you do? How could you just leave Roger like that and then take Franny and Dean with you?" I asked.

"It's business, and you're supposed to support me, not Roger. Thanks, Mary. Don't you think that was hard for me to do?"

"Don't you think we should have discussed this before you left your job?"

He stormed around the house, banging and slamming doors, and I yelled behind him. "Well, you have a right to do what's best for you, but what a shitty way to do it. He's been good to you. Besides, what can you do with just two guys?"

"My dad is coming to work for me too. I won't have to pay him much because he doesn't have any experience. He'll learn. My brother might come on board too. We'll be fine. I have some money saved, and we can get by for a few months. I'll have work by the end of the week. I'm working on it."

"That's great. It seems like you planned out everything except the part where you screwed Roger."

"Well, I'm an asshole. What can I say?" he yelled from the bedroom.

"That's great, Vince. Jesus, who are you?" I whispered under my breath.

Our arguments became more frequent and increasingly volatile. Sometimes I got so mad that I left. I packed up and moved in with my brother, swearing never to go back to him, but I did, and three months later, we started the dance all over again. After a big fight, he would smother me with affection, and everything would settle down like it was in the beginning. We had perfectly normal days laughing, cooking spaghetti, washing clothes, paying bills, hanging out, and watching movies together. This was our norm. He had never hit me or hurt me physically, and for the next few years, I accepted the craziness in my home. It was ridiculous. I never told Russ any details about the breakups, and he never asked. There was always a place for me to land, and unfortunately, I took advantage of it too often.

One Friday night after work, Vince suggested a date night. "Hey, sweetie, let's swing by the Moose Lodge for a drink tonight. My dad and Ruby are there, and I haven't had a chance to catch up with him this week."

I grimaced. "Honey, you know I don't like that place. It's a bunch of old guys drinking dollar beers and playing darts. They spend the whole day there, and by the time we get there, they'll all be drunk and flirty. It's gross."

"Yeah, I know you don't like it, but just one drink, and we'll go. I promise. I need to talk to Dad for a few minutes, and I'm sure he's there." He gave me the puppy dog eyes, dipping his chin and smiling slightly. "Please?"

"Okay, but just one drink," I said, charmed by his innocent look.

As the door to the Moose Lodge opened, the cigarette and stale beer smell hit me in the face. It was dark inside, and it took me a moment to orient myself.

"There they are," he said.

Vince held my hand, guiding me to the bar, where Tony grabbed me in a bear hug and kissed me on both cheeks, the stereotypical Italian greeting, even though he had never stepped foot on Italian soil.

Vince offered me the only remaining seat and stood behind me, shouting our drink order to the bartender. I sipped my whiskey sour, making small talk with Ruby, who was already slurring her words, while Vince caught up with his father. The jukebox wailed "Honky Tonk Women," and I lit a cigarette, relaxing into the good music.

Vince seemed restless, shifting from one foot to the other, crossing and uncrossing his arms over his chest.

"Are you okay?" I asked. "You're like a worm on a hot rock tonight."

"Yeah, I'm fine." He smiled, shoving his hands into his pockets, jiggling coins, removing his hands, and shoving them back in again.

I shook my head and turned my attention back to Ruby as Vince bent down to tie his sneaker. She gazed over my shoulder, smiling. I turned to see why she was grinning and found him on one knee with a small velvet box in his hand.

He thrust the closed box into my lap and blurted, "Will you marry me?"

My hand flew to my mouth in shock, clipping the pretty little box, which tumbled to the sticky barroom floor. Vince was sweating as he snatched it from the floor, opened it, and grabbed my hand. He put on a sweet smile as he slipped the ring onto my ring finger.

"Mary, you know we belong together. Will you marry me?"

I nodded furiously, my eyes welling with tears of joy. "Yes, yes, of course I'll marry you," I squealed, throwing my arms around Vince's neck and kissing his face.

Ten drunken men and women cheered for us while Ruby and Tony swallowed us up in hugs.

Vince's awkward, seemingly unplanned proposal was so characteristic of him that I found it endearing. It was clear that he needed the support of his father to risk rejection and ask for something that wasn't a guarantee. If I had said no, he might have spent the evening drinking cheap beers with him.

As much as I would have preferred a nice dinner at a fancy restaurant and champagne, what I wanted most was to have a great life with him, so the how didn't matter much to me. He was vulnerable, and I knew at that moment, looking into his terrified eyes, that he truly loved me.

Vince and I had been dating for four years and had been living together for three of those years, so the timing seemed right. Though we had never discussed it, the natural progression was marriage. Despite the presence of his family at the Moose Lodge proposal, our marriage, on December 3, 1988, would be the best day of my life. It was the wedding of every girl's dreams. The church was beautifully decorated in Christmas red and green for the evening candlelight service, and surrounded by our friends and family, I became Mrs. Mary Moretti.

We honeymooned in the Caribbean like movie stars; we spent lavishly and played hard, and I felt alive, lucky, and happy to be with my new husband. I felt like a fairy-tale princess—and Vince was my prince.

As if one week of tropical bliss weren't enough, we flew home, repacked our bags for skiing, and flew off to Colorado for a week, where I would meet Vince's mom, Janet. I was super excited to meet her. Because of her history with Vince's father, I secretly felt like she and I were kindred spirits, loving profoundly and enduring the often-foul temperaments of our husbands. We hit it off immediately, and soon she was teaching me to make proper Italian meatballs using the secret family recipe.

Janet was an intelligent, strong, well-spoken woman, and I had difficulty imagining her getting knocked around by anyone. I never told her about the picture in Vince's wallet, and we never discussed that time in her life, but there was an unspoken knowing between us.

I was married. Things would be different now. Vince and I were joined by God, and I would never leave him again. The days of stomping off to stay with Russ were over. We were family, and I would stay with him till death do us part.

# Chapter Three

IF WE HAD KNOWN WHAT WAS WAITING FOR US WHEN WE GOT HOME, we might not have come back at all. We unpacked our bags and were just getting into the swing of things when we discovered that the thousands of dollars we had received as wedding gifts had disappeared. Our accounts were overdrawn, and Vince was furious. Tony had managed Vince's construction site and men while we were gone, and he had agreed to deposit the wedding checks for us.

"What do you mean we're overdrawn?" I asked. "We should have plenty of money. I mean, assuming your dad had a chance to deposit the money for us. Maybe he didn't have time."

"Yeah, maybe," Vince answered, storming around the house. "I just started this business, and I have contractors to pay. I used the company money for our honeymoon, and these checks were supposed to replace that money. That was payroll money, and now we don't have funds to cover wages, and it's Christmas." His voice was loud enough for the neighbors to hear.

"Hey, relax. Call your dad. I'm sure he just got caught up and didn't get the checks deposited. He had his hands full with the crew and all. Why do you get all worked up over things before knowing what happened? We'll pick them up from him and deposit them. Everything will be fine."

"I already called him. He's not answering. I left three messages."

I had never seen Vince this upset. I watched him storm through the house with his shoulders reared back and his fists balled up. I could hardly make sense of his words through the cursing and slamming of doors. His face was red and sweaty as he yelled like a maniac, punching the walls. I wasn't sure what to say, and it seemed best to let him burn himself out, so I stayed out of his way and said nothing for a while.

I assumed that his dad hadn't deposited the checks, but the fact that he wasn't calling Vince back was concerning. We had plenty of money. I wondered if it had been a banking error that caused our account shortfall, but Vince's behavior seemed like dramatic overkill for a banking error. What wasn't he telling me?

"What the heck is wrong with you?" I finally asked. "We'll figure it out. I'm sure it's just a mistake. Jeez."

He stormed past me, squeezing his temples with his palms.

"Come on," I said. "We'll go to the bank and find out what happened."

He never answered, but climbed into the truck, sulking on the drive to the bank. On the way, I noticed his driving didn't reflect his mood. He slowed for stops and waved people on like they were old buddies, but the radio was off, and I could hear his ragged breathing beneath the straight-faced facade. It was eerie. He hadn't turned the heater on, and it was a cold day in December. As much as I wanted to turn it on, I sat shivering in the bitter temperature and tension, remaining agreeable and quiet.

We arrived and sat down in the matching orange swivel chairs reserved for customer service. Finally, a middle-aged woman wearing a skirt suit and too much perfume walked over to us, her hand extended in an overly friendly introduction. Vince fidgeted nervously, chewing his fingernail, refusing to make eye contact with me as Florence escorted us to her office.

She listened intently to a much calmer man than the one I experienced an hour earlier as she scooted up to a computer, checking our accounts.

"The checks weren't deposited into your account, sir. Do you know what branch they supposedly went into? If you can tell us who had access to them, we might determine what happened. In the meantime, we will begin the investigation for you. If someone has committed a crime, we'll see that they are prosecuted. Once it's all worked out, we'll take care of any overdraft fees, and of course, you won't be responsible for that. I'm sorry this happened to y'all and at such a beautiful time in your life."

She had an irritating southern drawl—annoying because it sounded fake and exaggerated to the trained ear. I had listened to Southerners speak my whole life, and she sounded like an actress reading for a part. Still, she was trying to help, so I was patient.

At this point, we were both confident that his dad was responsible for this mess, but Vince never told Florence about him, and I followed his lead. I didn't tell, but I wanted to, and if Tony had stolen our wedding gifts, I wanted to prosecute the bastard. I wanted him at least arrested and maybe hanged.

Vince was quiet, and when we climbed back into the truck, he sat beside me, staring down into his lap, breathing heavily, white puffs of fog gushing with every exhale. He ran his hands through his hair.

"What can I do? He's my dad," he said.

"What? What do you mean? 'What can I do?' You go and get the money from him."

Without looking at me, Vince said, "I'm so sorry. I don't know what to say. This is the most embarrassing moment of my life."

My heart dropped. I knew how that felt. I had bailed my mom and Jim out of debt plenty of times and understood how strong the ties of blood relations were and the shame it brought to bear. His father had let him down. There was no way I would rub Vince's nose in it.

He started the truck and drove off slowly, the tires crunching ice in frozen potholes, as I gazed out the passenger-side window, my breath fogging the glass. I turned on the heater and stopped mentally planning his father's demise, working up as much empathy as I could muster.

"We'll figure it out," I whispered.

It was a quiet drive home. Vince walked in the front door, a beaten man, subdued and vulnerable. He closed the door behind me, and I turned to face him.

In a soft voice, Vince began to explain. "He doesn't just have a drinking problem. He has a gambling problem too. I thought he was done with all that."

And that's when I knew it was gone. We would never get it back. I was overwhelmed with such a mix of emotions that I didn't know what to say. I mentally berated him: *Why didn't you tell me? Why the hell would you trust your drunken, gambling-ass father with six thousand dollars of our money?* I was pissed at his father and sad for Vince, but I had a hard time feeling empathy for the pain he felt at having to tell me this horrible truth about his father. I knew shame well enough to know it wasn't his to carry, and I settled. He was as much a victim as I was, but I knew we were going to struggle until we figured a way out of this mess.

I wrapped my arms around Vince, and we stood, leaning into each other until it felt like we had melted together. I wanted desperately to ease his pain, and I searched my own life story for anything that remotely prepared me for a response but came up short. I kissed him gently on the lips.

"It's not your fault. I love you. We will figure this out," I said.

"Thanks, babe," Vince said, his eyes still closed.

And for the first time, it felt like we were an average, healthy couple working together toward a resolution. I was blissfully unaware that I was alone in that feeling.

# Chapter Four

In the days that followed, we were less like team-building partners and more like drowning victims. Vince's dad had vanished, but not before passing out the payroll checks. Without the wedding gift deposits, there wasn't enough money to cover them. Things quickly spiraled out of control, and we were left with bounced payroll checks and angry construction workers, the kind of guys you wouldn't want for enemies. Cheap labor often meant hiring some of the criminal element, and Vince had a few guys on his jobsite who scared me. I knew I'd be looking over my shoulder until they were paid.

We had to cover their wages somehow, and generally Russ would be my savior at a time like this. He was always there for me, but his wedding gift to us had been a check for $57.68, which was probably the balance of his account. Russ became the unofficial man of the house when I was fifteen. He was only seventeen when he assumed the role of provider and father figure and took responsibility for his sisters' welfare. He represented the opposite end of the spectrum from Vince's dad—an incredible guy. He was, as they say, an old soul. My sister, Kena, was a year younger than me, and as a single parent, she was struggling to feed a newborn.

Aside from Russ, I was probably the most financially stable member of my small family, and I had no clue what to do about this. We spent somewhat lavishly on our wedding and honeymoon, anticipating that we would replace the borrowed money with generous gifts from our friends and family. It would have worked, too, if not for Vince's father, who had skipped town. We needed to find six thousand dollars and find it fast.

My dream of us conquering this challenge together was short-lived; it wasn't long before the bickering started again.

"Vince, this is absurd. Why don't you find your father and get it back? I mean, he's got to be drinking or spending it somewhere. What about your brothers? Can't they help? Your mom, maybe?"

Vince turned on his heel and slammed the door as he walked into the bedroom.

I was sitting on the front porch with my third cigarette trying to figure out a solution when Vince came out of the house, bummed a smoke, and sat down on the steps beside me. Seeing my teeth chattering from the cold December air, he huddled closer to me and took my free hand in his, blowing a warm breath on my palm. It brought a smile to my face, and for a moment we remembered that we were newlyweds.

"Honey, what are we going to do?" I asked. "We need to pay these guys. It's Christmas. I mean, I can handle our bills, but I can't make payroll. Do you know anybody who could? Maybe someone could give us a loan or something?"

His disposition had changed from anger to defeat. "No, I don't think so." He shook his head slowly. "Maybe Roger, but I probably burned that bridge when I left to start my own business. I can't pay them. They'll have to wait. That's all there is to it. If we lose the work crew and the contract with the builder, then so be it. We'll get another."

He stood, looking across the dirt road at the neighbor's house where twinkling Christmas lights flashed a not-so-subtle reminder that Christmas was only a week away. I cautiously made a suggestion, careful not to reignite his temper.

"Honey, I have an idea for how we might get things straight. As I see it, we have about a week before everything falls apart financially and we lose the crew."

He nodded.

"You know I have a special relationship with my Aunt Ruth."

He started shaking his head before I could get the words out.

"Wait, honey. Hear me out." I started slowly. "I'm pretty sure Aunt Ruth is financially comfortable. I don't think it would harm her in any way, and it would be a loan. I mean it. We would have to pay it back, but I'm pretty sure she'll loan us the money we need for payroll."

"No way," Vince fired back. "You want me to borrow money from your aunt? We've been married for less than one month, and Christ, I just met her at our wedding. What kind of a man do you think I am? What would your family think?"

"Vince, no one has to know about this, and it has nothing to do with you being a man. Besides, a man pays his debts, right? If you borrow money, then you pay it back. It's a business transaction. You owe it to your men to ask, Vince. I don't want to do this either, but we're desperate here, and this isn't your fault. I can't think of anything else. Can you?"

He stood in silence, gazing at the festive decorations that surrounded us.

"I know she'll help if she can. We aren't taking advantage of her. I don't want to lose everything we've worked so hard to put together."

He picked at his fingernails. I watched his jaw clench and unclench, watched him process what I had said.

"Vince, this is a temporary setback. Please, sweetie, don't let pride get in the way of a perfectly reasonable solution. Besides, she can say no. It's her choice."

He folded his arms across his chest, and I could tell I had said enough. After what seemed like an eternity of silence, Vince turned his back and walked away, shooting over his shoulder, "Okay, go ahead. I'm going to look for my father. I have an idea where he might be."

Aunt Ruth was my grandfather's sister, so she was technically my great-aunt. Her husband, Uncle Joe, had had a stroke and died soon after he retired, and she grieved his loss tremendously. We were close, and I visited her often after he passed. She had gumption, as the older folks used to say. She wasn't a woman to be trifled with, and I loved her sarcastic sense of humor.

Talking Vince into accepting a loan was one thing, but mustering up the courage to ask for it was another. I called Aunt Ruth and asked if I could come over, explaining that I needed her help. I met her the next day and explained what had happened.

"Oh my God. That son of a bitch. I noticed he drank a lot at the wedding, but I've never heard of anybody doing such a horrible thing to their kid."

We sipped coffee for an hour before she calmed down and I found the courage to ask her for the loan. She was quiet, and the tension was palpable as she slowly stirred her coffee with the sugar spoon. The trailer walls were closing in.

"Aunt Ruth, we will pay you back." My voice shook with nervous energy and I was talking fast. "Vince has a new house starting next week and the framing goes quickly. We could pay half of it as soon as he gets his first check. And then we could pay a thousand a month for each month after that."

I stopped talking and watched her expression for any hint of disgust or anger, finding none.

She spoke slowly. "I don't loan money to anybody, and that's because I don't trust people to pay it back. You're a hard worker, and if you say you'll pay it back, then I know you will. I'm going to loan it to you, but don't you tell anybody I did."

She hadn't even looked up from her coffee cup as she spoke, and I knew it had been a decision of the heart.

We spent the next hour in awkward conversation before I left with a check in hand. I had never borrowed money from anyone, and given how horrible it felt to ask, I would never do it again.

Vince had jobs lined up that would pay well, but it would take a few months to pay her back. We were relieved that his men were paid in time to prepare for the holidays and that the business didn't go under.

I expected everything to blow over and get back to normal, but accepting the loan from Aunt Ruth had been a hit to Vince's pride. Instead of being grateful, he was angry and sullen.

"We'll pay her back and everything will be fine. Why are you acting like a jerk? Maybe you could just say, 'Hey, thanks for asking, sweetie!' It was very kind of her to take a chance on us, don't you think?"

Vince shook his head and as he walked away, said, "I wish you'd just shut up about it."

Somewhere along the line, this whole mess had become my fault and not his father's. Tony had dropped out of sight, and Vince never mentioned him again, instead directing his anger toward me. We didn't always make our payments to Aunt Ruth on time, and each time we were late, I bore the brunt of Vince's frustration along with the embarrassment of having to call Aunt Ruth.

Within six months, we were caught up and had repaid the loan in full. The topic was still off-limits between Vince and me, and I knew we would never ask for money again. We had worked through a pretty big problem together, and I was at least happy about that. Things improved, and we fell into a routine that seemed like everyday married life, if there was such a thing.

Spring brought work and plenty of it. Our finances were back in order, and as business increased, the administrative responsibilities multiplied. Vince had a hard time juggling both, and he wasn't very good at managing the books, so he approached me with an idea.

"You don't need to work," Vince said. "Business is going great, and I need someone to handle the banking, the books, and the phone. I can't do it all. I need to be on the jobsite. Why don't you quit working at Wawa and help me? You work too hard there anyway, and they don't appreciate you. It'll be so much better for both of us." His enthusiasm was contagious, but I was a practical person, not known for financial risk-taking.

"I don't know, honey. It will be a huge drop in our income. I'm not sure we can get by without it, and what about benefits?"

He continued making his pitch. "Won't it be great to get up whenever you want and not work for someone else? Tell me you wouldn't love that. And business is great. We need to take advantage of it. Don't you trust me?"

He grabbed me around the waist and, with a broad smile, picked me up. I laughed as he spun me around in circles, saying, "Let's do it. C'mon, honey."

He put me down and began explaining how much work needed to be done, including advertising and tax preparation. He was right. It was too much work for him, but practical Mary was on high alert.

"Honey, of course I trust you, and I am tired of the long hours. We should probably think about this first though. I love the idea of working as a team, and I'd be thrilled to use my brain instead of breaking my back, but we need to crunch the numbers. And I don't know anything about accounting or bookkeeping."

My desire for that romantic knight-in-shining-armor feeling drew me in, and I slowly pushed away my doubts. I wanted him to sweep me off my feet like he had when our relationship was new. We had been through a lot. The more I thought about the possibility of working with him, the more excited I became. We talked it over for a few days and I conceded. Things hadn't been the same since our honeymoon, and I felt this might help us get back on track. It had been a harsh winter, but spring brought with it possibility, and business was booming.

We moved from the house we were renting to a townhouse about an hour away in Wallingford, Pennsylvania, about fifteen miles from

Philadelphia. It made perfect sense. Vince wanted to build houses in an affluent area, and the new townhouse was ideal. I loved the neighborhood. Even though I didn't know anyone, it was new and felt like a clean, fresh start. We could put all the start-up problems behind us.

We both had to make some sacrifices. Vince couldn't play drums in the house anymore. I loved that he was a musician, but I didn't mind the change as much as he did. It was probably the worst part of that move for him. Music was his outlet for stress, and without it he was miserable. I couldn't change it, so I pushed it to the back of my mind and didn't address it.

He made up for losing his creative outlet by throwing himself into his new business. He was finally working for himself. He was always a talented carpenter with the natural ability to create beautiful home designs. He had six men working for him, and they were loyal and respected his skills. I was proud of him and felt excited for us to be working together.

I took bookkeeping classes at night at a local technical school and learned how to incorporate the business, and how to set up and manage the company's accounts payable and receivable functions. I did not earn a degree, but I learned what I needed to know to start a business and manage the books. I didn't draw a paycheck, so we saved money by not paying for those services. Vince already knew how to bid jobs, but it was a competitive market and there wasn't a lot of wiggle room in the budget. We were always just barely making it, but we were making it.

The move was hard on me too. I was lonely, and being away from my family for the first time in my life felt like losing a limb. I used to talk to my mom, brother, and sister regularly, but now that we lived in Pennsylvania and they lived in Delaware, the calls were long distance. Calling was expensive, so they were always short. My sister was busy with a newborn. Her husband had left her as soon as the baby was born, so she had her hands full. Mom rarely called because she subscribed to the belief that kids are supposed to call their mothers. The drive was more than an hour, so there were no more pop-ins, and scheduled visits were few and far between. I convinced myself that it was a temporary plan, that once the business was up and running, we would move back to Delaware.

The summer months went by and wintry, snowy weather set in. The residential construction industry took the typical weather-related dive, and money became tight again. One cold day, Vince looked up from the checkbook and made a proposal.

"Sweetie, since you're working from home now, maybe you don't need a car. What if we sell it and then get you another car in the summer, something nicer? Business always picks up in the summer."

I looked up, a bit surprised at the question, and noticed that he looked exhausted. His hair looked like he had just rolled out of bed and his filthy Carhartt jacket had holes in it. He was right. I hardly went anywhere without him. I didn't know my way around the area yet, so it didn't seem like a huge sacrifice.

"Sure, sweetie. I think that'll be okay for a while. I won't need to go out much. I can run errands after you get home from work. I'd like to have a car by spring, though. Do you think that's doable?"

"Yeah, of course! It'll be perfect. Things are always booming in the spring and summer." He wrapped his arms around me and kissed me softly as a reward. We sold my Camaro Z/28 for more than I had paid for it, and it helped us get through the lean winter months.

Vince began working long days, trying to save money by doing more of the work than he had in the past. Everything was going according to plan, and we were confident that we would make it through.

It didn't take much time each day to do the company books, but I prepared for the days when it would. The phone wasn't ringing with offers for new houses to build, and I was bored. I didn't know anybody in the community. The parking lot was empty every morning, suggesting that most people worked during the day. With no one to visit with and the light winter workload, I tried to fill the time by cleaning the house more than necessary. But aside from that, I didn't know what to do with myself.

One day, Vince came home to find me still in my pajamas, smoking a cigarette, and looked at me with judgmental eyes. He didn't need to say what he was thinking. I knew. I brushed breakfast crumbs from my T-shirt and mussed my hair.

"I'm sorry, honey. I know I look like hell. I was just about to get a shower. It's just that I'm lonely, and I'm so bored I can't stand myself."

I gave him the boo-boo lip as a convincer, whining, "I feel like one day runs into another, and I haven't accomplished anything. I need to do something. You're doing all the work, and I'm not contributing."

His expression changed to one of compassion as he took the cigarette from me, took a long drag, and handed it back. "I know, honey. I'm sorry. It's because you're so smart. You finish the books in half the time it would take most people. It's temporary, babe."

He flipped through the mail and dropped it back onto the coffee table, grabbed a beer from the fridge, and flopped into a chair, switching on the TV.

He was right. It wasn't his fault, so I guiltily threw myself back into being the perfect housewife, trying to see things from a positive perspective. I became a regular Betty Crocker. Dinner was on the table every night by 6:00 p.m. I cooked and cleaned and kept the company books and cared for Vince's brother Jason who came to stay with us while he was going through a divorce and custody situation. It wasn't a bad gig. I liked Jason, and Vince was happy to have his brother for company. It lightened his mood. He hired Jason as a laborer, and they continued working long days. For us, though, money continued to be tight. We didn't have much left at the end of each paycheck for fun, so we watched rented movies and went bowling once a week.

Weeks turned into months, and I spent much of my days watching television or sleeping, and Vince began staying out late after work drinking with the boys. His father was working for us again, but Vince didn't tell me that until I saw the paycheck.

"What the fuck is this?" I asked, holding the week's checks in my hand.

Vince didn't answer immediately; he put his head down and began walking into the bedroom to avoid me. I was right on his heels.

"Hey, why is this check made out to your father? There is no way he's going to work for us. Not until he pays us back what he owes us."

Vince yelled back at me, "He's never going to pay us back. He needs a job, and I need a laborer, so I hired him back. He's back with Ruby and is doing better. He needs a job to stay stable."

"He needs?" I shouted. "What about what we need? What is wrong with him? Has he no pride? And what's wrong with you? How does he walk right back into our lives with no consequences?"

"Let it go. It's gone, and he'll never get another opportunity to do it again," he said.

Vince never mentioned the six thousand dollars his father stole from us again, but I stewed over it every week when I signed his father's check.

One afternoon, Vince looked over our checkbook and asked over his shoulder, "Would you mind not calling home to Delaware so much? The long-distance calls add up. I know you miss your mom and all, but it would be great if you could stop calling for a while, just until things pick up."

I held my breath and gritted my teeth, mentally bickering, *It would be great for who?* but said, "Of course." I felt like he had just cut my last lifeline.

I struggled to convince myself that it made sense, feeling a sting of resentment well up as my inner demons stabbed out all the reasons to say no. The sounder part of my mind prevailed just in time to recall the angry words before I spoke them. I assumed there would be more discussion about this change, but he walked away as if it were a simple afterthought, handing his brother another beer.

Glancing back at me, Vince saw the expression on my face and softened his gaze. "Never mind. If you can't, that's okay. I understand," he said.

A wave of guilt washed over me for overreacting to what now seemed like a minor request. "No, it's okay. That's fine," I answered, still feeling bruised.

"Are you sure? It'll be temporary, sweetie, just until we get back on our feet. I promise. Spring will be here soon, and business will pick up again. Trust me."

He smiled that boyish grin that always melted my heart, and I attempted a half-hearted grin in return, stuffing my feelings back into the sack reserved for things I wish I'd said. I crossed my arms, feeling the tug of resentment in the pit of my stomach. I couldn't help noticing I was the only one making adjustments and thinking, *Maybe things wouldn't be so hard if we weren't supporting your whole family. Or maybe if you didn't spend half of our paycheck buying drinks at the bar, I would have a car.*

# Chapter Five

Week after week of sameness was suffocating. Spring was here and I still didn't have a car and money was tight.

I decided to broach the subject with Vince when he got home from work, but he didn't come home. I paged him repeatedly but got no response. The dinner I had prepared was cold, sitting on the table, waiting for Vince and Jason, and I was angry when they both came in at eight thirty, drunk.

Vince came in the door first, laughing and shouting, "Did you see the look on that guy's face?"

Jason fell into him, stumbling in from behind, and slurred, "It was priceless. What a jerk. He should have known better."

I interrupted the levity, shouting over them, "Where have you been? I've been calling you all night. Dinner has been on the table for hours. Why didn't you call me back?"

Vince half grinned at Jason, saying, "I told you she was gonna be pissed. Don't worry about dinner, honey. We already ate."

They both stifled laughter as Jason staggered into what had become his bedroom.

Vince stayed behind, folding his arms, and said, "Okay, let's get it over with."

I felt the color drain from my face as I paced the living room, seething.

"Vince, this has to stop. You're out almost every night after work drinking. This is bullshit. I spend my days here alone, and everything I do revolves around you and our business. I cook dinner for you two every night and never know if you're coming home or not. I'm tired of this."

"Oh, stop. It's not every night, and he's my brother for Christ's sake."

Vince was yelling loud enough for Jason to hear, thrusting his chest out like he was boasting. He continued as he peeled off his T-shirt. "Why don't you get a hobby or something and stop being such a bitch?" He tossed the shirt in my face; it hung on my ear and over my eyes for a second before toppling to the floor. He laughed hysterically.

I snatched the shirt off the floor and slung it across the room, feeling his words like a punch in the gut. "Because hobbies cost money and we don't have any," I fired back.

"Oh, so it's all my fault. Right? Then why don't you stop being a bitch, you bitch?" he slurred. "Get a job or something! Or if you're gonna lay around all day, at least make yourself useful and put out!"

"Put out? You're such an asshole! Are you kidding me? You come home stinking drunk and pass out every night. That's sexy. Yeah, who wouldn't want that?"

I stomped into the bedroom crying, and he followed me a few steps, throwing his hands in the air. "I didn't mean it. Come on, you know I didn't mean it. Okay, I know. I'm sleeping on the couch."

The whole display was a show for Jason, who could only hear the blowup, and I knew they would both get a good laugh when Vince described the scene in the morning.

I slammed the bedroom door so he knew not to come in, but more so he couldn't hear me cry.

Jason had all the fun with Vince while I felt like a live-in maid. It was springtime and I had paid my dues. I was supposed to have a car by now, and business, which was just starting to pick up, was supposed to be thriving. I looked at the phone on the table, which hardly ever rang. The only thing that had changed since we'd sold my car was that we had another mouth to feed and Vince was drinking every day. The more he drank, the more we argued, and each disagreement was a bit more volatile.

Sometimes I initiated a conversation even though I knew it would push his buttons. He didn't want to talk about problems, but we needed to, and I didn't know how to get through to him. The more I tried talking, the longer he stayed out, and the less we spoke. Like water, the tighter I clenched, the more he slipped through my fingers. We were struggling financially and emotionally, and if we weren't arguing, we weren't talking at all.

My imagination ran wild when he didn't come home from work. Eventually, it didn't matter who he was with or what he was doing. He wasn't doing it with me. Vince mostly ignored me. He didn't want to hear anything from me, and the tighter the money got, the less we talked. We were building walls and no-talk zones around all the things we fought over. But pushing past me in doorways angrily, throwing things at me and hitting me with them, or almost hitting me, was new. They were always something innocuous like a towel or a coaster, never anything that would hurt me if it hit me, so I blew it off as if it were accidental. It only happened when he was drinking, and I gave him a pass. But these kinds of arguments were becoming progressively worse. The more volatile he was, the more I wanted out. The more I wanted out, the more aggressive Vince became.

# Chapter Six

VINCE FOUND AN OUTLET. HE BEGAN PLAYING DRUMS WITH A NEW band called Steam. They had a few steady gigs in local bars, and he liked to play with them for a little extra money and probably peace of mind. I was glad he was playing again, and even though the money was minimal, I hoped it would improve his mood. After a few months of him gigging with the band, they began picking him up, leaving me with the only car, which was a relief. I had underestimated how much freedom I would be sacrificing with the loss of transportation. Jason had moved back to Georgia when his divorce and custody arrangements were finalized, so Vince and I were spending more time together, and things leveled off.

Most nights, I took advantage of the opportunity to run errands or shop for groceries, but one night I stopped in the bar to watch Steam play. They were good. Vince had not seen me come in, so I found a seat in the back of the club near the door, waiting for his break.

He was playing well and had just started singing backup with the band. I noticed his sexy, raspy singing voice and smiled, reminding myself that that hot, sexy man was mine! My heart softened as his eyes found me, and he smiled into the blistering lights. I fell in love with him all over again. I smiled back and flagged down the waitress to order a drink, deciding to stay for a while.

They played a few more songs, ending the set with what I now considered my new favorite song, "When a Man Loves a Woman" by Percy Sledge. Vince continued smiling and nodding at me as he sang, and I knew the lyrics were heartfelt and meant just for me. He would do anything for me. The months of arguing faded away, and I remembered who we were when we were together.

It was a pleasant surprise to see his best friend, Franny, there too. He approached me with a warm embrace, but the worried look on his face told another story.

"Hey, how's it going, Mare?"

Franny already knew how things were going since he worked with Vince. I stepped back, confused, and answered, "Well, you know, Franny. How are you?"

He glanced away, avoiding the question, as we watched Vince strip off his shirt behind the drum kit.

"I know I shouldn't be telling you this, and he'll kill me if he finds out, but I'm worried. Maybe you already know, I don't know, but I'm telling you anyway. Vince has been using coke. I know I should have told you sooner, but I tried talking to him once and I thought he quit."

Noticing the shocked look on my face, he stopped talking and hung his arm around my shoulder.

"Wow. I didn't expect that at all, Fran. I think I was more prepared for you to tell me he had a girl on the side."

"Oh, hell no. I'd kick his ass myself, Mare. I told him if he ever messed around on you I'd kill him, so he'll never brag about that to me."

"I wish that made me feel better, Fran, but I don't know what to do about this." I shrugged, blowing out a lungful of air. The lighting dimmed and I leaned closer, straining to hear him over a drunk arguing with the bouncer escorting him out the door.

"He's a mess." Fran shook his head. "He's convinced that it makes him a better drummer, but it doesn't, and he can't handle it. He can't run with these guys, and they don't care about him. I'm afraid he's gonna kill himself. This group of musicians aren't from around here. I don't know them, and he won't listen to me. I don't know what to do, but I know he can't roll with these guys and keep running a business."

"Damn, I knew there was something wrong but couldn't put my finger on it. How do you know?" I asked.

"He told me. Actually, I asked him if he was using and he admitted it. Maybe you could talk to him." He stepped back and lit a cigarette off mine.

I hesitated, considering how much to tell Franny and deciding he needed to know.

"Talk to him? There's no talking to him these days. He breezes in from work, grabs his drum kit, and heads out. It's rare if he gets home before 3:00 a.m. and then he works and hangs out at the bars with his buddies. If he doesn't have a gig, he comes home late, eats a cold dinner, and goes to bed. I don't see him for more than twenty minutes a day. Everything is falling apart."

We stood awkwardly for a few moments, laughter erupting and beer bottles clinking around our solemn conversation. We hugged and Franny shook his head, grimacing.

"It's not you, Mare. I'm sorry. He doesn't deserve you. Let me know if I can do anything to help."

I kissed him on the cheek, and he smiled sadly as he slid away into the crowd.

I was worried. The idea that Vince was using drugs had never occurred to me, but it sure would explain where the money was going. Drugs had never been his thing, but Franny was right. I'd seen him playing, shirtless, soaked in sweat, his quivering jaw a new addition to his stage presence. I saw the signs, but I knew nothing about drugs; I was at a loss. Franny and Vince had been best friends since high school, so if he wasn't listening to Fran, he was in trouble.

The song ended and I drifted back to the smoky bar, waiting for Vince to towel off and make his way through the crowd to me. He put on a dry T-shirt and walked off the stage, weaving through the crowd, finding a seat at a table directly in front of me, but never once making eye contact.

I leaned forward in my chair, craning my neck to see who he sat down with. Had he seen me? I adjusted my position to see the face that went with the chair next to him. It was Amanda! He was singing to his ex-girlfriend! Their exchange at the table was intimate and flirty, their faces too close for friends as he slipped his hand in hers. He wore the same infectious, boyish grin that had melted my heart, but that look was focused on her, not me. She was cute, prettier than me, and I felt like a fool. I snuck out of the club before he saw me and made my way home. I stumbled inside awkwardly, all of my senses heightened as the door slammed behind me and I switched on the blinding living room lamp. My heart leaped as the prickly images of what they might be doing flooded my consciousness, my mind skipping and hopping from one raunchy prospect to another.

By the time he came in the door several hours later, I was all cried out. "What is going on?" I demanded red-eyed.

"What are you talking about?" he asked cautiously.

"I saw you with Amanda. How could you?"

"No, no . . . Stop worrying. We're just friends!" His eyes were wide with panic.

"You were holding her hand, Vince. I know what I saw, and it was not innocent. That's not a friendship. That's a girlfriend. You were almost in her lap for God's sake. I haven't seen you for days, and you're hanging all over your ex!"

My eyes began to tear, but not wanting to let him make me cry again, I changed the subject.

"And I know you're using coke! Your eyes looked like pinholes and your jaw quivered all night while you played. I know what that means and so does everybody else. Then I see you there with her, and—"

My voice had risen and he yelled over me. "I only tried it once. Tonight was the first time, and it was dumb! I didn't even like it! I won't do it again, I swear." He was begging and looked guilt-ridden.

"Amanda came in on her own." He softened his tone, pleading. "I didn't want to be rude, so I sat down with her. If I had known you were there, I'd have come right over. Why didn't you come over and say something? Honey, you know I love you."

He took a step toward me, close enough so I could feel the heat from his skin, and I leaned away from him.

"I'm sorry you thought it was something more. I can see how that might have looked, but I'm innocent here. I would never, ever cheat on you, ever!"

"Don't try to put this on me! I know what I saw." But before I could protest further, he pulled me into his arms.

"Sweetie, you know I love you more than life itself. She's my ex. I'm sorry. If I had seen you, I would have had a reason to avoid her, but I didn't."

I began to question my judgment, but I saw him holding her hand, and he had that smile, that same smile, the one I'd seen a thousand times.

"You have no reason to be jealous. Amanda is history. Mary, you're my everything. You're letting your imagination run away with you. You have to trust me."

"But the way you looked at her. You were smiling, and . . ."

"Mary, I love you." He took my hand, lifting it to his chest, placing it on his heart.

"This is yours, just yours. I promise."

Heat emanated from his body and I allowed him to pull me closer. He stroked my hair as he gazed lovingly into my eyes, kissing my forehead and cheeks, leaning into me, kissing my neck; his hands began caressing my body. His familiar lips and gentle touch made it feel like everything else was a lie as tears slipped down my cheeks. He lifted me into his arms, and I wrapped my legs around his waist as he carried me into the bedroom.

We made love well into the morning and I fell asleep wrapped in his arms, feeling the closeness I had been craving for so many months. It was relief that didn't last.

It was a short night, so when the doorbell rang at eight thirty the following morning, Vince stumbled out of bed, cursing.

"Oh shit! What time is it?" He pulled on a pair of shorts and stumbled to the door.

Vince's late hours made it difficult for him to get up for work, and some of his loyal men were covering for him, but he was losing their respect. He was a scheduling mess, making significant mistakes. Electricians showed up before they were needed and subcontractors were fighting on the jobsite.

Vince opened the door. It was Mike, one of Vince's carpenters, an easygoing, reasonable guy, a retired navy captain with a great sense of humor. "Dude, what's up? We got guys waiting on the job for you."

"Yeah, I know. I'm coming," Vince snapped, dressing as he shouted.

"Well, that's admirable," Mike replied sarcastically, "but you can't keep doing this shit, man. Even Franny's there, and he's always late." Mike chuckled, trying to make light of it. "Your dad was there, but he already left for the bar. He probably won't be back, but that's not too unusual. Man, you gotta get yourself together."

I walked halfway into the living room, close enough to see Vince slam his forearm and shoulder into the wall beside Mike, screaming. "Don't you think I know that? I'm busting my ass here! You need to mind your own fucking business! You work for me!" he shouted, inches from Mike's face. Mike, who was equal to Vince in size, didn't back down but instead puffed up.

They were both fit and strong, but Mike was the levelheaded

leader of the two as former captain of the USS *Kidd*, DDG-993, a time-honored navy destroyer.

"Vince, man," he said in a calm, even tone, "I'm trying to help you here, but I'm tired of it too. What do you want me to do?"

It was a stalemate. I stepped into the room, grabbing Vince's boots and briefcase.

"Mike, would you go back to the site and let the men know Vince got held up at the lumberyard, and he's on his way? Honey, I'll put some coffee on. It's Friday, so take the checks with you. That'll make them happy. Mike, please don't tell them any of this."

Dead silence stood between the men as they squared off like dogs raising their hackles at one another.

"Hey, c'mon. You're burning daylight," I said.

Both men shook it off, separating. Mike nodded and left. Vince avoided eye contact with me and went about getting ready for work, rushing off without so much as a goodbye.

I gazed out from the second-floor slider as they drove off, watching purple martins fly in circles. Their black-plum bodies were like fighter jets, spinning and plunging without warning, plucking insects from the sky; for a moment I wished I were so free as I began another day of worry, alone.

We were losing good contracts that kept the bills paid and key employees, too, and Vince was staying out even later with the guys, heading straight to the bar after work.

I was used to being busy and working hard, and as a type A personality, boredom was entirely out of my comfort zone. I had too much time to think. I suspected that Vince was cheating, and the last thing I wanted was to lose my husband.

I confronted him with these allegations of cheating during one of our quarrels.

"You're crazy! It's all in your head. I'm working two jobs, and you know I love playing. I have to talk to the customers, and yes, some of them are girls. It's all about selling the band. We need people to follow us," Vince said.

"I know you do, and if it makes you happy, I want you to play, but, Vince, you're more miserable now than you were before you started playing. You're never home. What's going on?"

"Nothing's going on," he yelled, turning on his heel, storming out of the house, and slamming the door.

I spent a long night alone with my thoughts, wondering if I was creating a dramatic world in my head for lack of an interesting one in reality. Vince crept in at daybreak, shedding his boots at the door, sneaking quietly into the spare bedroom that had once been Jason's. I didn't bother to confront him. It felt like too much trouble, so I put on a pot of coffee and went about my weekend routines, washing clothes and preparing for the next workweek. When Vince got up several hours later, he passed by me without speaking and poured a cup of coffee. He looked homeless with half a beard and dirty, matted hair, wearing a T-shirt full of holes, and warming his hands with his coffee cup. He slunk back into the spare bedroom, picked up the guitar, and strummed a slow version of "White Room" by Cream. He would spend nearly the whole weekend alone in that room, punishing me, and I wondered if this was the beginning of the end.

# Chapter Seven

It was May of 1990, just before Memorial Day, and I stared into the darkness alone again, hugging my pillow, infinitely waiting for Vince to come home. I had crawled into bed so long ago that I had lost track of time, but I'd been there long enough for the silence to become deafening. He didn't have a gig, so his whereabouts were left to my imagination. None of the potential scenarios left me feeling comforted, so I lay there listening for his keys in the lock, wondering what he was doing and who he was doing it with and getting worked up. After numerous trips to the bathroom and glances at the clock, I gave up.

I was twenty-nine years old and I was tired, beaten down to the point I no longer cared. But when the doorknob turned, I strained to hear his heavy work boots scrape across the floor. My pulse quickened. It was 3:00 a.m., and I stumbled out of bed in my underwear, dragging myself into the kitchen. He was drunk again, and judging by his pupils, he was high on something. I shuffled past him, groggily opened the refrigerator, and grabbed a container of orange juice, as I gave him a sideways glance. I poured myself a glass as he leaned against the counter, his arms folded across his chest, a belligerent look on his face. He was puffed up, threatening, and his glare dared me to say something.

This kind of antagonism was exhausting. I wanted to yell in his face to stop but thought better of it. He was messed up, and I wasn't sure what reaction I might get. I slipped past him, noticing how he towered over me, one of the things I liked about him, but at that moment his height was a little unsettling. I stepped aside, giving him a wide berth. He stared down at me intently, clenching and unclenching his jaws, dropping his hands to his side, and balling up his fists like he wanted to hit me. I stepped back, rolled my eyes, shook my head in disgust, but said nothing.

Seconds later he wrapped his hands around my throat and shoved me backward with two long strides into the kitchen, plowing my head into the microwave and against the kitchen counter, choking me. My bare feet were slipping and sliding in orange juice and broken glass, and I couldn't stand or pry his hands from my throat. My head vibrated as I twisted out of his grip, his hands finally slipping off my bare skin so that I could breathe.

I half ran, half staggered into the bedroom with him just a step behind.

"Leave me alone! Get away from me," I screamed, tripping around in the dark, falling over furniture as he grabbed me around the waist, picked me up, and tossed me onto the bed like dirty laundry, growling.

He jumped onto the bed, straddled me, and pinned my arms over my head, howling at me and pausing between each word for emphasis. "Shut, up, bitch! Just, shut, up! I should just . . ."

Rather than finish the sentence, he spat in my face. Saliva ran down the bridge of my nose into my eyes. His whiskey-soaked cigarette breath overcame me as he hovered above me, panting and holding me down by my wrists in the darkness.

Bile crept into my throat, threatening to escape, but humiliation turned to rage, and I swallowed hard instead, screaming, "What's wrong with you? Does this make you feel like a man? You're a real tough guy, aren't you? You're a coward! That's all you are."

I struggled, squirming helplessly, trembling beneath him, trying to break free, shouting, "Coward, you're a bully. Get off me!"

My energy drained, and my wrangling slowed as he kept my

arms pinned above my head and trapped my legs under the weight of his body. Thoughts of a rescue permeated my mind as I prayed one of the other tenants in the building would knock on the door or at least call 911.

A guttural howl rose from his throat as his fists pounded into the mattress beside my ears, his hands inching closer and closer to my face with each blow, threatening to bash my skull. His red, contorted face rained perspiration on my body, my skin slippery with sweat. I hated him more with each muffled thud in the mattress.

Veins in his neck bulged with exertion, his face burning crimson as his mouth undulated silently like radio static. I shuddered, closing my eyes as tightly as possible when, with no warning, like a carnival ride, everything stopped. He climbed off, just crawled off, almost trancelike, as if nothing had happened. I quickly rolled off the bed and sprawled on the floor, sucking in a healing gulp of air. I unsuccessfully willed my heartbeat to return to a reasonable rate, and instead my brain busied itself with a slingshot of random words: *car keys, clothes, purse.*

I shook my head, boosting myself to my trembling hands and knees, with a renewed intention to get out unscathed. Scavenging around the floor in the dark, I frantically searched for clothes, anything I could wear to get out. My heart raced in the darkness like the victim in every horror show I'd ever seen waiting for the monster to pop up again out of nowhere. I fumbled in the darkness, listening. All I could hear was my own heart hammering away in my chest, which didn't help restore my confidence. I grabbed a shirt off the floor, feeling victorious, and inched toward the door, my light at the end of the tunnel. It was quiet, almost too quiet. I stood.

A splintering shock to my head spun my body weightlessly in the air, and I was hurled face down onto the mattress. My surroundings faded to gray like an early morning fog. The scream I heard in the darkness was my own but sounded like it came from far off. Like watching a movie when the sound doesn't match the picture, my mind couldn't catch up with the events that were quickly unfolding. My face was dripping with blood, but its origin was unknown. My slow-motion thoughts couldn't work out the details. My ears were ringing when he grabbed my hair and jerked my head back so he could glare into my face.

My eyes were on fire; I cupped them in confusion and pain as warm blood streamed down my neck. I struggled to get to my knees but couldn't manage it on the unsteady surface as he dragged my body off the mattress by my hair. I yelped, and his grip loosened. I rolled away from him, crouching between the bed and the wall, collecting myself. Seconds passed before he hoisted me up by my wrist and roared into my face.

"Now, what the fuck's wrong with you?"

They were some of the few words I actually heard him say, and I was terrified. My arms flailed in a desperate attempt to ward him off and struggle free, and I silently took a mental inventory of my body parts as I dangled by one arm. I gritted my teeth in anticipation of the next blow. He was close. Eyes closed, I could smell the stench of sweat and alcohol as his face came within inches of mine. Nausea overcame me as the metallic taste of my own blood crept into my awareness. I cowered, shielding my face with my free hand against another attack, straining to open my eyes and see what was next, but nothing happened.

It was quiet. He wasn't dragging me. His grip loosened, and gently he helped me up, placing his arm around me, slowly escorting me. My mind darted about. He led me into the bathroom, still breathing heavily, flipped on the light, which left me momentarily blind, and seated me on the commode lid. He turned on the water in the sink and left the room. I sat in silence with my eyes shut. He returned within a few seconds, gently mopping blood from my forehead with a cloth, dabbing my already swollen eye. He caressed my face with his hands like a lover, tending to a gash between my eyes as if he had no idea how it had gotten there. My thoughts began to slow.

He cradled my head in his hands, kissed my face, and whispered, "I'm so sorry, my love. I never mean to hurt you. It was an accident. Hold still. I'll fix it."

He stooped down in front of me, wiping blood from my near-naked body, swabbing my shoulders, breasts, and legs as if he were performing a sacred ritual, and I was relieved. My breathing slowed, and my heart returned to a more regular rhythm. I was grateful to be alive, and as he stroked my skin, I clung to him like he was a superhero come to my rescue, and silently thanked God.

Every minute felt like an hour, and as he left the bathroom, I could hear him pacing. I waited for the next round, fearing the horror wasn't over. I stared into the bathroom mirror at my bloody face. His fingerprints were appearing on my neck, my hair was soaked in sweat and blood, and my face was pale. A nasty slash between my eyes proved to be the source of the bleeding, and my right eye was bright red and swollen shut. I listened for his return.

I could hear him talking to himself, pacing, and occasionally passing the bathroom, where he periodically peeked in to check on me. I couldn't make out complete sentences, but as he passed by, I heard clips and phrases like, "They're just gonna . . . what the hell was she . . . there's no way I could . . . maybe I should . . ."

He didn't know what to do. It was clear that I needed a doctor. He came back into the bathroom with clothes, dressed me in shorts, a T-shirt, and socks, and carried me to the car.

"I'm taking you to the hospital, love. Don't worry. We'll get you fixed up."

The nearest hospital wasn't far, but it seemed to take forever. The car in front of us stopped for a red light, and Vince leaned over and kissed my cheek, stroking my hair. "I love you so much. You know that, don't you? You know I would never hurt you on purpose, right?"

I shifted my weight away from him, avoiding the contact as he tugged me closer by my shirt. I hadn't answered before the light turned green and the car behind us blared the horn.

Vince yelled out the window, "I'm going, asshole!"

Every stoplight was an opportunity for him to profess his love, but I was quiet. He noticed, and it caused him to up his game. His voice softened, and he turned on the puppy dog eyes as he kissed my face and whispered, "I love you so much."

The words that used to melt my heart descended upon me like a tsunami.

# Chapter Eight

WE ARRIVED AT THE HOSPITAL, AND EVEN THOUGH I WAS PERFECTLY capable of walking, Vince carried me into the emergency room and up to the desk where an intake nurse sat behind bulletproof glass. It was a quiet night, and nobody was waiting but me.

The nurse, a woman in her sixties, looked up over her reading glasses and asked, "What happened? You get in a bar fight?"

Vince answered for me. "No, I hit her in the face with a fucking table! You got a problem with that?" He was still breathing heavily from carrying me inside and looked like he might explode. The nurse's face registered shock. I stiffened, too, as I listened to him spew the details of how I had been injured.

"There was an X-Acto carving knife on the nightstand. The knife must have hit her in the eye somehow. I think the table hit her here." He pointed to the gash on the bridge of my nose. "The blade might have sliced her eye because it swelled up right away. I don't know. Just get a doctor."

The nurse looked down at her papers in obvious alarm and said, "Have a seat."

Now it made sense. It was dark in the bedroom and I couldn't make out what he had hit me with. It felt like a club or baseball bat, but I knew there wasn't a bat in our bedroom. I could envision it now. He had picked up a small nightstand, one of two that sat on either side of the bed. They were made of heavy oak wood. He swung the table at me, and the hardwood tabletop struck me between the eyes just at the bridge of my nose, where the slash appeared. I now remembered seeing the X-Acto carving knife, used to sharpen carpentry pencils, on top of the nightstand and panicked. *Am I going to be blind in that eye?*

Receiving no support from the hospital staff, I allowed him to carry me the few steps to the waiting room. I felt pathetic, a grown woman gazing helplessly over his shoulder like a wounded dog, silently begging the nurse behind the glass to save me, but she never looked up from her work. I slumped onto a bench next to Vince in the cold waiting room, wrapped in his jacket. I had just allowed the man who had beaten me to comfort me, and not only did I allow it, I was relieved. What was wrong with me? He held me in his arms until the nurse called me back for treatment.

"Mary Mazetti?" the nurse called.

I looked up and Vince answered, "Here we are."

"Okay, are you Mr. Mazetti?" the nurse inquired, looking intently at the clipboard she carried with her.

Vince smiled at her. "Yes, I'm her husband," he answered as he stood up, assisting me to my feet, escorting me in the general direction of the nurse.

"Mr. Mazetti, you'll have to wait here for now. We'll bring her right back after she's seen the doctor."

I felt Vince's body tense as he tightened his grip on my hand. "No, I'll go back with her and keep her company until the doctor comes in." He was glaring at the nurse, his eyes peering into her threateningly. I stood paralyzed, waiting for her response.

She shifted from one foot to the other, looking to her left and right for staff support. Vince watched her intently, glancing around, noticing that he and I were the only ones in the waiting room except for the lady behind the glass, who watched the situation unfolding but did nothing.

He shook his head. "No. She's my wife. I'll go with her."

Vince began walking in the nurse's direction, never slowing his pace, anticipating she would show us to a room, but she stood her ground.

"No visitors are permitted beyond this point," she said.

I noticed the clipboard shaking and Vince did too. He smirked.

At that moment, a young, well-built man in scrubs walked toward the nurse, took the clipboard, and said, "I think this is my patient. Thanks, Jane, for helping me out. Mr. Mazetti, why don't you have a seat? We'll get you a cup of coffee while you wait. It's pretty late, and I'm sure you're exhausted. As soon as she has seen the doctor, we'll fill you in. She might not remember everything, so we'll be counting on you to take care of her. We'll have you guys out of here, lickety-split. How do you take your coffee, Mr. Mazetti?"

Vince loosened his grip.

"Besides," the man said, "we'll need insurance information from you, so you can help speed things along."

Vince turned to me, leaning down, and in a low voice whispered, "Are you okay if I stay here and wait?"

I couldn't will my lips to move, so I nodded assent, trying my best for a comforting expression. Vince raised my hand to his lips and kissed my wedding band, then lowered my hand, letting go without ever losing eye contact with the man.

"Okay, sweetie, I'll wait here." The tension in the room evaporated as Vince shot over his shoulder, "Cream and sugar."

I strode over to the man in scrubs like a hostage just released, and trailed behind him to the exam room in my bloody blue socks, limping from the still bleeding cuts on my feet. I climbed onto the table as instructed and the man left. My legs dangled as I hung my head, looking between my knees and then gazing at my reflection in the stainless-steel paper towel dispenser. I looked like a prizefighter with one eye nearly swollen shut.

I blinked back the blood and tears; a nurse came into the room, took my vital signs, and made small talk as she asked for the details of what brought me in. It seemed pointless to describe the events again, knowing Vince had already told the nurse at the front desk. I was sure she had told everyone, so I gave her the thumbnail sketch.

The doctor came in fairly quickly after that. "You're going to need a few stitches to close the laceration between your eyes, but we'll have to take a closer look at that right eye. If you have a corneal abrasion, you'll need to see a specialist at Wills Eye Hospital," he said. "Your husband did this?"

I nodded and he pursed his lips, looking at my chart rather than at me. The exam took just a few minutes, and the eye drops they provided relieved the pain and scratchiness immediately.

"Yeah, unfortunately you've got a significant abrasion. It's more than we can manage here, so the nurse will give you instructions and schedule an appointment for tomorrow. Can you do that?"

"Yes," I said, having no idea what I could do or whether Vince would let me go.

I could feel the doctor's disdain as he prepared to close the cut between my eyes, a frown on his face. He jerked each stitch into place until he finally dropped the cold steel implement, letting it clang onto a metal tray, and stalked off, seemingly to let me know that I wasn't worth his time. I didn't disagree.

Another nurse came in, checked my bracelet, and introduced herself as Sarah.

"So, that's your husband in the waiting room?"

I nodded.

"Did he hit you in the face with a table?"

I nodded again and muttered, "I guess so. I don't remember, but that's what he said."

"What happened to your eye? Did he punch you?"

"I don't really know. It was dark. He said there was a knife on the table. He hit me with the table and the knife hit me in the eye or something."

"What else happened?" she asked.

I shrugged and she read the doctor's report, confirming that everything else was accurate. I expected to be discharged right away, a reward for my honesty, so I waited patiently, shivering behind the curtain.

Nurse Sarah tapped her pen on my chart like she was thinking about something and pulled up a chair to sit, facing me, inches away. "Don't leave the hospital with your husband," she said.

I bit my lip and bowed my head. She spoke softly and slowly, like she was talking to a child, and at first it was annoying, but then I realized that I needed it and found her slow, methodical speaking and soft tone comforting. My mind had been racing. Her voice was soothing, so I sat and listened, and though I didn't hear half of what she said between the blipping machines and intercom messages, I felt safe with her. I didn't mind staying there for just a little while until my head cleared. She talked to the top of my head as I gazed at the floor, resisting when she cupped my chin in her palm and slowly raised my head until our eyes met and she spoke.

"Honey, you don't deserve to be treated this way. It isn't normal. This is not your fault."

I didn't respond, but her compassionate use of the word "honey" caused my eyes to well with stinging tears.

"Mary, what can I do to keep you from leaving with him? Can I call someone to pick you up? I'm worried about you. You don't have to live this way."

She continued talking, and she seemed genuinely concerned about me, which was something I had not experienced for a while. She was resolute, so unwavering in her insistence that this was in no way my fault that I began to wonder if there might be some truth in her words. Maybe I did have options. She was adamant, completely unconcerned with my lack of a response.

"Please let me call someone to pick you up," she said, reaching for my hand, gently squeezing, waiting for an answer as she leaned forward, looking into my downcast eyes.

"My family lives in Delaware, and it's the middle of the night," I said. "Besides, my brother is the only one I might be willing to call, and he just had surgery on his knee. He can't drive."

"Let me call him anyway," she begged. "We'll figure the rest out as we go. Let's take it one step at a time, Mary. Does that sound okay?"

I shook my head no. "I can't. If I don't leave with him, he'll kill me," I said.

Even to me, my words were jarring, but if she was stunned, it didn't show.

She shook her head. "No, no. Don't you worry about Vince. He's fine and we'll take care of him," she swore, talking faster now. "You won't even have to see him. Please, honey, let me call your brother. We're here for you, now. You're safe. What's his number?" She paused, looked into my eyes, and enunciated, "You are not alone anymore. I am not leaving you."

She couldn't possibly have known how much I needed to hear those words. The room clouded as tears gushed from my stinging eyes and rolled down my cheeks, dripping onto my bare legs. Sarah reached for a box of tissues on a nearby table and leaned into my pain. Pink, murky tears stained the pant legs of her white scrubs as she closed the space between us, placing her hand on my shoulder. She stayed. More than a half hour had passed since she first sat down with me, and I imagined she must have better things to do, but if she did, it didn't show. She explained Stockholm syndrome, a survival mechanism where the victim cooperates with the abuser to avoid being injured or killed. Time ticked on and I bit my lip, fighting tears as she continued talking to me, explaining that this kind of thing happened a lot and that it could stop now. She stayed. I wiped my running nose and took deep breaths, forcing oxygen to my brain until I was ready.

"Okay," I said finally. "Can you call my brother?"

I wasn't entirely sure I meant those words or that I would go through with it. Maybe I just wanted to hear how they sounded in my ears, but she didn't give me a chance to change my mind. She bolted off to make the call.

My heart thumped wildly in my chest as I imagined what Vince would say when he learned that I wasn't leaving with him. Sarah was relieved, but I was overwrought. They had no idea who they were dealing with. He was going to explode, and I wondered what he might do and how they would handle it. Sarah walked away to talk to some people but hurried back, settling back into the chair, facing me. I was momentarily relieved.

I strained to hear what was happening just a few feet away. I couldn't hear the conversation, but I knew the exact moment that they told him because I heard glass shatter. It was deathly quiet after that, and the suspense was killing me. Sarah seemed completely unaffected as she sat expressionless, peering off into the distant corridor, and I wondered briefly what would happen next. Finally, a security guard with gray hair and glasses pulled the curtain aside and entered the small room.

"Ma'am," he started, "I'm going to need your name and address and your husband's too. He threw a chair through the emergency room sliding glass doors, and you guys are going to be responsible for that."

I looked at Sarah, and for the first time since she had sat down with me, I saw a flash of anger cross her face. She glared at the guard and pulled him aside to talk to him, out of my earshot. I don't know what she said, but the cranky old guard shuffled away, notepad in hand.

"I'll be right back," she said.

Soon, other hospital staff members peeked into the room, presumably to see the girl who had caused all this drama, like nosy neighbors. I sat there, still amazed that Sarah had come to my defense, and then quickly snapped back to reality.

She had called my brother to pick me up, and I waited for what seemed like years, trying to imagine what to say when he arrived. I cared what he thought about me. Who would I be if I stayed with a guy who treated me like this? He would want to know how long this had been going on, but I knew I couldn't give him an answer and I dreaded his arrival.

Sarah stayed with me for the better part of the next hour, writing notes, offering support, and letting me know what to expect next.

"Mary, because your husband assaulted you, the hospital has a legal obligation to notify the police. You're under no obligation to press charges for what he did, but I want you to think about it. The police will file a report anyway, so whether you decide to have him arrested is up to you. They'll be here soon."

Shit. Why didn't she tell me they were going to call the police? I hadn't considered having Vince arrested, but now it seemed obvious, and I began regretting my decision, feeling just a little betrayed.

"What will happen to him if I do?" I asked.

"I think you should direct those questions to the officer. That's their area of expertise. I'll be right here with you unless you want me to go, and I can do that too."

Twenty minutes later, a police officer arrived with a note-pad in hand. Sarah sat with me, nodding appropriately while he asked questions and I explained what happened to the best of my recollection.

When he finished writing, he looked up from his notes. "Well, ma'am. What happens next is up to you. Do you want him arrested?"

"What will happen to him? Will he go to jail?" I asked.

The officer frowned. "Well, probably not. It looks like your injuries are minor, and you aren't likely to have any permanent disfigurement, so it'll be a misdemeanor. If the injury to your eye turns out to be more serious, which I hope it doesn't, it would be a felony, and then he might be in a little more trouble. He'll be arrested and arraigned before a judge, who will issue a restraining order, but either way he'll probably be out of jail before I finish writing the report."

"Then what will happen?" I asked.

"Well, he'll have to go to court. You'll go and tell the judge what happened, and he'll tell his side. The judge will decide what happens to him. Does he have a criminal record?"

"No, not that I know of," I answered.

"Well, then he'll probably get probation for a first-time offender."

"So nothing will happen to him?" I asked.

"Well, he probably won't go to jail. I'm sorry. I wish guys like this got what they deserved, but it doesn't often turn out that way."

"Okay, then, no. I don't want to press charges, but can I just get the restraining order?"

"No, I'm afraid not. The only way you can get a restraining order is to have him arrested. They go together. Some states offer what is known as a PFA, or Protection from Abuse order, but we don't get involved in that much. Does he have any weapons?"

"Yes, I think so. He had a sawed-off shotgun, but he told me he got rid of it."

"Well, you might want to get a lawyer and look into the PFA."

The officer didn't say much more. He collected his papers and wished me good luck.

It was the most humiliating moment I'd experienced in my life. For reasons I couldn't explain, I sat, patched and stitched up, worried mainly about my pride and what my brother would think of me, terrified of what tomorrow might look like.

Russ was a good man and one of the only positive role models in my life, and I knew he would be upset for me. I felt like a disappointment. When he arrived, I left the hospital and Sarah behind and climbed into the passenger seat of his car, dressed in my shorts, a T-shirt, and bloody blue socks, looking like I'd been in a bar fight, beaten and humiliated at the hands of my own husband.

It took him forever to settle himself in the driver's seat with his leg in an Aircast, and though I offered to drive, he opted to drive with one leg rather than letting me drive with one eye. I was ashamed and at a total loss for words when he asked, "What happened?" I had more than an hour to consider my response but still nothing came. My first words sounded adolescent. "I don't know."

Russ would have had every right to criticize me for my lame response, but before I had time to collect myself, he gently asked, "What happened tonight?"

In the hour it took to drive back to his house in Delaware, I explained as much as I could recall. He sat quietly, listening and nodding or taking in deep breaths and blowing them out again. Sharing the details of months of abuse in the darkness of his car felt like a confession, the occasional bright lights of oncoming cars accusatory. My head hung in shame as I told him about Vince's father stealing the wedding gifts and how things had gotten progressively worse over the last seventeen months leading up to this moment. Finally, he shook his head and asked, "What are you going to do?"

I let him know what the doctors said about my prognosis and felt that a short-term answer might be best, because I had no idea what I would do. I hadn't planned for this.

"Do you think you could take me to Wills Eye tomorrow and then back to the townhouse so I can pack up my stuff?"

"Yeah." He nodded as we pulled into the driveway and hobbled out of the car and into the house. I hadn't even asked Russ if I could stay with him while I figured things out. It was understood. He had provided for my sister and me for much of our adolescence and now adult lives, and this would be the last time he ever needed to do that for me.

I went to the spare bedroom and flipped on the light. The twin bed that was flush against the wall was a welcome sight, but daybreak wasn't far off. I fell onto the bed and stared at the ceiling, then bounced back up to look in the mirror at the bruises on my neck and the black marks now appearing under both eyes.

I thought of Sarah and how supportive she had been. She reminded me of a childhood friend, Sue Kennedy, the morning after a pajama party. The night had been a rare glimpse of a perfect childhood adventure, but the morning brought with it a completely different experience. I awoke quietly mortified to see neighbors gawking at county inspectors who were searching our backyard for rats that had taken up residency in the broken-down cap from a pickup truck my stepfather called a shed. It was part of the junky clutter that had accumulated over the years and that included not only bicycles, old car batteries, and other random shit but also apparently vermin. A rat skittered from the shed to the neighbor's trash can as I sat paralyzed in my shorty pajamas. My friends watched in horror, but Sue broke the spell, becoming my new best friend as she walked the fence line in bare feet and pj's, holding out her hand.

"Okay, people, pay up or move on. Nobody gets to see the show for free." The girls laughed, encouraging her, cheering until my neighbors slunk back inside their homes. Sue stood up for me when I was too ashamed. This night felt a little like that same freak show.

When I fell asleep, I slept in a state of peace I hadn't felt in years. I was safe.

The visit at Wills Eye the next morning was hopeful.

"You'll be fine," the doctor began. "You're going to need to wear that eye patch for a couple of weeks, but you're a pretty lucky girl. If that abrasion had been just a bit deeper, we'd be having a different conversation. I'm sending you home with some drops. Follow the dosing instructions, no makeup, and come back in a week for a follow-up visit. In the long term you may have some scar tissue, but that can't be avoided. Like I said, you're a lucky girl." He smiled, looking into my good left eye with an assurance he had probably given thousands of people before me.

Nothing in the doctor's instructions limited my mobility, so Russ and I went back to the townhouse with two police officers to collect my belongings. I prayed that Vince would be gone as I walked into what used to be my home. Looking around, I couldn't believe what I saw. It was a crime scene with broken, overturned furniture, blood all over the bedding, and bloody footprints smeared on the floors. I didn't remember it looking like that when Vince carried me out in the dark. Goose bumps raised on my arms when I saw the broken table and carving knife lying innocently on the floor. I stepped carefully over broken glass and dried orange juice still a sticky mess on the floor, evidence of the violence of that night.

I made my way back to the bedroom through the long hallway, and like I was seeing it for the first time, the scene replayed in my mind. I saw myself cowering between the bed and the wall, trying to crawl to safety, and I began to sweat.

"Ma'am, we've only got about an hour. Can you speed it up?" one officer asked.

I shook off the memories and began packing. Revisiting last night's horrors with my brother and the police was demoralizing, and I felt less like a victim and more like a loser. Russ stood quietly watching me gather my belongings, occasionally making small talk with the police officers. He remained stoic as I went slinking from room to room, shoving belongings into bags. I avoided eye contact with the officers, who were talking about how many times they had been to my house for prior complaints as if I weren't there. I had never called the police, but I didn't bother to engage with them. I was glad they were helping me and conceded that I deserved whatever judgment they dished out.

I gathered clothes and everything I could carry out within an hour, packing my whole life in trash bags, which seemed appropriate. The drive back to Russ's house where the guestroom awaited was quiet. I knew that Vince wouldn't try to contact me there, and there was no other way for him to reach me. Russ was more than six feet tall and athletic looking, but it wasn't his size that caused most people to be wary of him; it was his quiet, calm demeanor.

I flipped up the eye patch for a better look in the guest-room mirror, examining the matted curls that recklessly framed my pale face. What would I tell everyone? Where would I begin and who deserved to know? Vince would not give up that easily. I was sure of it.

# Chapter Nine

BEING ISOLATED IN PENNSYLVANIA FOR ALMOST TWO YEARS WITH no car and very few long-distance phone calls, I had lost track of most of my friends and family members, but in all honesty, I wasn't looking forward to sharing this ordeal with them. In the days that followed my escape, most people I knew were horrified when they saw me. They were pissed that Vince would hit me with anything, let alone a table. Maybe the injuries just seemed worse because they were on my face, very visible and personal. Bruised arms or legs were dismissible because you couldn't see them, but black eyes were undeniably hard to look at.

Contrary to what most people might have thought, the black eyes and other physical injuries weren't the worst things that happened to me. The bruises and stitches on my face were a gift. They eliminated my excuse to stay because they were so visible. They were my escape because I looked at myself in the mirror and saw them every day, a constant reminder of why I had to leave. My secret was out. I couldn't hide it anymore. But the hardest part of it all was the emotional damage that had been done. The real work of emotional healing would take time.

The stress of my physical and emotional injuries, of leaving, was taking a toll on my body, and I wasn't surprised when the next day my stomach roiled. It was Memorial Day weekend. Vince and I should have been at Cape Henlopen Beach together. We had reserved a room at the swanky Henlopen Hotel in hopes of reigniting some of the intimacy we had lost over the last stressful year. But instead of sunning on the beach, I was unpacking clothes from plastic bags like a hobo, wondering where Vince was and who was with him. This kind of torturous thought cycle didn't make me feel better, and I began to wonder if I should see a doctor. It didn't matter. It was a holiday weekend, and I had no medical insurance; it was something Vince and I hadn't gotten around to. I twisted my wadded Kleenex beyond recognition, stunned at how much had changed in just a few days.

I lay around, watching TV in the living room, smoking cigarettes, and moping. Russ walked past me numerous times, avoiding eye contact, and I did the same. Before Vince and I were married, I moved in and out of Russ's home repeatedly, each time swearing it would never happen again, that I would never go back to Vince, but I did. I always went back, and I wasn't sure this time would be different. I had promised God I would never leave Vince, but I had left him. I had broken my marriage vows, and I couldn't guarantee I wouldn't go back to him this time too.

I made it through the long weekend with enough pain in my abdomen that I decided not to wait for an appointment to see a doctor but instead flipped through the Yellow Pages to find a free clinic nearby. I drove with one good eye, found the building, and hobbled in from the parking lot, stopping just inside the door so my eye could adjust to the light. It seemed like everyone stopped talking and turned to watch me walk in as I took my place at the check-in counter.

For a moment, I wondered what they were looking at, but as my eyebrows scrunched together, the pain reminded me that I looked like a pirate.

I sat down and waited my turn, noticing my surroundings between waves of pain. The small waiting room, cluttered with chairs and children's toys, smelled like dirty clothes and the dank walls needed paint. There were screaming kids and loud parents, and the room was dreary. Some of the light bulbs were burned out but hadn't been replaced. The radio softly played elevator music, which didn't match the environment. Patients were herded in and out like cattle as the office staff managed the chaos. It was like an assembly line, which, despite the atmosphere, seemed to function seamlessly. I waited for about an hour, and when my turn came, the cramps had subsided, so I walked upright without drawing too much attention.

The doctor, a bald older man, and his nurse, a stern, matronly woman, came into the room and began the examination process with a litany of questions.

"Young lady, what happened to your face?" the doctor asked.

"I was in a car accident last week. Guess I should have been wearing a seat belt," I answered, shrugging.

Neither of them batted an eye, so I decided to use that one again. I explained the reason for my visit and answered the next stream of questions about when the pain started, where it was focused, and the level of pain, along with my personal and family history. The doctor started the physical exam, pressing on my stomach and listening with a stethoscope. After some more prodding and questions about the accident and the steering wheel, our eyes met.

With a benign gaze and monotone voice he said, "We're going to need to do an ultrasound, Mrs. Mazetti."

My senses tingled. I nodded, but my mind was busy sorting out his advice. I couldn't hear their words as I continued formulating questions that I never voiced. The stern nurse softened her gaze.

I undressed, put on a hospital gown, and waited.

The probing continued for several minutes, and the cramping began again. I held my breath through the worst spasms until the doctor stood, pushing the sheet up farther, exposing my stomach. I felt the warm gel spill down my belly and get smeared around by the probe as the doctor glared at the monitor tilted just out of my view. A few minutes later the nurse toweled the warm jelly from my abdomen.

"We're going to need to do an internal exam," he said.

As soon as my feet were in the proper position in the stirrups, the doctor patted my foot, and the nurse returned to witness the exam. I could see myself reflected in a mirror hanging from the ceiling behind the doctor. My face was pale. My mind ran laps as I looked at my own bright-white, skinny thighs trembling under the exam lamp with a strange man invisible beneath a sheet between my legs.

The doctor reappeared from time to time until finally warning me, "You're going to feel a little pressure."

I winced in pain as the nurse held my icy hands.

"So, what did you do for the holiday weekend? Anything special?" she asked.

I didn't respond.

Finally, the doctor rolled his chair away from me, turned off the light, took off his gloves, and abruptly said, "Mary, you're pregnant," and with as much compassion as he could muster, added, "And I'm afraid I couldn't find a heartbeat. I'm sorry to tell you this, but the baby is dead."

He kept talking as if he needed to fill the silence, but it was too much. My brain stalled at the word "pregnant." Before I could get my head around the thought of being pregnant, like a clap of thunder I realized he said the baby was dead. As he continued, I scrambled for understanding, mumbling something unintelligible, then just lay there, listening.

"I'd estimate it was only about eight weeks along, so you probably didn't even know you were pregnant. You'll be scheduled for a D&C tomorrow morning. The cause of death could have been any number of things, including the car accident, none of which are your fault."

His face looked empathetic, but his voice lacked compassion, and it was clear that he had not only done this many times but that he hated it.

"You and your husband can try again in a few months, but for now, let's take care of this and let your body heal. It looks like you've been through a lot already."

As he left the room, the nurse took over, speaking softly. "Honey, you and your husband will need to come back in the morning for the procedure. You'll be sedated, so you'll need a driver. The whole process will take a few hours. Take some time and work through it. I know right now it's a shock. You'll need some time to digest what's happened. We would prefer that you have some quiet time tonight. You'll be better off with just bed rest, but that's not required."

I nodded my understanding and sat silently as they began prepping the room for the next patient.

"You go ahead and get dressed now and meet us in the office just outside this room to the right. You can't miss it. Take your time."

She patted my arm on the way out, seeming genuinely sorry for me.

I had assumed that my poor diet or maybe too much smoking was the reason for my abdominal pain. I had never dreamed I might be pregnant. Since I took birth control pills and Vince and I so rarely had sex, it didn't immediately come to mind. Had I missed a period? I couldn't remember.

I sat up quietly, scooting to the end of the examination table—my legs dangled; I slumped over, the cold steel stirrups now resting on my knees.

I continued sorting information, observing my questions like an outsider rather than trying to divine answers, until I realized I wasn't alone. The nurse had come back into the room to check on me, maybe because I hadn't made it to the office in the allotted time. She found me just as she'd left me, naked from the waist down with a drape over my shoulders and my eyes glazed over.

She recognized the despair on my face and came over to comfort me, or maybe to move me along.

"Oh, honey, I know this is so hard, especially not knowing you were pregnant. It's a lot to comprehend all at once, but you'll get through this."

She reached down and gently stroked my sheet-covered shoulder.

"Come on into the office and we'll get you the names of a few therapists in case you want to talk to someone further."

I shook my head. "Wait." I gently touched her arm as she walked past me. "I wasn't in a car accident. My husband did this. He knocked me around and hit me in the face with a table. I was in the hospital last night and got stitches. I'm sorry I lied. I didn't know what to say, but I don't have anyone to come here with me tomorrow. I don't know what to do." I bit my lip as tears welled in my eyes.

"Oh my gosh, honey. I'm so sorry. Okay, you sit tight. I'm going to get the doctor and see how we can help you."

A new protocol took over. People began moving around me with purpose, heightening my anxiety level until the doctor came back into the room. He looked annoyed.

"Mrs. Mazetti, it seems maybe you left out a few things when we spoke before. Let's talk about options. We can still do this tomorrow and you can bring anybody you want with you. You will need a driver, but whoever you choose for comfort is up to you. If you prefer, we could perform the procedure here today, but if you choose to do it now, you won't have anesthesia. We'll numb the area so you won't have any pain. The upside is that it would be dispensed of quickly, and you'll be able to drive home from here in a few hours. It's up to you."

I never considered coming back with a support person or taking the time to weigh my options. I nodded in agreement as the nurse shoved a clipboard and pen in front of me with a practiced smile of compassion on her face, asking me to sign next to the X.

"I'd do the same thing if I were you, honey," she whispered. I silently wished she was me as I signed the papers.

I sat alone waiting until the nurse poked her head in to check on me after about an hour.

"We're ready if you are," she said as they wheeled me down the hall to another room. It looked like a sterile operating room, but on a smaller scale. I never imagined such a large room in what seemed, from the front office's appearance, to be a small building. It was spacious and empty like a dance floor before 10:00 p.m. but with intense lighting like a football stadium.

The nurse and a few other people arrived, all wearing scrubs and masks over their faces, talking about what they had done over the holiday weekend. I became lost in thought. Vince was probably getting home from the beach and sobering up. I resented having to go through this alone, but I already felt like such a failure that I didn't know if I could handle the judgment that might come from telling anyone else. I wanted to be alone but not lonely.

This was to be my first-ever medical procedure, and it wasn't how I had envisioned my first miraculous experience of pregnancy. I listened intently as the nurse walked me through the procedure; I pulled the sheet around my shoulders as she talked, embarrassed by my nudity. A lump in my throat prevented me from speaking, so I just nodded each time the doctor asked a question that required a response. This process wasn't much different from the exam aside from this new wave of emotions. The drape across my thighs slipped slightly down my calf, and two bright, round halogen lights shone so brightly that I was blinded even through the sheets. My body trembled.

The procedure was about to begin.

"You're going to feel a pinch now, honey," the nurse said as she held my hand and hovered at my head, smiling sweetly down at me.

The cramping was immediate, excruciating even with whatever numbing agent they had used, and I squeezed her hand, wondering if they had begun too soon.

With each wave of pain, I squeezed, taking a deep breath, and she squeezed back and whispered, "You're doing fine, sweetie."

She coached me through each wave as I listened to the sounds of the machines and watched my legs tremble. I wept quietly.

I tried in vain to pinpoint the exact time of conception, knowing our romantic relationship had become infrequent, with intimacy happening only out of either duty or desperation. Having sex to avoid an argument left me feeling cheap, the act itself fake and unfulfilling. Physical connection seemed like the only thing I had to offer, but going along with Vince's advances had left me feeling violated, and resentment built up around our sex life. I needed intimacy to connect sexually, and he needed sex to feel intimate—a terrible catch-22. *How did it get so complicated?* I wondered, staring into the lights.

The nurse smiled, murmuring, "You're doing fine."

It was too early to determine the sex of the baby and no birth certificate would be issued to legitimize its existence or my misery. Alone in what I assumed was a recovery room, I listened as people shuffled around outside. The friendly banter ticked along for everyone but me. I drifted blindly through the fog like a wayward ship seeking a lighthouse until I ran aground into the present moment, voices growing louder as they approached with discharge paperwork.

Three hours later, I walked down the sidewalk toward the car I had borrowed from my brother. I carried prescriptions in one hand and a fistful of papers in the other, describing what I should expect and what to do in case of an emergency. I passed people in the parking lot and felt like they all knew my secret; I made a conscious effort not to make eye contact with anyone. None of the papers I carried out of the clinic that day told me how this event would affect my emotional state, and somehow, I knew my body would never bear another child. I climbed into the car, turned the key in the ignition, and drove away, stopping at red lights, using turn signals, and maintaining a reasonable speed until I pulled into the driveway like nothing ever happened.

I would never have thought anyone could love a child that had never been born, having no memories or life experiences to grieve. Maybe it wasn't love but regret, or perhaps just me feeling sorry for myself, but whatever it was, I will never forget the depth of my emptiness and how mismatched it felt compared to that beautiful, sunny day.

# Chapter Ten

I was fortunate to find an accounting job with Carlton Construction, a nearby residential home-building company. It was a small, family-owned business and a good job. It would help me get back on track.

The construction industry was close-knit, and word spread fast among jobsites, so it wasn't long before Vince's growing reputation for being a hothead left him without labor and new contracts. He had his ear to the ground, too, and within a week of my taking the job with Carlton, he knew where I worked. He called the office relentlessly, and ignoring him became increasingly difficult.

Each call was an attempt to convince me to come home. Even though my body was still healing from the loss of a baby at his hands, I struggled. Part of me wanted to tell him about the baby, so I would not have to go through the pain alone, and the other part of me wanted him to feel guilty for what he had done. I wanted to hear his pleas for forgiveness, and I wanted him to hurt like I was hurting. I was aware of how messed up that was. I wanted to believe his promises, and during weaker moments, I still had hope. I was a wreck, a bona fide basket case. Talking to him and holding out hope was like having a loose tooth. I knew it would hurt, but I couldn't stop wiggling it.

One of those particularly hopeful days, Vince called, begging to see me; his calls were wearing me down.

"What's going on?" my boss, Anne, mouthed to me, seeing the expression on my face as I stammered, trying to get off the phone.

Muddled explanations and defensive pleas gushed. "He's been calling and begging me to come back almost every day. He won't take no for an answer. I don't want to talk to him, and I need this job. I'm sorry. I know it's been interfering with my work, but I'm making progress. I'll threaten to call the police or something."

I gave her a thumbnail sketch of how my life had been going. When I finished, she draped her arm over my shoulder and escorted me to see Mr. Carlton, who gave me the day off and promised to intervene on my behalf from an employer's position.

I don't know what Mr. Carlton did for me, but I never received another call from Vince. Finally, my wounds began to heal. The eye patch came off, the stitches were removed, the bruises healed, and I started to at least look normal again. Having a job helped me to feel normal on the inside; the healing came slowly, but it came.

As the weeks passed I grew stronger, and the scars became a reminder right between the eyes, literally and figuratively, of what I had gone through. Well-meaning friends and family members shared their concerns, but with no clue about what it was like to be in that situation and without checking their filters, said things under their breath that did more harm than good. The coffee talk went on without me but about me. I listened in horror, shocked that I could be related to some of these people, and resolved myself to check my freaking DNA at some point.

"I would have kicked his ass."

"She should have left him a long time ago."

"That never would've happened to me."

"What the hell is wrong with her?"

I had done my share of judging, so I guess I didn't blame them, but when you go through trauma without a solid, supportive family, you learn to just buck up and move on.

I made it a point to focus on what I needed to do. I needed a job and a place to live. Russ was great, and his door was always open, but

I had imposed upon him so many times during my turbulent relationship that I had started calling his Delaware house my summer home. I didn't want to impose upon him again, but I had nowhere else to go, and family is family, so until I finished licking my wounds, I had a safe place to be, and I was grateful.

My head cleared, and I began the process of figuring out what would come next. I hired a lawyer in August, just three months after the assault, using settlement money I received from a car accident that had happened over the summer. I wanted to be sure I didn't back out again. And for me, asking for help was progress. I walked into the law office having no idea what to expect. It was a storefront property that sat on a four-lane highway. The office lobby was sparsely furnished like they might need to pack up and leave in the middle of the night, but they met my budget. I walked up to the receptionist's desk.

"Hi, I'm Mary Mazetti. I have an appointment."

She picked up the phone, letting someone know I was there.

A middle-aged man in a good suit and bad toupee appeared, escorted me to a private office, and motioned for me to sit. He slid a business card across the table and began his pitch.

"Mrs. Mazetti, I'm Mark Wilkins. I understand you are seeking a divorce."

I nodded.

"Let me tell you a little about how the process works. Divorce proceedings in Pennsylvania require a two-year separation period unless we can prove fault. Some people don't want to wait either because children are involved or they are disputing property, such as the primary domicile. These cases can take longer to resolve. If you choose to move forward now, we can do that, but it will require a hearing where we will have to prove cause. If you can wait, it will be a lot easier and cheaper. Did he do that to you?" He motioned to my face while jotting down something on a notepad. I nodded and started to speak, but before I could, he continued.

"Then we shouldn't have any trouble proving fault. We'll need some pictures of your injuries to present as evidence. Mr. Mazetti will have the right to be in court, and he can present any evidence in his defense that he feels is pertinent."

He continued gathering information over the next half hour, then put his pen down.

"Well, since you rented the house and you don't have any real property, investments, children, or cash, it won't be complicated. So, you can wait two years or we can move forward with proving fault."

I shrank back in the chair as he evaluated my net worth, but I knew I didn't want to wait. I chose to move forward immediately. I explained that there had been a police report to support my injuries, but that Vince hadn't been arrested. Mr. Wilkins didn't react but just slid some papers in my direction for a signature. I signed, handed over the last bit of money I had, and left. As hard as it had been to describe the details of my relationship with Vince to him and to hear them reflected back to me, I felt empowered and supported. I was taking control of my life.

# Chapter Eleven

AUNT RUTH'S CANCER DIAGNOSIS SEEMED UNFAIR, BUT AFTER SPEND-ing more than my lifetime smoking cigarettes, I suppose she wasn't surprised. She had always been unflappable, swearing she didn't need anything even with her illness, but I sensed an uncharacteristic loneliness in her.

Deciding that neither of us should be alone, I packed up and moved out of Russ's house and into the spare bedroom at Aunt Ruth's. She lived in a small town in Pennsylvania, which was closer to my work. We both felt abandoned, angry, and resentful, and since misery loves company, we leaned on each other for a while. She was good company for me, and taking care of her took my mind off my problems. Our afternoon errands soon became a snapshot of our relationship.

"I need to stop at the bank and get some cash," Aunt Ruth said.

"Don't you have a debit card?"

"Yeah, I have one."

"Then how come you need to go to the bank?"

"My card's in my safe deposit box."

"Oh, how are you gonna—" I stopped myself and chuckled. "What do you want to do today?"

"Well, I always wanted to go to a museum. I think I would enjoy that, but I'm too tired today. I need to go to the bank."

"Okay, did you need to get your debit card?"

"No, it's safe right where it is. I need to make a withdrawal. I'm going to pay for karate lessons so you can defend yourself in your next relationship."

She had a great sense of humor, and I never saw the jokes coming. We drew lots of attention, laughing on that sunny afternoon as we pumped gas, which she had never done before since Uncle Joe always pumped it for her, but when he passed, she paid a little more to have the attendant do it. Now that she tried it for herself, she felt it was overrated.

She was a modest woman and was not prone to outward displays of affection, but there was a moment that night after our errands when she hugged me, just for a second and then let go. It wouldn't have been significant to most people, but to me it was as warm and vulnerable as I ever remembered her being, and I will always cherish that moment. She taught me a few things about living while she was busy dying.

As her last days came nearer, she was made as comfortable and pain-free as anyone who's dying from lung cancer can be. She fought the good fight, as they say, until November 16, 1990, just six months after her diagnosis.

Aunt Ruth's passing and the months leading to it taught me how important it was to plan and balance working, laughing, living, and being grateful. She left me with the awareness that money won't make you happy unless you already are. She died with plenty of money and a shortage of good memories, which made me sad but left me determined to learn from someone else's mistakes for once in my life. Her son, Jerry, who lived nearby with his wife, contacted me a month later regarding her estate. Aunt Ruth had made good on her promise to leave money for karate lessons. She always had to have the last laugh.

Without Aunt Ruth to care for, I temporarily moved back in with Russ. He was gracious as usual, but it was time I relieved him of the perceived responsibility of caring for his sisters. I couldn't stay in a perpetual state of recovery, going from one set of crappy circumstances to another and using him as a safety net; he deserved to move on with his own life.

The six months I spent with Aunt Ruth had been healing for me, and I launched into my newfound freedom by renting an apartment. The drive to Exton, Pennsylvania, for work grew old quickly, and I was happy to land an accounting job closer to my new home in Newark, Delaware. My new job paid enough for me to afford rent and buy a cheap used car.

The repeated commercials I saw for tae kwon do were divinely inspired, as if Aunt Ruth were paying a visit. Though I knew she had been joking, self-defense training seemed like a good idea, and images of Vince easily tossing me around motivated me further; besides, it looked like fun, something that had been missing from my life for a while, so I signed up.

Being a pack-a-day smoker, I was an unlikely candidate for martial arts training. Each time I lit up, I thought of Aunt Ruth, which bothered me. Weirdly, cigarettes were the one constant in my life. Being out of cigarettes was one of the few things that would drag me out of bed at three in the morning to drive to the nearest Wawa. I tried everything to quit—gum, pills, patches—but nothing worked. Every time I tried, I went through ugly mood swings, overeating, guilt, and self-judgment; I was constantly disappointed in myself.

Cigarette addiction was something that controlled me. Finally, I decided I hadn't ended an abusive relationship only to beat myself up, so I chose not to smoke, and that's how I finally walked away from smoking a few months after her passing. I left an entire pack of cigarettes on my dresser. I had a choice every day to smoke or not to.

Mr. Wilkins couldn't locate Vince to serve the divorce papers, so he placed ads in newspapers in every town and state where he might be living, advising him of the divorce hearing.

I had all the confidence in the world in my decision until the court date, June 5, 1991. I sat in the courtroom picking my nails until they bled.

"Do you see Mr. Mazetti here, Mary?" Mr. Wilkins asked.

"No, he's not here."

"The judge will wait an hour for him. If he doesn't show in that time, then we will present our case to the judge without Vince, and the judge will decide. That's good for you."

"Great," I said, smiling uneasily.

For the next excruciating hour, I scoured the courtroom, jumping out of my skin each time the door opened or closed, praying Vince wouldn't show. Mr. Wilkins wandered away, leaving me alone in a room full of divorcing couples who were trading barbs and being admonished by the judge. I watched how quickly two people's lives dissolved into nothingness, waiting my turn to prove I shouldn't be married.

When my name was called, Mr. Wilkins returned to my side and told the judge we were ready to proceed. When Vince's name was called, no one responded and the judge considered whether to reschedule. Mr. Wilkins approached the bench, offered evidence that he had made every effort to serve Vince notice, and submitted the photographs of my injuries as his motive for ignoring the summons. The judge was moved by the photographs and the accompanying police report and addressed me directly.

"Mrs. Mazetti, when is the last time you saw your husband?"

"It was on the night of the assault, sir," I replied.

The divorce was granted, and he even added terms stating that Vince would be responsible for all remaining marital bills since he had not felt it necessary to tell his side of the story.

I wasn't surprised that Vince didn't show. He did all of his fighting with me. He wouldn't have been as confident standing before a judge in a courtroom full of men in suits. I wondered if Mr. Wilkins, when seeking him for the divorce, had gotten close to finding him and had rattled his cage.

The divorce was finalized on September 13, 1991. I took back my maiden name, Sweeney, filed the papers in a shoebox, placed the box on the top shelf in the back of my closet, and moved on. The time from the wedding day to the divorce decree was just shy of three years. My marriage, and everything that came with it, was over, and it was already beginning to feel like something that had happened to someone else.

I started training two or three nights a week in tae kwon do, and my body ached after every class. I met lots of new people and learned the curriculum quickly. I was desperate for structure. Everything in my life was a disorganized mess, and I needed the order that tae kwon do offered. With it, I fell into a steady routine.

My new life began with a fitness plan and tae kwon do competitions. I felt silly at my first competition because I stood about three feet taller than most beginner competitors, who were all under twelve years of age. I wandered around the gymnasium watching the others compete until my turn came. A fellow yellow belt nearly tripped over me as I bent over to straighten my pant leg. It was Franny! I hadn't seen him since Vince and I separated.

"Hey, watch it, clumsy," I said, laughing.

Franny staggered a bit with a look of confusion, but then grabbed me in a bear hug and swept me off my feet with a beautiful toothy grin.

"Wow! What are you doing here?" he asked as he put me down.

"Isn't it obvious? The outfit is stunning," I joked. "Vince isn't here, is he?"

"No, he moved to Colorado after you guys broke up. It's great to see you! You are a sight for sore eyes," he added. "Last I heard, Vince was staying with his mom. He's afraid he'll get arrested if he comes back to Delaware, but he should be more worried about what I would do to him. I can't tell you how sorry I am about what he did to you, Mary."

The sensitive nature of the conversation was out of sync with the echoing shouts and smacking slaps of hand and foot gear connecting with their intended targets. I smiled a thank-you, and he smirked, shaking his head.

"He was such a fool," he said.

I changed the subject. "I didn't know you took tae kwon do. When did you start?"

"Oh, I've learned a few things here and there, but I just started taking lessons about six months ago. As you can see, I'm sporting this very impressive yellow belt." He laughed.

We watched one another compete and it was clear that we were both beginners, but we each had some natural athletic ability. Franny cheered me on from the sidelines and it felt euphoric. I knew it was something Vince would never have done. We chatted after the competition, and as we walked outside, he lit a cigarette. I smiled, secretly feeling better about myself, and finding it interesting how little we talked about Vince. I didn't care what that meant. We hugged, and he kissed me on the cheek as we exchanged phone numbers, promising to keep in touch.

Franny was roguishly handsome, like Mel Gibson, tall with curly brown hair and light-green eyes. He was the best man at my wedding, in more ways than one. We began seeing each other casually, and I battled feelings of guilt over whether Franny was my get-over or get-even guy. I didn't want to use him, but he was easy to be with, so I pushed those thoughts from my mind, deciding to enjoy him for however long it lasted. Having just ended a relationship himself, he felt the same way. Being with him was comfortable, and I needed someone sweet who understood me and wouldn't ask for more than I had to offer. With all of his charm and our undeniable chemistry, Franny was a link to my past. I saw him as the bad boy I never had, wild and unpredictable, and to him, I was the settled, responsible partner he was searching for. He wanted to be more like me, and I wanted to be more like him.

There wasn't an exact end date for what we had. There was no breakup. We just drifted away like clouds in the sky, maintaining an intense admiration for each other. It was healing. Things might have been different if the timing had been right. We would never know.

# Chapter Twelve

I looked forward to going to tae kwon do and took every class I could make. The dojo smelled like dirty sweat socks, and the bright fluorescent lights paired with the wall of mirrors made the room appear much larger than it was. One Tuesday night I checked my hair in the mirror as I carried my gear bag containing my spongy red head, hand, and shin protection inside, anticipating an opportunity to spar. I stopped and looked through the glass doors to watch the end of one class and see who would teach tonight.

Maria Friswell was a super talented black belt who taught a few nights a week. I watched her classes and the dynamics between her and her male counterparts with awe. She was so skilled that some guys didn't want to spar with her, but some couldn't wait. I had never seen men show this kind of respect to a woman before, and it was inspiring. When I heard that she had earned a wild card spot in the Barcelona Olympics, I understood why they respected her and why they didn't want to tangle with her. No man wanted to be knocked down by a woman. She dropped them to the mat with thighs the size of tree trunks and dished out black eyes like badges of honor; her opponent would return to their feet, bow at the waist, touch gloves, and thank her for the beating they had received.

Her sense of humor and ready smile caused people to underestimate her abilities. She made the sport look easy, and I tried to make it to the gym on the nights she taught classes. Her warm-up drills were consistent. We did tons of push-ups, kicks, and stretches before learning any new material. That Tuesday night, we worked on blocking kicks and punches with our hands and arms.

"Keep your hands up," she hollered at me for probably the fifth time. "You let them drop when you kick. Don't do that. You're exposing your face."

Her voice echoed through the gym as I shouted back, "Yes, ma'am."

She stepped in and took over for my sparring partner, placing my hands in the correct position once again, in front of my face with my elbows nearly touching my rib bones. As we sparred, my gloved hands lowered little by little until they were nearly at waist level again, and Maria landed a roundhouse kick, pounding me above my weaker right eye.

The impact knocked me to the floor, and my goofy, red head protector swiveled to the side like it was on a cartoon character. Maria helped me up, and I shook off the hit, bowed at the waist, and touched gloves with her, slurping spit through my mouthpiece.

"Oh my God! Are you all right? I'm so sorry. I tried to pull my kick, but I had already committed. I'm sorry. Are you hurt?" she asked.

"No, ma'am. Thank you, ma'am. I guess I shouldn't block it with my face, huh? Bet I won't do that again."

She took a bit of razzing from some of the class for beating up a lowly yellow belt, which she took gracefully, and we became fast friends. Unlike boys, girls don't typically get into schoolyard fights, so knowing that I could survive being hit in the face and get back into the fight would serve me well in the future.

Maria was an officer with the New Castle County Police, and I was curious.

"Hey, how long have you been a cop, Maria?" I asked.

"Oh, almost three years," she said. "What do you do?"

"I do accounting work for a construction company."

"Oh, that's interesting," she said, her head bobbing up and down.

"No, not really. It's boring."

"Hey, if you're bored, apply for a job with us. You'll never be bored again and we're hiring."

"I'm not sure I'm cut out for that kind of work, but I'm flattered that you think I could do it. If I wanted to, though, how would I go about applying?"

I was making conversation more than actually considering the possibility of working with the police department, but she walked me through the process anyway.

"Why don't you start by doing a ride-along with me? You'll get to see what it's like firsthand and then decide whether it's something you might like to do."

"Sounds exciting," I said. "I didn't know they did that sort of thing."

"Yeah, all the time. No better way to see if it's right for you. Some people want to go back to headquarters after the first hour; they've seen enough. But some folks know then and there that they love it. You should try it and see for yourself."

I signed up for a ride-along on an evening shift in the spring. At almost ten o'clock at night, I arrived in the police station's lobby and waited until a chatty young man in civilian clothes came to get me.

"Right down this hallway, Ms. Sweeney. We call this area 'mahogany row' because staff members with mahogany desks have offices here. This building used to be an elementary school. We need a new building. This place is too small."

Once he mentioned it, I could envision classrooms along both sides of the long hallway that were now offices. The brown, wood-paneled walls reminded me of my grandma's house, complete with the musty smell I remembered from my childhood. Trophy cases that once displayed only the best science projects now housed mannequins wearing uniforms and police equipment—old stuff from many years ago.

The polite young man handed me off to a uniformed police officer, and I sat down in the last row of what turned out to be the roll call room. It was noisy and crowded, with thirty-seven uniformed cops sitting in the rows ahead of me and three men, who were supervisors, seated at a table facing us. It was just like *Hill Street Blues*, and I smiled to myself in anticipation.

I signed a liability waiver, agreeing that no one would sue if I got killed, which wasn't very reassuring but I figured it was a formality. Maria sat beside me in uniform and described what was happening in a low, whispering voice.

"Okay, so we have roll call every night. Each squad rotates with the same officers every week. This is A squad. The men up front are the supervisors, also referred to as white shirts, for obvious reasons, and the rest of us in the rows are road cops like me," she said.

At just that moment, one of the men in a white uniform shirt stood up. "Line up!" he barked.

The officers lined up for inspection along the wall, snapping to attention. Their uniforms were freshly pressed, light brown slacks with yellow stripes down each leg. Their shirts were chocolate brown, and their buttons, snaps, and badges glistened gold. The black gun belt carried all sorts of accessories and looked heavy. I was immediately taken in by how they all stood the same, shoulders square and straight, eyes forward, like marines at boot camp. They exuded confidence. I wondered for a moment what I would look like in the uniform, doubting I could pull off the same fearless appearance. There was an air of superiority among them that made me feel like the outsider that I was. I wondered if it was their confidence or my lack of it that created that feeling. It was probably both.

Some officers wore rows of stripes on their sleeves and various medals on their chests while others had none. The presence of decorations or lack thereof seemed to coincide with their ages. Officers without decoration looked like teenagers, barely old enough to drive, while the others sported gray hair and extra weight around the middle. All the officers clutched their campaign hats in their left hands with small gold badges facing out, their faces stoic.

The room fell silent until the head guy shouted, "Weapons inspection!" and everyone quickly drew their guns out of their holsters, pointing them straight up in the air—a bit startling, at first. I sat still, watching wide-eyed as they unloaded their guns, and the lieutenant checked them inside and out.

"He's looking for imperfections," Maria whispered as he walked around each officer, looking at their shirts and trousers, flicking lint off hats, and asking them questions at a level I strained to hear.

"Jackson, that looks like the same tie you got right out of the academy fifteen years ago. Get a new one for God's sake. It looks like hell."

"Yes, sir," the officer responded, his eyes still glued to the imaginary spot on the wall in front of him.

This process continued until he made his way to the end of the line and, in a normal tone, ordered, "At ease. Take a seat."

Jackson got a death stare from the other officers as they made their way back to their chairs, and I felt empathy for him for being singled out.

"The lieutenant will brief us on what happened since we last worked," Maria whispered.

I listened excitedly to details about people stealing from cars, committing burglaries, and robbing a pizza delivery guy until one of the officers made an off-color joke, and the lieutenant yelled at him.

"Hey, joker, watch it! We have a civilian in the room tonight."

My heart stopped. The lieutenant was referring to me, and my face blazed red as everyone turned around to look, smiling and laughing at the joke I hadn't heard; I felt stupid but smiled knowingly, trying to look like I got it but wasn't offended.

"Check the front desk for returned paperwork before you leave. Right turns only," the lieutenant said, ending the roll call.

I noticed the front desk, littered with police reports that needed to be corrected, as officers crowded around looking for their names, making faces in disagreement or annoyance. The entire process was over in about fifteen minutes and we were out the door.

"What does right turn only mean, Maria?"

She laughed and explained as we walked. "Well, the parking lot is out the door to the right. Lieutenant is telling them not to fool around but to get their butts out of the building and go to work."

Maria and I waited for a man to appear from behind a cage, and she explained, "There aren't enough shotguns to go around, so if you want one, you have to check it out of the arms room. It's first come, first served. We'll be working up north and backup can be a while getting to us, so I always get a shotgun if I can." The arms officer recorded the serial number, sliding the gun through a small opening in the cage along with a box of ammo.

"There aren't enough cars to go around either, so we have to share them, and getting out of roll call quickly usually gets you a better car. The shifts are staggered, so when one shift ends, another begins, and the previous shift turn their cars over to the next squad. We're the next squad to take over." She gestured to our car.

It was chaos, like a supermarket parking lot the night before Thanksgiving. The oncoming shift inspected their vehicles for new damage and ensured the horns and sirens worked. It was loud, and I jumped each time a siren blared, my heart racing even though I knew they were just being tested. I imagined what it would be like to be in a situation where they were needed and wondered if I might find out tonight. The officers joked with each other and made small talk throughout the process, chattering about sports and weekend entertainment. The uniforms made them look serious, but their demeanor was lighthearted, and I was surprised that they seemed like ordinary people.

It was a beautiful spring night, and the sweet smell of honeysuckle drifted from somewhere along the fence line. Maria fiddled with the keys, handing me a bulletproof vest just before I climbed into the passenger seat, the two simultaneous experiences in direct conflict with each other.

"Here, put this on over your shirt," she said.

"This piece of fabric, less than an inch thick, is going to stop a bullet?" I asked, pulling it over my head and tightening the Velcro straps. I took the spare set of car keys she handed me, and she placed the shotgun in the trunk.

"Let's hope we don't find out," she said.

I estimated the weight of the vest, flashlight, uniform, boots, and handgun to be about thirty pounds. With all that and the gun belt, I would weigh 140 pounds, which was almost a 30 percent increase in my weight. How could anyone function with this much added weight and bulk?

"If anything happens to me tonight, get in the car, push this button, and call on the radio '10-40' for help. Can you remember that?"

"10-40," I repeated, wondering if the paper I signed wasn't a formality.

"Good. 10-40 is police code for officer down or officer needs assistance, and they'll come like manna from heaven. At that point, grab the shotgun from the trunk and defend yourself," she said.

"Won't I get in trouble if I shoot your shotgun?"

"Better to be judged by twelve than carried out by six," she answered. A sobering thought.

I looked around the car, surprised by how cramped it felt inside. A steel cage separated us from the back seat, and with all her equipment, law books, flashlights, lunch box, and boxes of paperwork, there was barely room for us. We had just gotten situated in the seats when the first call came in on the radio.

"It's a domestic complaint," Maria said.

I had no idea how she got that from the garble I just heard on the radio, but she scribbled the address on a notepad suctioned to the windshield, and we were off. She described the call to me as she drove.

"A lady just called and reported that her boyfriend was hitting her and pulling her hair. We get lots of these kinds of calls, but it's hard to tell what's going on until you get there."

I knew how fast this kind of situation could get out of hand based on my experience with Vince, and I had an uncomfortable feeling in the pit of my stomach. Filled with trepidation and dread, I wanted to get there faster to help the poor lady. We arrived within two minutes, which seemed like an eternity as I replayed scenes from my own experience. Adrenaline shrieked through my body as we jumped out of the car and ran toward the apartment. I sprinted alongside Maria, but couldn't keep up. Just ten feet from the apartment building's entry door, a man wearing dirty jeans, a wifebeater, and no shoes ran out the door toward us.

Maria yelled, "Stop."

Her hand bolted to her side, resting on her handgun still in the holster as the sweaty man stopped abruptly in front of her, ten feet from me.

"Slow down now. Let me see your hands."

Her commanding voice and rigid posture were at odds with how I knew her, and I was surprised to notice that I stopped, too, frozen in place. My hands trembled as adrenaline coursed through my veins, and everything seemed to unfold in slow motion.

He shoved his hands at her, palms up.

"Good—keep them where I can see them. What's your name, sir? What happened in there?"

Maria quickly moved closer to him and began patting down his pants pockets while talking to him in a slow, calm voice.

My heart pounded and my mouth was suddenly parched as I watched and listened in silence. When other officers arrived, I nervously backed out of the way, and they walked up the grassy hill to help. They didn't know who I was, and Maria waved them off. It was clear that I probably shouldn't have been in this situation, but I was wearing a vest, so they passed me by as one of the good guys.

*Take a breath, Mary*, I told myself, which settled me enough to hear the man explain his side of the story.

"We had an argument," he yelled. "I didn't touch her! She's inside. Go see for yourself. She does this all the time. You guys are always looking for something on me, but I didn't do nothing."

The other officers rushed inside the apartment to check on the woman. I stayed with Maria, who began asking questions.

"Then why were you running?" Maria asked, which now seemed like a brilliant question that I hadn't even considered.

"I've got a bench warrant." He turned his head and spat on the ground. "It's just traffic shit. It's no big deal, but I don't want to go to jail, and I ain't got no money, so I ran. Don't lock me up, man. It's Friday night, man. If you lock me up tonight, I won't get out till Monday. I didn't touch her. She just wants me out—I swear, seriously. Give me a break, man. I'll leave. I won't be no trouble. I promise."

I didn't notice Maria pulling the handcuffs from her belt, but she had him cuffed so fast, he didn't have time to protest. All the while, she spoke to him in a smooth, even tone, asking questions and acknowledging his responses.

"Relax, buddy, we'll figure this out."

The first thing I noticed was that she didn't seem like an adversary. They were just two people talking. I listened intently, absorbing her tone, style, and manner. Whatever happened in the apartment didn't call for an arrest, and the whole thing ended with the other officers taking the man to court for his outstanding warrant.

For a moment, I wondered what would have happened if I had called the police on one of the nights that Vince had pushed me around. Would he have been arrested? Would I have gotten out sooner?

It was beginning to get dark as we walked back to her car.

"I have a ton of questions, but I need to go to the bathroom," I admitted sheepishly.

"It's the adrenaline rush," Maria explained. "There's an all-night coffee shop up the road. It's a clean spot, and they're police friendly. It's the only thing open all night. Grab us a cup of joe, and we'll relocate to a park up the street to do the paperwork."

After I relieved my bursting bladder and we both had coffee in hand, Maria began to explain what she had done and why. I fired questions at warp speed, and she laughed at my excitement and inexperience.

"Why didn't he get arrested? Why didn't you read him his rights? Was she hurt? What if he hadn't stopped when you told him to? Is it always like this? Where did those other cops come from, and how come one was wearing a blue uniform?"

By the time Maria began answering my questions, my heart rate had returned to normal. I was astonished at how fast that whole thing had unraveled. I was also completely hooked! Maria had the power to make a life-changing decision for that lady. Thankfully, no force was necessary, but at that moment, Maria was a superhero. Those officers really made a difference in that situation. Maybe the woman would never see that guy again, I didn't know, but there would be a record of the incident in case something happened again. Maria wasn't alone; there was a team working together for that lady. I wanted to make this kind of difference, to be a part of that team. *This job was for me.*

Maria interrupted the questioning with a few directives.

"Hey, I probably shouldn't have let you get out on that call, but I've seen you spar and felt like you would be all right. I might not let you out on a different call, so don't be insulted if I tell you to stay put. If you have to stay in the car, I'll brief you when I get back. Remember our call sign, fourteen Adam one, and listen for me on the radio. Got it?"

"Hey, thanks, Maria." I nodded vigorously. "I learned a lot and kind of figured you put yourself out there for me," I said. "Thanks. I'll try to stay out of your way, but I'll be there if you need me." I probably should have told her that I had been paralyzed and couldn't have moved if I wanted to.

The rest of the night was a mix of traffic stops and disorderly conduct disputes, and according to Maria, it was a slow night. For me, each complaint was the Lindbergh kidnapping, dramatic and exciting, compared to my boring accounting job. Each call was unpredictable, and the variety of problems kept me intrigued. At six in the morning, the end of our shift came too soon, and there was no way I would sleep. I had no idea that people walked the streets at 4:00 a.m. while I was tucked safely in my bed, but they did.

"So, what do you think, kiddo?" Maria asked, already knowing the answer.

I never hesitated.

"I love it. I want to do this for a living. I've never been in any trouble, not even a traffic ticket. There's no college requirement?" I asked.

"If you want to do this, you should get a degree because the hiring process is competitive. There will be a thousand applicants for about forty jobs. It would be a good time for you to get in, though, because affirmative action is in full swing, and the county police is recruiting women big-time."

I smiled at her and shook my head. "That might be the first lucky break I've ever had, but why would they hire me? I would love to be a police officer, and I'm excited about the idea, but what do I have to offer? I've never done anything like this. I've managed a store, and I've done accounting work, both of which bored me to death, but how does that make me a good candidate for a police officer position?"

"Well, you're thirty years old and have plenty of life experience, unlike some of the kids coming right out of college," she said. "You're fit and can take care of yourself, having martial arts training. I hate to remind you, but your experience with Vince gives you a personal perspective on domestic violence situations. Who can tell you what that's like? Nobody! Don't sell yourself short, kid. It's one thing to read about it and quite another to have lived through it, but I don't need to tell you that. Listen, don't worry about it. I didn't have any experience before I started the job either. If you get hired, they'll teach you everything you need to know in the police academy."

Maria was so encouraging and supportive that I began to consider it possible. Why not me? It was worth a shot. It would be the first time in my life that I had done a job I really wanted to do, and that would be refreshing. I stayed up most of the day, reliving each moment and imagining what it would be like to redefine my life. Maria was right. I considered my personal history a deficit, but that was a mistake. It was a valuable experience to take to the table. Maybe I could create a new life for myself, one of confidence and personal power. If I could do this for a living, maybe I could help someone the way Sarah, the nurse on that awful night, had helped me. Maybe I could help some poor soul get out of an awful relationship and save her years of grief.

I knew I needed to develop healthy lifestyle habits, but I had no idea what that might look like. Martial arts became the first step, and it seemed like that was all it took. I took one step forward, and even though I wasn't sure it was the right step, the action itself was empowering. Delaware Technical Community College became the next step, and from there, one tiny step at a time, everything changed. Things were going well, and I was reasonably happy. More importantly, I had a goal and I was going for it. There was no way I could have looked at the whole picture and proceeded with confidence. It was too big, but I could take that one small step. That was doable.

My relationship with Del Tech was a love-hate one, but it was not without its charm. I found the college atmosphere a great social experience. Meeting new people was a refreshing change after several years of being isolated. I was exhausted by the end of each day, but my grades were good, and the work came easily. College life also helped me to ease back into the dating pool. I didn't know what I wanted in a relationship, but I knew what I didn't like, so that became my new standard. My life was packed with school, tae kwon do, friends, and the occasional short-term boyfriend.

One of my professors quoted Mark Twain, who said, "The two most important days in your life are the day you were born and the day you find out why." This rang true for me. Meeting Maria, someone who was doing the job she loved just because she wanted to, was inspiring and allowed me to dream that the same might be possible for me. Once I took that first step, the next one presented itself with clarity and seemingly little effort. I approached all of this with absolute certainty that I was where I should be. I was sure to be hired as a police officer. *I just knew.*

# Chapter Thirteen

I MOVED STEADILY THROUGH THE RANKS IN TAE KWON DO. DOUG, a new martial arts instructor with impressive, undeniable talent, came into the program. He was the kind of guy that made tae kwon do look natural—like it was a gift, rather than the result of years of hard work; his moves looked so crisp and clean. He didn't catch my eye at first, but something about him intrigued me. I think it was the way he carried himself with confidence, not with a swagger, but more like a purposeful walk, with no wasted energy. His perfectionism defined the term "martial artist." He was graceful like a dancer or a figure skater, and I enjoyed watching him move.

I started taking classes with him, and most of the time I felt awkward, like a gangly teenager who doesn't know where her feet are yet, stabbing out moves that looked rigid rather than fluid. I watched him train, performing the same move over and over until he got it right, no matter how long it took. When he worked on a technique, he didn't notice anyone else in the room, just him and his desire to be perfect. I watched him like a stalker, pretending to stretch, praying he was unaware of my presence as he broke down each series of moves and put them back together again. It was a thing of beauty that I had never seen.

Doug was reserved. Though he chatted with the other instructors, he didn't socialize with anyone else. Still, students flocked to him at the end of every class, asking questions. Clearly, they wanted to be with him. He joked and laughed, but his face turned red, and he seemed uncomfortable with the attention. *How endearing*, I thought.

Doug taught classes every Friday night and I noticed that every other Friday, a woman dropped two kids off at the gym. She was young and attractive but always looked tired. Doug approached her, and I noticed the body language between them was tense. I watched him as he stood with his arms folded across his chest, avoiding eye contact, nervously shifting from one foot to the other. She handed him papers and kissed the children. They were adorable little buggers, timidly clinging to Doug's leg as he nervously chewed his top lip and looked around the gym as he and the woman spoke; there were no kisses on the cheek between them. It looked like a custody exchange.

What would my life have been like if I hadn't lost the baby? I wondered. Would I have had a lifelong relationship with Vince, trading off the baby every other week, like Doug seemed to be doing? I shook my head, clearing the image from my mind, glad that Vince was out of my life.

Doug didn't teach often, so I trained with John and his wife, Barbara, most of the time. They were both competent instructors and beautiful people with huge hearts and a soft spot for the underdog. John was a big guy with long black hair that hung down the middle of his back in a ponytail and a full beard and mustache. He was covered in tattoos and looked like a biker, the kind of guy I probably would never have had contact with if it weren't for having met him there. He and Barbara became good friends to me.

One night John shouted to me from across the gym. "Hey, Mary, Mary! How are you doing, sweetie? Where ya been? I've missed you."

He always said my name twice. He was a bear of a man, with a ready smile and a great sense of humor. I shouted back, "Aw, you know, work, school, homework. Same ole, same ole. You teaching tonight?"

"No, Barb's teaching. I'm just hanging out." He took a swig from a bottle of Maalox. I'd seen him do this a hundred times, and it made me wonder how the business was going.

I had never worked so hard at anything in my life and I loved leaving the gym soaking wet and feeling good. I progressed through the ranks and loved assisting in classes for students with less experience. After class one beautiful July night, Doug walked toward me, seemingly with a purpose. I stopped and gave him my full attention.

"What are you doing Saturday night?" he asked.

My mind searched the schedule for a class that I hadn't noticed, assuming that he needed coverage for something.

Confused, I answered, "Um, nothing special. Did you need something?"

"Yes, a date," he responded with a reddening, but confident face and a cute grin beneath his cheesy mustache.

I was startled and at a loss for words. He never showed any of the typical signs a guy does when he's interested in me. There had been no flirting, joking, small talk, or special attention of any kind. I was shocked and unprepared. I looked at him with what was surely a confused expression while I processed his request.

Caught completely off guard, I mumbled, "Um, I don't know. I, well, maybe you could call me, and we could talk."

I finally spit out my number, which he scribbled on his palm. I shook my head at how poorly I had handled things and wouldn't have blamed him if he ran to the bathroom and washed his hands with bleach, but he raised his eyebrows and waved with the phone-numbered hand as he walked away.

I wasn't sure how I felt about dating him at first. He was quiet and not the type I typically noticed. He was about five-seven with long hair that fell below his shoulders in a ponytail. It seemed a bit adolescent since he looked to be in his late twenties. More recently, I had gravitated toward tall, clean-cut guys. At five-eight, I was tall for a woman and self-conscious, often feeling like a giant in heels if my date wasn't taller than me.

But after minimal consideration, I realized that this might be a good thing since my type had been a disaster so far. Barb and John were friends with him, so I approached them.

"Hey, guys, what's the lowdown on Doug?"

"Why?" John asked, cocking his head.

"Well, he asked me out."

John looked surprised and said, "Nope. I love you, Mary Mary, but you do not have my permission." He laughed, and I couldn't tell whether he was serious or not.

"Well, what's his deal? Is he married, divorced, kids, what?" I asked.

Barb jumped in. "He's divorced and has two kids, so he'll never be rich." She laughed. "He works in a restaurant somewhere. I don't remember where, but he's a damn good instructor here."

Neither of them offered anything further, which seemed odd.

When he called two days later, I was better prepared for his question and agreed to go out with him. He picked me up for our first date in an old blue Chevy panel van, wearing a long black trench coat and a fedora, which screamed either confidence or serial killer, I wasn't sure which, but I liked the look and hoped it wasn't the latter of the two. He was the perfect gentleman, opening doors and helping me out of my coat as we sat down for dinner at a local chain restaurant. The waiter asked if we'd like to order drinks.

"No, thanks," Doug said and looked at me for a response.

I could tell there was a story there, so I ordered an iced tea, smiling awkwardly.

"I'm sorry. I should've told you that I'm a recovering alcoholic. I don't drink. I hope that doesn't bother you. You can have a drink if you like. It won't bother me," he added.

"No, I'm fine not drinking. I don't drink much anyway," I said.

I was naive and had nothing close to what anyone would call street smarts, so I had no idea of the gravity of what he had just told me. I drank socially, but I had no frame of reference for what alcoholism was. I knew how alcohol had affected my marriage, and I needed no more education than that. What I got out of it was that we wouldn't be hanging out at bars, and I didn't mind that.

Doug was funny and even a little silly when we were alone, sometimes making goofy faces. He didn't care what other people thought, and I found it refreshing. He had two kids, a girl and a boy, and had recently divorced; he had visitation with his kids every other week, like many fathers. What I knew about him was that he was always at the gym, and he seemed like an attentive dad. He had a great sense of humor, and my impression was that he was genuine and down to earth. Though he never said an unkind word about her, he seemed to have the typical tenuous relationship with his ex-wife. He enjoyed spending time with his kids, and I liked that. We didn't have much in common except that we were both divorced and loved martial arts. It was enough, but I wasn't ready to plan a destination wedding.

I met his children, Dustin and Megan, after one of the weekend drop-offs.

"This is Miss Mary," Doug said. "Say 'hi,' guys."

They were both shy and quiet, clinging to his legs.

Megan buried her face deeply into Doug's tae kwon do dobok while Dustin answered in a low voice, "Hi, Miss Mary."

His response prompted Megan to sneak a peek as I shook his hand.

"Very nice to meet you, Dustin."

I knelt closer to Megan's eye level and, smiling, said, "I love your Mickey Mouse sandals, Megan, but I'm not sure. Which princess is on your shirt?"

Megan was quick to correct me. "Her name is Ariel, and she's a mermaid."

"Oh, I see. So, she's not a princess. I didn't know that," I said.

"Well, she is a princess, but at first she's a mermaid, and then the prince comes, and she falls in love."

She went on a long, animated rant, most of which I didn't understand. Being childless, I had no experience with Disney characters, and she babbled along for a while before Doug grinned and shook his head.

"Well, you wound her up. We may never stop her now."

Megan play smacked her dad, and he tickled her in return, guiding both children to a sofa where they unloaded their backpacks and settled in to watch the tae kwon do classes.

Megan and I were fast friends, but Dustin would take a little more time.

Doug began introducing me to things I'd never tried, like running and fishing. As a rule, runners don't smoke and smokers don't run, so I never considered trying it. But I had quit smoking and Doug was so encouraging that I started running with him, and at first, it was horrible.

He ran backward in front of me singing a cadence, "Left, left, left right left. I had a good home, but I left. C'mon, sweet pea, you can do it."

"I *am* running. This is as fast as I go," I choked out between spasms.

He was utterly unconcerned about my bursting lungs and fifteen-minute mile. He was fit and could run forever, and I was completely ill prepared. I didn't even own running shoes and walk-trotted my first two miles in hiking boots.

"Sweet pea, we have to do something about those shoes. They look like combat boots. You're going to ruin your feet in those things. Trust me, you'll do much better once we get you some running shoes."

He hugged me to seal the deal and I kept at it. It became more natural, and within six months, I learned to love it. I had all the gear, a Nike shirt, running shorts, and authentic Saucony running shoes. We started entering 5K races together on the weekends, and soon I ran with or without him. I had a routine that included running three days a week and training in tae kwon do on opposite days. I was in the best shape of my life, and I felt great!

Doug was a fisherman. I had never fished from a boat before, so he took me out, teaching me everything I needed to know, like what to catch and where, and what kind of bait to use for what type of fish, but he laid down the law immediately.

"Okay, sweet pea, let me show you how to cast. I don't mind baiting your hooks, but you have to cast on your own."

He put a thin slice of squid on the hook and feigned wiping his slimy hands on my shirt.

"Hey," I yelled, laughing.

Doug stood behind me, my body between his arms and the fishing pole in front of us, and he began the lesson. He nearly fell into the water as the two of us teetered with rods flailing, laughing hysterically as a strip of white squid swung back and forth on the hook in front of my face. It was more like a Kama Sutra pose than a casting lesson, and we both giggled at how poorly it was going. He was a good sport, exaggerating his awkwardness, nearly tipping the boat over. A right-handed man teaching a lefty to cast is no small feat and required lots of patience. We lost a ton of tackle that day trying to figure it out and spent more time baiting hooks than fishing. He was so proud when I caught my first fish.

"Oh my God! What is this? It looks like an alien!" I screeched.

"It's a flounder," he said, laughing.

"It's got two eyes on the same side of its head! Is this normal? What's in this water? Is there a nuclear power plant around here or something?"

"It's perfect! It's a keeper. Excellent job, baby! You caught dinner," he announced, planting a kiss on the top of my head as we bobbed around.

Over the next several months, we took that small craft farther out into the Delaware Bay than we had a right to fishing for flounder, shark, or whatever came along, and we routinely ended our days with plenty of fish for dinner.

I loved the serenity of being on the water in the middle of nowhere with him, and the days we didn't get a nibble were some of the best. It was peaceful. The smell of salty air and watching the sun go down on the water at the end of the day as we headed back to shore were my fondest memories. I found God again in the sunsets and peaceful moments with Doug on that water. I rarely called on God when things were going well. I typically came sliding in on my knees when things were a disaster. In tears, I'd beg for His help, blaming Him for not being there for me, but things were different on the water, and it was good to have Him back in my life.

Doug had a regular commitment opening a local church and setting up for AA meetings, which he attended several days a week. He seemed happy enough doing it, and I was impressed by his commitment to staying sober and helping other people do the same.

He was smart, but he didn't seem to know it, and he was open to learning new things.

I talked him into skiing in the Pocono Mountains not far from home. It was his first time, and I was excited to introduce him to the sport like he had introduced me to running and fishing. I wanted him to love it. As a natural athlete, he picked it up right away, which annoyed me since I worked hard at being an average skier. I secretly wished he would fall so I could rest a bit, or maybe so I would feel better about myself. It was a cold, windy day, and as the blowing snow stung my face, I silently wished we could stop in the ski lodge for a drink, like all the other couples. It was the first time that his alcoholism had come up for me, but I never mentioned it to him. I remembered him sharing this metaphor many times: "If you keep going to the barbershop, eventually, you're going to get a haircut."

I didn't want him to drink, so we never went in, and I dismissed it without too much disappointment.

Doug and I spent all our free time together. His easygoing manner helped me feel safe again. There were no raised voices when we disagreed, and whatever the dilemma, the priority was always to resolve the conflict peacefully and respectfully. I told him about my marriage to Vince, and he assured me that Vince was wrong about a healthy relationship. Other couples fought, but we didn't. The longer we were together, the safer I felt, and the less I thought about Vince and the horrible way our marriage ended. Months rolled into years as we planned and lived our lives together. Nothing could go wrong. Or so I thought.

# Chapter Fourteen

I WAS THIRTY-ONE WHEN I STARTED A NEW JOB AT THE CROWELL Corporation in 1992. It was a paper tape manufacturing company, and I was responsible for the accounts payable invoices. I worked in an office with a receptionist, a payroll clerk, and six customer service representatives, all women in their midforties who had worked for Crowell for many years. They all got along well and seemed content, even after many years of sameness. I wanted to fit in but I don't think I ever really did. It wasn't an exciting job, but it was what I knew, a stepping stone to better things, and I was glad to have work until I finished school and was hired by one of the police departments. All in all, things were going well.

One Monday morning, I needed clarification on an invoice, so I walked out to the factory to discuss it with the shop supervisor, Mark. The factory machines were deafening, so I shouted over the crunching and clanging metal to make myself heard. Before we could resolve the issue, my name blared over the intercom. "Mary Sweeney, please respond to the front desk."

Mark cupped his hands around his mouth and shouted, "Go ahead. We can work this out later."

"No, that's okay. It's probably just somebody looking for money. They can take a message."

I continued explaining the questionable invoice when a second page came through. Mark smiled and I shrugged, leaving him with the invoice.

I walked the few steps from the factory and shoved the heavy door to reception open, and as it closed, the factory noises hushed. I looked up to see Doug wearing his favorite blue fishing hat, turquoise Jams, and a white tank top. He stood at the receptionist's desk with a red face, a big smile, and a beautiful bouquet of flowers in his hand. I rushed to him, in excitement.

"Hi, sweet pea," he said, smiling.

"Oh my God! Hi," I said quietly. "What are you doing here? Is everything okay?"

He shoved the flowers awkwardly at me along with a small bag from Dunkin' Donuts.

"I brought you your favorite donut, chocolate frosted," he said.

My smile broadened as I accepted the gifts, scanning the office staff for reactions.

"I don't want to interrupt your day. I just wanted to stop by and say I love you."

"This is *not* an interruption," I said. "Thank you so much. What a nice surprise."

We were center stage, and I could tell he was deciding whether he should kiss me. I turned to the receptionist, who had been listening to every word as she dusted her telephone, and said, handing her my gifts, "Doris, would you set this on my desk, please? I'll be right back."

She smiled an ornery grin. "I sure will, Miss Mary."

We walked outside to the parking lot and Doug beamed with joy over the embarrassing display he had made. I laughed and hugged him.

"Thank you, sweetie. This might be the nicest thing anyone has ever done for me."

"You deserve it. You look hot, by the way."

"Do I? Are you sure this skirt isn't too short? When I came into the office this morning, Evelyn looked me up and down, and I'm pretty sure when she turned her back, she rolled her eyes."

"Too short? Well, it's too short for Evelyn, but not you, baby."

With a quick peck on the cheek, he winked and shuffled off. "I have to run, or I'll miss my meeting," he said.

I floated back into the office, and all eyes were on me. Shirley, the office mom, was the first to say anything.

"He's cute. That was so sweet of him. My husband wouldn't have done that in a million years. You're a lucky girl, sweet pea!"

The girls erupted in laughter, and I squeezed my eyes shut, my cheeks hot, but I walked on cloud nine for the rest of the day.

Doug made it a point at least once a week to hand-deliver flowers or a chocolate-covered donut with a smiley face and "sweet pea" handwritten on the bag. He became popular with the office staff, who lavished him with attention. The pet name embarrassed me in front of the girls, but I secretly adored it. My heart swelled at how courageous he was to openly show his affection for me, knowing Vince would never have done that. I couldn't imagine my life without Doug.

One sunny day in April 1993, our relationship entered a new phase. I said goodbye to my first solo home and we moved into an apartment together. It made weekend visitations with his kids easier, but it was a massive step for me, having not yet recovered from the sting of an awful, dysfunctional marriage. Living with Doug was much different from dating, but he was attentive, and I trusted him. We'd been living together for about three months, so we were still learning about each other, when my past reared its ugly head.

Doug had been out all day. It was getting late, and I hadn't heard from him. He hadn't called, and I couldn't reach him. I was frantic—worried about where he was and why he hadn't returned my calls. My knee-jerk reaction was to feel anger and suspicion, but it was unlike him to ignore my calls, and I was afraid that something had happened to him. I battled the voices in my head, reminding myself that he was not Vince and he had never given me any reason to doubt him.

It began pouring rain, and I worried he had been in a car accident, imagining a crumpled car and him lying on the side of the road in a pool of blood with water washing over him. I called everyone I could think of, pacing wildly, and as the time dragged on, the story I told myself changed. He wasn't coming home. He was with another woman or hanging with the boys, drinking.

When he came through the door that evening, I jumped on him with questions. He laughed nervously, trying to settle me. "Hey, hey. What's wrong? Are you okay? Are you mad?"

"I've been worried sick," I whined, sounding a little more angry than worried.

"Oh, I'm sorry, sweet pea. I'm sorry I'm late. Dad and I were out on the boat, and a storm came in. We sat under a bridge waiting for it to subside."

His excuse sounded right to me, but I'd gotten myself so wound up, I wouldn't let it go. I had waited and worried for hours, and I had earned the right to be mad. He couldn't just say "I'm sorry, babe," and make it go away.

"You couldn't call and let me know?" I asked accusingly.

"Honey, I didn't have a phone on the boat, and it didn't make sense to stop and call. We were only three miles away."

He walked toward me for a hug, and I stepped back. It was a slap in the face to him, and I saw his expression change.

"I'm not sure what to do with that, Mary," he said, backing away.

I'm ashamed to admit that I didn't say what I should have said. I didn't ask, "How could I know you were safe or that you were with your dad? How was I supposed to know you were fishing?" I didn't say, "For just a moment, I forgot you were Doug. You were Vince, and it was a long night of worrying. It was three o'clock in the morning all over again." That's what I should have said and didn't. He might have understood my response then, but he didn't, and we spent the rest of the night in silence. He wasn't lying, and I knew it.

I sat lost in thought, feeling guilty for mistreating him, but I was too proud to explain or apologize. He didn't even get angry. All he said was, "I'm not sure what to do with that." He met my doubt with patience and love, and I loved him more because he made me raise my relationship bar to meet his, but I never verbalized that to him, so I'm sure he had a different experience than I did.

Our life was evolving quickly. Doug's ex-wife moved away, resulting in changes to his custody agreement. Instead of having the kids every other weekend, we would have the kids for the whole summer. I was an unofficial stepmother! Dustin and Megan would be my and Doug's shared responsibility, which scared the hell out of me and, at the same time, made me deliriously happy. I had no idea how to relate to children, but they were sweet kids, and I'd already fallen in love with them.

That fall I would start my second year at Del Tech and decided to take classes straight through the summer months to get finished sooner. An associate's degree in criminal justice would improve my chances of being hired as a police officer, and I had never felt more accomplished in my life. I was happier and healthier than I had ever been.

Doug and I got along beautifully, and I never dreamed that life could be so simple. If Doug and I argued, it was about money. He had never learned to manage money, and when you don't have a lot of it, that is an essential skill to have. I was at the opposite end of the spectrum so the subject of our finances came up often. Having support payments for two children cut a massive hole in our budget, but I respected him for meeting his obligations. I was frugal, always saving for a rainy day, but every day was a rainy day to Doug. He wanted toys, and though they were never extravagant, much of what he wanted was, in my opinion, other people's junk: an old motorcycle that didn't run or a bigger motor that he was sure he could fix for the boat or a bigger boat that just needed patching up. I wanted to save for something new, but he didn't have the patience, and the cheap stuff always cost a fortune in the long run. All of the fixing, selling, and buying cut into the time we had to share.

Doug was always trying to do better. He found a new job as a manager for a shoe distribution company and cut off his ponytail, going for the professional military buzz cut. He jumped through the front door one day shouting, "Ta-da! What do you think?"

"Oh my gosh! I can't believe you did that! I love it! What in the world made you cut it all off?"

He smiled and raised his eyebrows, trying to look debonair. "I just thought I might look more like a manager with short hair," he said.

"I didn't think you could look any sexier, but there you are, an absolute Adonis!"

I smothered him with kisses while helping him out of his suit jacket as proof of my approval. The new job suited him, and while we weren't rich, we had everything we needed.

Soon our lives settled into a routine that included having the kids in the summer. They loved training at the gym with us, and they were adorable in their little tae kwon do uniforms. We traded the small boat for a bigger one to take the kids fishing on weekends. They joined us for our running regimen, and we entered them in local one-mile fun runs while we competed in the occasional weekend 5K race. They were easy, well-behaved, healthy kids of five and seven, and if they weren't with their grandparents, they were with us. With frequent visits from us and the grandchildren, Doug's mom and I became closer.

My feelings about losing my first biological child faded in the light of those two beautiful souls. I couldn't believe I was doing the obligatory birthday parties and Christmas prep. I was even fixing lunches, strange since my idea of lunch had always been coffee and a cigarette. Our lifestyle was becoming comfortable, and I felt I could get used to it.

One night as I dragged myself in after school, slamming the door shut, Doug hollered from the kitchen, "Hey, sweet pea, what happened to those peppers I brought home today?"

"I chopped them up and put them in a salad for dinner."

"You what? Those were jalapeños. They're not for salads."

"Well, I know that now. I thought they were banana peppers. I rested my chin in my hands at my desk tonight, and look!"

"It looks like someone slapped you across the face," he said, laughing and then grabbing me around the waist and hoisting me into the air. When my feet touched the floor, he brushed my hair back and kissed my face, lingering over the red streaks. He leaned back and whispered, "Yum, they taste pretty good. Can I fix you something to eat? A salad, maybe?"

"Um, no. I'm good. Thanks, sweetie. Hey, I got a message from the bank today that one of our checks bounced. The girl from the bank said we were overdrawn by two hundred dollars, but I don't see how that's possible. Do you know anything about that?"

He looked at me quizzically and said, "I'm sorry, babe. I spoke to the lady. It was my fault. I didn't get my check in on time, and then I took money out today before it cleared. It's taken care of."

"Oh, I thought you were working today."

"I was supposed to, but my days got switched. I took the kids to Chuck E. Cheese. We spent the day playing air hockey and eating pizza, so I'm not really hungry, but I'm happy to make you something."

"I thought your mom had the kids. Where are they?"

"Yeah, she did. I picked them up to go out and dropped them off with her afterward."

"Well, shoot. Why didn't you just bring them here?"

He shrugged and picked up the spatula, swatting at my behind. "I wanted to spend the evening with my girl."

It was just another night in my new life. Doug was a great cook, and it seemed to me he had missed his calling. I looked at the tempting dishes he served, astonished that I had the ingredients somewhere in my kitchen to make these gourmet meals. I thought of the nights that Vince had never bothered to come home for dinner, and I was grateful for Doug. He was a simple guy who didn't need much to make him happy. He was fit and attractive but not hunky or arrogant. I was pretty sure I had hit the lottery with him. How could my life get better than this?

# Chapter Fifteen

IT WAS 1994. I WAS NERVOUS AND EXCITED ABOUT MY BIG DAY. IT had taken me four years to earn my black belt in tae kwon do. The testing process was grueling, but I had trained hard and knew that I was ready for this. Doug was there for support and snuck a kiss before the ceremony began. I flashed him a toothy grin before putting on my game face.

The first part of the test was simple. I completed the technical skills required to pass for the first-degree black belt without any struggle. The second portion involved a demonstration created by each testing student that showed an ability to use what we had learned and synthesize the skills we knew. Music, costumes, weapons, or anything else needed to enhance the presentations were fair game. I created a mime routine using "Man in the Mirror," Michael Jackson's musical hit, and Doug was my partner. We had worked together for years and made a pretty good team. For my performance, we painted our faces white, donned black uniforms, and took to the floor.

My weapon of choice was the bo staff, a long stick made of rattan. I was not yet proficient with it, but I was learning, so I kept it simple. After months of practice, Doug and I moved in near-perfect tandem, and I was excited at how polished it looked. Our choreographed routine represented a warrior's internal struggle with themself. For me, it had meaning. Over the last few years, I had taken a deeper look into my soul than at any other time in my life. I understood that becoming my best self was an ongoing internal battle requiring reflection.

We began the demonstration facing each other, holding our staffs, and bowing at the waist, never breaking eye contact. We straightened up, placing our free hands together, and made a circular motion as if cleaning the steam from a bathroom mirror. And then, grabbing the business end of the staff and stepping back into a fighting stance, we spun our bo staffs in tandem, slamming the stick onto the gym floor, causing a loud crack. The crowd jumped as we turned back-to-back, swinging our staffs into the air and catching them with our hands approximately a foot apart, and then quickly jumped into the air, landing in a fighting stance again, swinging the staffs in a circle over our heads. The rattan weapons whooshed through the air, and cracking sounds echoed through the gym with every strike until, right on cue, my mirror image missed a step. His misstep left our weapons opposite one another, revealing that the reflection was not me. The impostor transformed into attack mode, encouraged by jeers from the crowd. His face was an angry display of rage as he swung his weapon at my knees. I jumped high enough to clear it, causing his forward momentum to lurch him off balance and knock him to the floor, where I pinned him with my staff. Doug dramatically writhed in agony while the heroine, which in this case was me, was left standing.

The demonstration ended and we stood, bowing at the waist to one another, and then to the audience of about fifty people. My eyes welled with tears. It wasn't nerves, upset, or even joy, as most people might have assumed. It was a release of energy. I had done it! After four years of blood, sweat, and tears, I had accomplished this great thing. My inner critic didn't get to jeer at my failure—not this time. The audience stood, cheering as I stood stoically with my shoulders back while the gym staff prepared the final test. Several assistants unloaded concrete blocks in stacks on the floor in front of me. I had to break one to earn my rank. I trembled at the sight of the two-inch-thick slab and paced in circles around my nemesis. I had tried several times but I had never succeeded in breaking a block with my hand.

I wasn't sure I would be able to do it this time, and I was afraid this would be where I would fall short. I felt my shoulders sag as my confidence waned at the thought of failing to break the block in front of the whole class. Doug knew what I was thinking. He set up the blocks with the other instructors and approached me, bowing at the waist. I bowed, returning his respect as was the practice for greeting an instructor. He reached out to shake my hand in the traditional martial arts manner with his off-hand palm down under his extended hand, but he hesitated for just a moment before letting go. It was just long enough for me to notice, and our eyes met. His nonsmiling face was stern. His wasn't the expression of a boyfriend humoring his girlfriend. He was honoring me. Closing his eyes, bowing his head in respect, he said nothing. When he released my hand, I felt empowered and worthy, and my confidence returned.

I physically felt the shared energy from him surge through my chest, and my heart thumped wildly. I stepped forward, choosing to break the concrete block with the palm of my hand. I turned to face my instructors, who granted me permission to break. Once again bowing respectfully, I returned to the block balanced atop a stack of other concrete blocks. I bristled at the disparity between the two-inch brick and my girlie hand. If I failed to break, I would have to start the testing process over again, and I desperately wanted to see the block smash into pieces on the floor.

I forced a deep breath and closed my eyes, concentrating all my energy to a point the size of a postage stamp on the heel of my palm. I allowed my mind to drift away from the audience, from the belt, rank, status, boyfriend, and accolades, leaving nothing but the concrete slab, this mass of energy to separate with my energy. I opened my eyes, took a deep breath, and summoned all my inner strength as I raised my arm high into the air and my hand careened toward the bricks. Time stood still as I watched the scene play from somewhere outside myself. I felt electrically charged, my body tingling as my heart pounded within the confines of my tiny frame. I was invincible. My focus was not on the concrete but rather on the space beneath the obstacle, the place I wanted to be. There was no barrier, no block at all, just energy to be moved.

My palm penetrated the brick with no hesitation, stopping only when my forward momentum and inertia naturally came to rest. I watched the blocks separate into two pieces and land at my bare feet, and watched them move seemingly in slow motion, tumbling to the floor. The audience erupted in applause.

I looked at my hand, brushed off the dust from the concrete block, turned to face the three judges, and bowed at the waist as they respectfully nodded their approval. I did it. I looked again at my hand in amazement. I had tried and failed other times, my hand exploding with pain, swollen and bruised for days. I understood now. It wasn't breaking the brick that had caused the injury but hesitating, doubting, and backing out at the last minute. I had never fully committed. Apprehension caused the pain. A flashback from *The Karate Kid* movie came to mind. It's the part when Mr. Miyagi tells his young protégé, Daniel, "You karate do 'yes' or karate do 'no.' You karate do 'guess so' *squish* just like grape." I allowed myself to feel joy and bowed to the audience with my newfound wisdom. I knew I would apply Mr. Miyagi's metaphor to many other areas of my life.

I would never be the shrinking violet I had been when I was married to Vince. I had changed, but in that split second, I wondered how our marriage might have turned out if I had asserted myself, refused to acquiesce to his suggestions to move, quit my job, give up the car, stop calling my friends and family. Would things have ended the same way, worse, or not at all?

The ceremony continued with the presentation of black belts. I turned my back to my masters, removed the brown belt, and replaced it with the coveted piece of black cloth, turning to face them once again. I returned to my spot on the floor and took my place sitting cross-legged as Doug took center stage, requesting everyone's attention. He held a stuffed rabbit, but not just any rabbit. This bunny was wearing a red tae kwon do uniform, white canvas pants, and a black belt. It was adorable. I was already embarrassed, not knowing what to expect but suspecting it had something to do with me.

Doug reached out his hand, inviting me to stand. When I stood, he took a knee, and I felt a sudden wave of excitement as I realized what was happening. He had a microphone in his hand, and he began to talk.

"Mary, I've known since the day we met that you are special. Today I'm so proud of you and stand in awe of your beauty and power. I love you. Make me a happy man today. Please say you'll be my wife."

He reached for my left hand and I covered my mouth with the other as he slipped a diamond ring on my finger.

I looked down at him and choked out through tears, "Yes!"

He stood, and I buried my face in the crook of his neck, whisper kissing a barrage of I love yous. A sea of well-wishers surrounded us, and the intimate moment evaporated. It was the best day of my life.

# Chapter Sixteen

We married that June of 1994, just three years after having met. At thirty-three, I began my second marriage to my soulmate. We had a simple afternoon wedding with a small reception, and no alcohol. After the reception, we had the evening to ourselves, so we left early for our honeymoon near Virginia Beach, where we fished for hours in the sunny, warm Chesapeake Bay. Doug was unusually quiet, but the excitement of fishing in unknown waters perked him up.

I would be graduating college soon. I had applied for positions with the two largest police agencies in Delaware, and because the process was competitive, I reapplied yearly, retaking the entrance exams to better my chances of getting in, as more qualified candidates were being hired ahead of me. My test scores improved each time I applied and having a degree in criminal justice I hoped would tip the scales in my favor.

Doug took a management job at a Wendy's hamburger joint and was happy to be making more money, but his schedule was unpredictable. I didn't like it. He was working evenings, and was always working late to cover for somebody who called out sick. His clothes reeked of french fries, and no matter how many times I washed them, they still smelled greasy.

Doug stopped volunteering to open the AA meetings and attended only sporadically. He still talked to John, who was his sponsor, but he seemed distant, different, and maybe a little secretive, which he had never been before. Was I being paranoid? I didn't like the feel of things, and his schedule wreaked havoc on our time together. He seemed off, but we were both busy, so I chalked it up to stress. Between having the kids to take care of and my school schedule, we didn't spend as much time alone. The worst part was the nighttime inventories when he stayed after the restaurant closed and came home in the morning. Those nights reminded me of the all-nighters I spent waiting for Vince to come home, and I always woke up feeling anxious and tired.

Whenever we had a free weekend together, we fished or took tae kwon do classes together. To some people this might sound boring, but I was happy, and for the first time in my life I was truly content. Before we knew it, we had been married for a year, both working toward our goals and enjoying life.

My homework was so involved that my time at home wasn't my own. The pace and stress were starting to show as I began having stomach issues and started losing weight that I couldn't afford to lose. There was no doubt we were both doing too much, but I kept telling myself it was temporary, and I wondered if the little bit of extra money was worth the time we lost together.

One typical Friday night, Doug called home at the end of his evening shift.

"Sorry, sweet pea, I have inventory tonight, so you'll be sleeping alone. I'll be dreaming about you though," he said.

"Oh no! Not on a Friday night. Really?" I complained.

"I know, sweet pea, but I'll be home in the morning. I'll sleep a little, and we can take the boat out. It's supposed to be a beautiful day. What do you think?"

"All right," I said, whining a little.

"That's my girl. I love you, baby," he chirped before hanging up.

I jumped back into my term paper with a vengeance, determined to finish it, which I did. I called the store to brag about my accomplishment and say goodnight before bed.

When the clerk answered, I asked for Doug, and he told me he wasn't working. I explained that he was doing inventory and asked if he stepped out, so he put me on hold, and when he came back to the phone, he said they didn't know anything about an inventory and they hadn't seen him since Thursday. His tone was wary, as if he knew something but didn't want to say more and he quickly ended the call.

I was numb. I spent the night pacing the floor, dreading the moment when I would find out where he was and who he was with. *Here I go again.* I was swept back in time five years, wringing my hands, waiting for Vince to come home, the anticipation of a fight fueling my anger one minute, and then trying to convince myself that Doug was not Vince the next. I didn't sleep. I paced at breakneck speeds around our little home trying to imagine what he was doing and what I would say. The longer I waited, the more devastated I felt by his apparent betrayal and the more hopelessness crept in.

Just before daybreak, the door opened slowly and he came in, crying. His face was tearstained and red, his eyes bloodshot. He was still drunk, reeking of beer, and he looked like a sloppy mess in a filthy T-shirt and shorts.

"I'm so sorry, sweet pea," he slurred.

I cut him off. "No, don't you call me that," I shouted. "You don't ever get to call me that again! I'm not your sweet pea! I don't even know what I am! How could you? How could you lie to me and throw it all away like this? Where have you been? Who were you with?"

As soon as the words escaped my lips, I regretted them. I had had all night to figure out what to say, and here I was, a stammering, venting fool, which made me even more furious.

Through his tears, Doug sobbed out the story of how he had fallen off the wagon.

"I was with my cousin at his house. We drank beer there all night, just the two of us, and then my uncle came in. I'm sorry, baby. Please forgive me."

Tears and mucus ran down his face, falling to the floor as he sat down on an ottoman, covering his face with his hands.

"Tell me everything," I demanded, dry-eyed. "When did this start?"

"I've been with my cousin Ray. He used to be my drinking buddy, back in the day, and he's been trying to talk me into going out with him since we got married. I kept refusing, but he would always say it was only a matter of time and that I would never stay sober. I had four years clean, and now I don't know if I can do it anymore. Oh my God."

I didn't recognize the man before me. He was a sniveling mess, slurring his words and whining. I had never heard my sweet, confident husband whine. He was freakishly different from anytime I had ever seen him as he wiped fluid from his face with his arm.

"What did you do?"

"We filled a cooler with beer and went fishing, but we drank more than we fished," he said, and it came out sounding more like *vished*. "I was trashed, so I went back to Ray's house and crashed for the night. I couldn't face you, so I put off coming home. I drank until I passed out."

Between gasps for breath, I made out that he had been meeting his cousin for weeks, sometimes fishing, and sometimes hanging out at his house where they'd drink themselves blind until they both passed out. I could smell the beer on him from six feet away and it was an unwelcome, foreign odor in our home that reminded me of days gone by.

"Each time we drank, I swore to myself I'd never let it happen again. I meant it, and I tried to stay clean, but hiding it from you was violating all the tenets of my sobriety, and it just got worse. I knew it would come to this if I didn't stop, but it picked up momentum fast and I couldn't control it."

Doug's shoulders sagged, and he looked exhausted. I wanted to be pissed, but he was so distraught that I couldn't. Seeing him cry was gut-wrenching, but the deception changed something in me and I couldn't muster up the compassion that seemed warranted. He was a broken man, and I could feel his helplessness as I pulled him into my arms and held him while he cried, his desperation palpable. The rank odor of beer emanated from his breath and the putrid smell of fish slime seeped from his clothes. He shared the details of his treachery and I held on to the only bit of relief I could find. He hadn't been unfaithful, but doubt crept in as I half listened and half planned my next steps. I knew how to end a marriage and began retracing my steps with Vince, preparing for the end, just in case.

I was scared for us, and for the first time in our relationship, I didn't trust Doug. I always expected that he was doing what he said he was. How could I maintain the crazy pace of my life and watch him too? It had taken longer than I had planned, but I was finally getting through my last few months of college and I felt helpless to do anything for him, with homework and papers to write and a full-time job.

The feeling of betrayal was the worst. As much as I knew it wasn't about me, Doug had lied to me. All those trivial things that didn't make sense, like missing money and blocks of time, started to fall into place. Was he really covering other shifts, or was he drinking? Did he take his kids to Chuck E. Cheese, or had he been partying with his cousin? I cursed myself for not paying better attention, for not trusting my instincts. After only one year of marriage, this was a problem that I couldn't fix. I was powerless to do anything to make him stop drinking. I was losing control of my life again, and this far down the rabbit hole, it would take some doing to shake off the doom and despair.

Doug was an emotional wreck too. He immediately started attending daily AA meetings and talking to John, grasping at straws for lack of a plan. I couldn't look to him for support because he couldn't even help himself.

Having no idea how to deal with this, I started attending Al-Anon meetings for people involved with an alcoholic at John and Barbara's recommendation. It wasn't a big help. I resented wasting time listening to people complain when I felt like I could be doing something productive. The overriding message I received was you can't help the addict. The other ideas I took away from the twelve-step program reminded me of the Ten Commandments, which reminded me of God, which reminded me of how pissed I was at Him too. I was doing my part, so where was He in all of this?

Trust between Doug and me was compromised. I wasn't sure it was fixable, and I wanted to try, but how do you try to trust? You either believe someone or you don't, so I was at a loss for some action to take. It seemed like we needed to get back to where we'd been, so we looked for familiar things, anything left that wasn't already broken, and did that. We began eating meals together as often as possible and took tae kwon do classes together or went running when I wasn't committed to schoolwork.

Doug still had a job, and no one knew what had happened that weekend except John and Doug's cousin and me. He was clinging to me like I was his lifeline. I loved that he had chosen to lean on me rather than drifting back to his cousin or coworkers, and it gave me hope that we could get through this.

Things settled down, but the atmosphere remained strained. He wasn't the same in the way he talked to me or in the relationship he had with his kids. They soon returned to their mother for the winter, so Doug didn't have that healthy distraction or motivation to stay sober. He quit coming to the office with flowers and donuts, and the intimate touching and general playfulness all but stopped. I was helpless, like I was on the outside looking in and couldn't reach him. I didn't like him working at Wendy's and suspected he had been

partying with some of his coworkers, but I didn't have the inclina-
tion to follow him around, watching to see if he was messing up. As
helpless as it felt, I let him be. I had a full plate and no time to run
around behind him making sure he was doing what he said he was.
The choice was his, and I had to accept that. This was growth for
me, and it was the only thing I could point to that suggested that no
matter what happened, I would be okay.

One Friday night in July 1995, I answered the phone, and it was
my college friend Iva calling to catch up. "Hey, Mare, how's it going?"

"Hey, Iva, good. You know, busy as always. How about you? Have
you almost finished the semester? You ready to graduate?" I asked.

"I should be. I'm about three classes away, but hey, I'm calling for
a reason tonight. Um, is everything okay between you and Doug?"

A wave of crushing "oh noes" washed over me, and my breath
quickened. My mind raced, trying to figure out how he and Iva could
have crossed paths. Was he drinking again? Did he get fired?

"Mare, are you there?" Iva prodded, tapping the mouthpiece of
her phone.

"Oh, yeah. I'm sorry. No, we're not really okay, Iva. We're having
some problems."

"I figured you guys must be separated." And before I had time to
respond, she added, "I saw him with a girl at a martial arts event in
Newark today. They were arm in arm, and it was obvious they were
a couple. What an asshole. I can't believe you didn't call me," she
fussed.

I couldn't shut her up or absorb her message fast enough to
respond.

"Yeah, I'm sorry. I should have, but I didn't know until this
moment. Thanks for telling me."

"Oh, holy hell." She blew out a sigh. "That fucker. He didn't even
try to hide it from me. I thought you knew. I'm sorry, Mare."

Iva tried to backpedal, suggesting that it might have been a friend, but I stopped her. I was done hearing my friends tell me how sorry they were for me, so I gave her absolution, cut the call short, and promised to call her later.

I didn't need convincing, but if I had, I received it when he didn't come home that weekend. I packed his bags and put them outside the door. When he came home on Sunday morning and found his belongings waiting for him, he cried, and the process of trying to regain my trust and get another chance began again.

For me, infidelity was the deal-breaker. No way! I wasn't hearing any of his stories, and I sent him out the door to stay with his parents, and he vowed to quit drinking and come back a better man. I was angry, inflexible, and incapable of any outward emotion except rage. It wasn't about what he might be able to do. It was about what I could do, whether I could or even would get past the infidelity. We weren't perfect together anymore. It didn't matter how great our relationship had been. This changed the playing field. Other women had the advantage because they could do something with him that I couldn't do. They could drink. What if he loved drinking more than he loved me?

I believed we were soulmates with all my heart, so when I hadn't heard from him after the first week apart, I called and invited him to come over for dinner to talk. I hoped he missed me and was sure our being together would help him summon the courage he needed to commit to his sobriety.

I showered and dressed in a pretty blue blouse and white shorts, hoping to look fresh and attractive. When Doug came through the door, he averted his eyes, and the smile faded from my face. He looked sullen.

He didn't have dark circles under his eyes like the ones growing darker underneath mine. His skin glistened from having showered too soon after a run, looking radiant, and while I looked haggard, he looked healthy. He didn't smile but opened his arms, and I closed the gap between us. To me, it was as if no time had passed, and I couldn't let go. Our primal instincts took over, and we connected passionately with the familiarity of longtime lovers. He was as tender and loving as he could be with my vulnerable heart, and our bodies responded but felt desperate. I held onto him as he pulled away. The heaviness between us let me know my feelings were one-sided as he averted his eyes and drifted toward the door, uttering his final words: "I love you, baby."

I collapsed onto the floor, pulling my knees to my chin, weeping. I had lost the battle, but no one had really won, and just like that, he was gone. I smelled him on my skin, inhaled his scent for maybe the last time, and allowed myself to feel the loneliness without judgment.

# Chapter Seventeen

It was a crisp, sunny Saturday morning in late November when I pulled into the parking lot of the new martial arts studio John and Barbara had opened called J&B Self-Defense Academy. I volunteered for them. Earning my black belt came with specific responsibilities, so as an assistant instructor, I took on the Ninja Turtle class. My adorable students needed help tying their belts and came up to my waist. I taught the same kids every week, and I loved it as much as they did. That Saturday, I had a group of about twenty-five, and they would be learning tumbling exercises.

The tumbling days were one of my favorite things in life. The kids came into class wearing white tae kwon do uniforms that resembled pajamas, complete with jelly stains that ran down the fronts of the jackets, which hung loosely around their small frames. They looked anything but menacing running around the gym in bare feet wearing bright-red headgear that made them look like bobblehead dolls. They giggled and screeched as they chased one another around on the hardwood floors strewn with blue wrestling mats, rolling and air kicking in mock sparring matches. The Ninja Turtles, both boys and girls, were between four and six years old, the perfect age for learning anything. They were full of life and always made me laugh, but that day, there was a slew of them. Thank goodness I had Sheree, a teenage assistant, to help manage the chaos, or at least kick the kids back into play when they got distracted.

As the class was just about to start, the gym grew louder with laughter and the sounds of bad actors landing tae kwon do blows. It was almost too much for a Saturday morning, and I shook my head silently, sending up gratitude to the coffee gods, who prepared me for this pandemonium every weekend.

I almost didn't hear the phone when it rang, but picked it up, motioning for Sheree to get the kids lined up and seated on the floor as was the ritual.

"Good morning, J&B Self-Defense Academy. Can I help you?" I shouted above the background noise.

"Hey, sweetie," John shouted into the phone.

"Hey, John." I could barely hear him above the din.

"You sitting down, Mare?"

"Am I sitting down? Are you kidding?" I chuckled. "You know what Saturday mornings are like. I'm just about to get started. What's up?"

He was unusually somber, and the long pause got my attention. Quietly and slowly he almost whispered, "Doug's been arrested."

"What? What are you talking about? Doug who?"

"Your husband, Doug."

My voice was shrill and cracking as I barked into the phone. "No way! Stop messing around. That's not funny."

He didn't answer.

"John . . ." I hesitated. "That's ridiculous. For what?"

He was quiet for a moment more, waiting for me to digest what he had said, and I shouted, "Arrested for what, dammit? What are you talking about?"

"There are lots of charges, Mare, but the one I remember is attempted murder."

He stopped talking. The silence on the other end of the phone was deafening, and as my knees turned to jelly, I slid down the wall, still holding the phone to my ear.

Just a moment ago, squealing children and laughter filled the room, but it turned to white noise as I processed what I had heard. My heart clapped against my rib cage, threatening to escape its confines as the tan phone cord twisted around my elbow, cutting off circulation. For a moment, I wasn't sure whose turn it was to talk, and I sat holding my breath, praying it wasn't mine since I couldn't find any words.

John was the one to break the silence. "Doug stabbed a man in the chest and he's on the run from the police."

I sat on the floor quietly, motionlessly, holding the phone to my ear as if it were a lifeline.

"Mare, you there? You okay?"

"No." I stared into space as the phone clattered to the floor and called out to the gym, "Sheree, I need you to take over the class."

"Yes, ma'am." She smiled, bowed courteously, and scurried excitedly back into the gym.

I dragged myself to my feet, stumbled outside, and doubled over, feeling suffocated, trying to catch my breath. My body tingled the way it does when you've narrowly avoided a car crash, and a heaviness descended over my limbs. I searched my memory for guidance, but nothing came. I don't recall making a conscious decision, but I knew I needed to expend some energy before my heart exploded. I walked fifty feet to the roadway, began trotting, and then picked up the pace until I was sprinting. I ran like a gazelle, as fast and as far as I could, right down the shoulder of a two-lane highway. I ran until my lungs ached, pushing them to their limit as the cold air stabbed at my chest and raked my throat. Wind tears flowed from my blurred eyes mixing with saliva and mucus as the cold November air stung my reddening cheeks. Cars passed by, traveling at highway speeds, blowing their horns at what looked like a crazed beast galloping down the shoulder of the roadway in white pajama bottoms and a red smoking jacket.

My legs soon joined the protest, and I slowed my pace about a half mile from the gym. I stopped and bent at the waist, catching my breath in the cold air.

My mind raced to Doug's defense. I needed more information. I turned and started walking back to the gym. It was brutally cold, and my breath appeared in white puffs with each exhale. I froze all the way back to the studio while screaming at God and talking to myself.

It was a mistake—a case of mistaken identity, someone with the same name or something. Cars stopped as drivers made sure I was okay, checking to see if I needed a ride. I looked like a lunatic, waving them off as I continued walking, talking, and screaming.

By the time I reached the dojang, I collected myself and took over my class, smiling, laughing, and teaching. I locked up the gym immediately after class and went straight to see John and Barbara. John would know what was going on by the time I got there. He had been Doug's sponsor for years, and if anybody knew what had happened, it would be him.

I parked in front of their house, made my way through their cluttered, junked-up front porch, and barged inside like I always did. John and Barb were sitting in the living room wearing sweats, drinking coffee, and waking up. They looked tired with bedhead and dark circles under their eyes. We hugged hello, and I unloaded laundry and dogs from the sofa and found a spot to sit down while John prepared to explain what he knew.

He was slow to start, offering me something to drink and attempting small talk. My expression revealed urgency, and he began.

"Mare, Doug didn't just fall off the wagon with alcohol. He's been smoking crack. I'm sorry, sweetie. I'd give anything not to have to tell you this."

I was silent for a moment. I knew that Doug was a recovering alcoholic, but drug usage was news to me.

"Doug was supposed to be calling me every night as part of his AA commitment, but he hasn't called lately, so I knew that he was drinking again. I've called him over and over, but he doesn't answer the phone when he wants to drink—but that's not all, Mary." John hesitated before he continued, and I knew this would be worse. "He's been sleeping with someone else. I don't know who, and he wouldn't tell me because he was afraid that I might tell you, but it has been going on for a while. I wanted to tell you, but I couldn't break confidence. You know what I mean? I'm his sponsor, so I couldn't tell you."

I understood the AA sponsors' responsibility to keep conversations confidential, but I still felt betrayed. I was angry and had a sudden urge to take back my hug.

"You knew Doug was sleeping with someone else and coming home to me . . . Fuck your honor code, John!"

He sat with his head down, riddled with guilt, unable to meet my glare.

"I've been so conflicted," he said. "I'm sorry. Doug was remorseful and promised me he would never step out of line again. He cried and begged me not to tell you. Dammit, Mary. I'm so sorry. I swear I didn't see this coming."

I was still questioning our friendship but decided this wasn't the biggest problem I had right now, so I set it aside and listened.

"All right, what else?" I asked.

There was no way to prepare for what came next. John went on, "I knew he was beyond my help when I learned that he was giving blow jobs for money and drugs."

It felt like a punch in the chest. John's eyes widened, seemingly praying that I wouldn't ask any more questions. He spoke dryly as I speechlessly waited for the next shoe to drop, searching his face for answers.

"How long was he doing that? Was he doing that and coming home to me?"

I couldn't even say what "that" was, and I was so afraid to know the answer that I excused myself to the bathroom before he had a chance to respond.

I didn't want to face them. I hung over the toilet, feeling like I needed to vomit, but my stomach was empty, so I began dry heaving. I paced frantically in circles in the tiny bathroom, looking at my ruddy face in the mirror, dreading the trip back to the living room, afraid I hadn't heard the worst. I wasn't ready, but after a few minutes, I washed my face and stumbled back to the sofa for round two, determined to get through somehow.

I asked John what had happened last night and he explained that Doug had gotten too far into debt with his drug supplier. He couldn't get any more credit from him, and he made a deal. In return for a supply of crack, Doug was supposed to collect a debt from some guy who owed the dealer more money than he did. The plan was for Doug to go to the motel where the guy was staying and collect money, but if the man refused to pay or didn't have the cash, Doug was supposed to cut his fingers off. Things didn't go as planned, and Doug stabbed the guy in the chest. He was in critical condition, and if he died, the charges would be bumped up to murder. As of that morning, he was wanted for attempted murder and all sorts of other charges, and he was on the run.

"John," I stammered, not finding the words to describe my fractured understanding of what had happened—of someone completely different from the man I knew. "Doug isn't violent! He could not have done this. There must be some mistake. Could it have been somebody else? His cousin, maybe?" I hadn't accepted any of this as truth and I was looking for validation from John. I got none.

John lowered his head and shook it. "I want more than anything to tell you it wasn't him, but I believe it was."

"What do I do now? Where is he? I need to do something, to talk to him."

"I don't know, Mare. I've called him a bunch of times but he won't answer."

"Maybe he came home. I'll go home. I'll talk to him and make sense of all of this and help him figure out how to handle it, but there's no way he stabbed anybody." I had a plan, and I rushed to the door fiddling with my keys. John and Barb hugged me and sent me away, making me promise not to get myself into any trouble, a promise even I wasn't sure I could keep.

# Chapter Eighteen

ON THE DRIVE HOME, A DARK CLOUD DESCENDED. MY FACE BLAZED red, filled with the physical evidence of pent-up anger and shame. I took the highway rather than the back roads to blend in with other people's chaos, pressing the accelerator until I was sure it would drop through the floor. Speeding faster and faster, I tried to keep up with my racing mind and heart. I weaved in and out of the three lanes of traffic on the verge of recklessness, in a hurry to get somewhere but having nowhere to go. I didn't know where I might end up, but at that moment, I wasn't sure I wanted to arrive alive.

Rapid-fire questions filled my head, skewing my judgment as the red Honda ahead of me, one lane over, tried to enter my path, swerving back at the last second to avoid hitting me. The near miss heightened my senses but did nothing to slow my speed. The lump in my throat spontaneously erupted, followed by the welling of tears, causing the yellow marker lines to blur. My foot lifted slightly from the pedal, proof that I wanted to live, but questions continued burning through the puddles in my eyes. *How could two men who seemed so right turn out to be so wrong?*

I exited the highway, and traffic forced me to slow my pace as my brain played a mental tango with options. It would be all over the local news. My family would want to know everything, so I needed to tell them quickly, but I was beyond capable of making decisions. I braked suddenly at that thought, and the driver to my right looked over into my car, noticing my tears. He shot me a concerned look, which felt too intimate, and I shoved sunglasses on my face, changing lanes to avoid his pity. Tired of feeling like a victim, I turned up the radio as loud as I could stand and navigated the last few miles with purpose. I got home safely. All was quiet. He wasn't there, so I decided to lie low, waiting for the storm to come to me rather than chasing it.

The following morning, I jogged to Wawa for a newspaper. The headlines in giant block letters read "Knife Wielder Hunted." Over the next few weeks, I read about what had been happening in my life while I wasn't paying attention. I wallowed in it. The humiliation alone was hard to endure, but I had the added benefit of press coverage. My phone rang incessantly with people wanting to express their concern or, more likely, get the inside scoop, but I couldn't answer their questions. My answering machine was full every night with messages from people I hadn't seen since eighth grade, along with new college classmates checking to see if I was okay. The only ones that hadn't called were the police. I wondered briefly why they hadn't contacted me and wondered if Maria had run interference. I tied my sneakers and doubled up on my nightly running regimen, ignoring the calls, sweating the pain and confusion away mile after mile until my legs refused to perform. Sacrificing limbs for sanity was a great trade, and it became a ritual that helped me feel normal when I didn't feel normal at all.

John had been right. According to the papers, a drug dealer named Nichols had hired Doug to collect a debt from a man named Osbourne. Doug owed the dealer $370 and would receive $500 if he collected the debt. When he arrived at Osbourne's, a scuffle ensued, and Doug stabbed the man several times in the chest. I closed my eyes, envisioning this horror, and slammed them open again to ward off the mental images. His cousin had driven him to the motel where the victim lived. I knew the area, and it was seedy, the kind of place that sits on a major highway renting rooms by the hour and has prostitutes hanging in front all day and night. The newspaper reported that Doug was positively identified as the assailant by a prostitute who witnessed the crime. Why would a prostitute know him by name? I didn't want to think about any of this, but I couldn't turn my mind off.

Getting new information became an obsession and one that would leave me feeling dissatisfied. I was relieved when I learned that the man would survive, but that fact didn't seem to help Doug much. The state charged him with multiple offenses, including attempted murder, which potentially carried the same penalty as an actual murder—life in prison. I was baffled that I didn't know the people named in the articles or the stabbing victim. It was as if Doug led a double life, one with me and the kids and one that included a dark side that I never knew existed. The man I knew was a loving gentleman who lacked the emotional ability to attack someone intentionally, and thinking about it made me queasy. Though I knew he had the skills and capacity, I couldn't conceive of him emotionally being able to enact that kind of violence. I was conflicted and needed a logical explanation to create order for myself.

Everything seemed normal until a few months ago, when he didn't come home on what should have been an average night. He hadn't spent that much time out of my sight, and I wondered how I had missed it. How did he tank so fast? I racked my brain but couldn't think of anything that felt so completely out of whack that I should have seen it and intervened. I spent countless hours sifting through routine days, searching for clues and coming up empty.

I ran to the store for a paper to look for news of his arrest. I grilled Maria for further information, and she dutifully filled me in on anything that wasn't privileged police information.

My friends and family didn't know what to say or do. They made comments like, "I never trusted that guy," "At least you found out now rather than later," and other remarks that left me feeling like a two-time loser. I guess in all fairness, there were no manuals that explained what to say to the wife of a man who just tried to kill someone. None of us had ever had scrapes with the law, and this was over the top. They were trying to support me, assuming I'd agree, but they didn't know the Doug that I knew, and it didn't seem like a good time to share that information with them because it was looking like maybe I was the one who didn't know him so well.

It was my second failed marriage, but this ending was different. Doug was good to me and we were perfect together, before he fell off the wagon. I steeled myself against any feelings I might still have for him, not wanting to look like we were a great couple anymore, and feeling guilty about that too. He was my kryptonite. I skipped between embarrassment, shame, anger, sadness, and love in nothing flat, trying to make sense of this mess. Then, suddenly and from nowhere, it occurred to me that this would probably ruin my chances of being hired by any police department. With a sudden fury burning in my belly, I saw my future flash before my eyes and disappear in a puff of smoke—all the dreaming, planning, studying, praying, and hard work for nothing. I had probably lost everything.

Doug finally turned himself in at the police station and was arraigned before a judge. It was an anticlimactic end to a dramatic story. His bail was outrageous, and his mom put her house up as collateral, allowing him to be released from prison and placed on home confinement. He was living with his mom less than a mile away from me, but I didn't hear from him, which left me feeling glad and sad at the same time. Knowing that he was out on bail and living close by was distracting, and I wanted to call or visit, but it seemed a little like supervised visitation with his parents being there.

I wandered around in shock, not knowing how to do life without him. Everyone said I was lucky to be free of him, but I didn't feel lucky. I still loved him, and I was sure we would work things out when this nonsense passed. I missed our life together but couldn't say that to anyone without looking like a psycho. I desperately wanted to wake up and have my old life back with all my plans intact.

Sometimes I secretly wished he had been killed in a car wreck and was grateful that no one knew my thoughts. I wanted the empathy associated with the complete loss of a spouse. I'd lost him just as surely as if he were dead. Instead of empathy, compassion, and understanding, I received nothing in terms of support, not even acknowledgment. It was yesterday's news. People stopped asking about him, and my phone stopped ringing. Mentioning his name was met with silence. I didn't know how to grieve him without support, but none came. I was a widow without a funeral, no tears, and no loving family members stopping by with a pot roast.

Some days I stayed in bed. The pain was too much, and the idea of doing something, anything, was an anchor around my neck. I couldn't cry. I couldn't will myself up. I knew I should get up, shower, and fix something to eat, or at least throw away the uneaten takeout from the last few days, but I couldn't.

I needed to be angry. I functioned much better when I was mad. This enveloping mudslide of emotions wasn't sustainable, but anger, yes—anger motivated me to get things done. I needed to get up and get something done, but I couldn't find an important enough reason. I couldn't even muster the energy to be angry with God for abandoning me again. Instead, I was ashamed to have been fooled, and just when I had opened my heart and let Him in again. I wondered in desperation how God could bail on me a second time, but one glance in the mirror at my dirty hair, smeared makeup, and mismatched pajamas was enough to convince me not to blame Him either. I was a mess, and even God couldn't be held responsible for the degree of useless that I felt I had become.

Doug's arrest and incarceration meant Dustin and Megan were ripped from my life, and I was powerless to change it. I had no voice, and it was crushing. My life had a before-the-arrest and an after-the-arrest feeling. Everyone I saw for the first time after the arrest reacted to me in one of two ways: they either didn't think he had done it and suggested we hire a good lawyer and sue the police, or they *just knew* there was something about him and were glad that it happened early enough in our marriage that I hadn't wasted too much time. Both types took a long pause before answering, hoping a look on my face or tone of my voice would clue them in so they would know which direction the conversation should go. Each time it happened, it was a crapshoot as to which Mary they would get, because most days, I didn't even know how I felt.

# Chapter Nineteen

I STAYED IN A STATE OF MENTAL ANGUISH FOR THE REMAINDER OF the semester, but after taking four years of night school to graduate with a two-year degree, that cold December day at the end of the semester in 1995 was a celebration to me. I graduated at the top of my class, and my good grades were tangible proof that I might not be a total disaster.

I needed a change, so I changed one of the only things I had control over. I moved out of the apartment Doug and I shared and into a new one. I had chosen it myself. I didn't choose it so my partner could play drums or because it was perfect for weekend visitation with the kids. I picked it because it suited me. The neighborhood was lovely, and the location offered shopping, decent restaurants, and nightlife. It was a small third-floor one-bedroom suite, but the rooms were light, and it had a balcony view of a golf course. Decorating was fun. My childhood fantasy had always been to own horses. The picture of galloping horses hanging over my sofa was a reminder of that dream. The sunflowers in the kitchen were bright and happy, but the Thomas Kinkade print in my bedroom was the greatest extravagance for my meager budget. Kinkade, also called the painter of light, was very popular. I fell in love with his print of a whimsical cottage surrounded by trees and was sure if I concentrated hard enough, I could dip my toes into the stream running by it and be reborn again. I was starting over.

Not long before Doug was arrested, I had applied to the New Castle County Police Department, and just after graduation, I applied for a position with the state police as well. The hiring process with the police department was drawn out and the wait was horrid. If either department hired me, I would go through a six-month police academy, but I needed something to occupy my time while I waited. Paul, a friend and fellow martial artist, was a trooper with the Delaware State Police. He had worked for New Castle County before transferring to the state police, and he offered to help with the hiring process. He knew the situation with Doug would make getting hired by anyone challenging.

I signed up for a ride-along with him to compare the two agencies. It was another exciting night of bar fights and extreme conditions, and by the end of the shift, I felt the same excitement and rush of adrenaline that had sent tingles up my spine on the ride-along with Maria.

I decided that I wanted to work for New Castle County as opposed to the state police, though I don't think the state police were sold on me anyway due to their ongoing criminal case with Doug. The domestic service calls on ride-alongs reminded me of my history, speaking to me in a way that a street brawl or traffic accident didn't. I had been in the shoes of those domestic violence victims, and I knew how it felt. I remembered how the intake nurse at the hospital had sized me up and treated me as though I were beneath her, the clanging of implements on the metal tray as the doctor relayed monotone instructions to the wall. I was invisible to them, maybe even dispensable. I wanted to change the system that shortchanged the victims.

Days slipped by, and I settled into a new norm, deciding the only thing that mattered was what I did, not how I felt. I focused on my goals and refused to give attention to anything else. It had been almost three months since Doug's arrest, and there were no more articles about him in the newspaper. I was no longer reliving the heart-wrenching story or being consumed with thoughts of him, and my heart began to heal.

It was Super Bowl Sunday, and I settled down to watch the game alone in my apartment. Not having a dog in the fight, I rooted for the Steelers but the Cowboys were winning, so I turned off the TV and went to bed before the end of the game.

A knock at my door bolted me out of bed at seven o'clock in the morning. I searched for clothes and checked my hair in the mirror, wondering who it could be. I shuffled to the door and looked out the peephole. State troopers stood on either side of the door. I opened the door slowly, allowing my blood pressure to return to normal. I recognized one of the men, having met him while on the ride-along with Paul.

"Oh, hi. How are you? Come on in," I said.

The trooper didn't recognize me, so I reminded him about the ride-along. "What's up?" I asked excitedly, thinking they may be conducting a background investigation for the job.

He and his partner came inside.

"We're looking for Doug Willis," he said.

I began stuttering out an explanation. "Um, I don't know where he is. We've been separated since November of last year. I haven't seen him, haven't even heard from him. I, um, I think maybe he's staying with his mom, but I'm not sure because I haven't spoken to him since November. We're separated." Repeating myself sounded defensive, and realizing that made me feel self-conscious.

"He's been visiting a mutual friend of yours, Scott, who lives a few miles away," the trooper said.

"Oh yeah, Scott Palmer," I said.

"Do you know where Doug is? Has he been here?" the trooper asked, and it was clear that my answer made it sound like I had been aware of the visit.

"Oh, no! Geez, I haven't seen him or heard from him. We've been separated, and he hasn't lived here for months."

"Well. He's in trouble. Do you know where we might find him?

He's not at his mother's house, where he should be. Maybe there's another family member or friend he might stay with?"

"I think I have the guest list from our wedding here somewhere. It has all his family members on it. What did he do? I mean, is he in trouble for something new, or is this related to the guy he stabbed?"

The troopers didn't answer but wandered around my tiny apartment, looking from room to room, presumably for Doug, speaking to each other in hand signals as I searched through desk drawers for contact information for his family. I found the guest list and checked off a few names for the troopers. Then they headed for the door, thanking me for my help.

On the way out the door, one of the men yelled over his shoulder, "You might want to find a place to stay for a few days until we pick him up. You might not be safe here." And they left, never telling me what had happened or why I might not be safe. I couldn't be sure, but it looked like they felt sorry for me as they both left with their heads down, looking at their shiny black shoes.

I shook my head, folded my arms across my chest, flopped onto the sofa with my head between my knees, then buried my face in my hands, feeling like someone had hit instant replay. Having the same trooper I'd met on the ride-along arrive at my door was like having my parallel universes meet. Shame swept me back into the riptide that was my life. I swam against the current as a flood of emotion and dread washed over me, threatening to pull me under, and my mind sent up rapid-fire defenses, reminding me that I hadn't done anything wrong.

My shoulders straightened as I kicked at the sneakers lying intentionally in my path, beckoning me to run, while feeling guilty for thinking about how Doug's problems would affect me. The phone rang. It was Scott.

"Hey, Mare, are you okay?" he asked.

"Yeah, physically I am, but I'm not so sure about the mental part. What's going on? The police were just here," I said.

Scott went on to explain that they had just left his house and apologized for giving them my address.

I asked him what had happened, and he explained that he and his girlfriend were watching the Super Bowl when Doug and his cousin Ray showed up uninvited. They were drunk and came in to watch the game like they were old buddies. When the game ended, they didn't leave, like they were stalling.

"So, what happened?" I nearly shouted.

"Doug knows I have guns I use for target practice, and he asked to borrow one."

"Oh my God. A gun? You didn't give him one, did you?"

"No way! I wouldn't give him a gun, but that scared the shit out of me. Mary, I didn't even know the Doug that showed up last night. That wasn't the same guy I used to know. He was dark and quiet, and it seemed like he had something up his sleeve the whole time he was here. He was nervous, constantly pulling at his mustache and tapping his feet. I honestly thought he was going to rob us."

"Jesus! What did you do? How did you get rid of them?"

"Well, it was getting late, and they still hadn't left, so I staged an emergency phone call. I told them they had to leave. They got back in the car and left. The next thing I knew, troopers were knocking on my door. They said Doug and Ray had gotten into an argument in front of my house and drove off together. The rest of the story is sketchy, but I've pieced together that they left here, drove back to Ray's house, and the argument escalated. Apparently, Doug lost his temper and stabbed Ray, leaving him for dead in the driveway. He took off with the car they had come in and somebody called an ambulance. Can you believe it? His own cousin! I'm not saying he threatened you or anything, but he is unpredictable right now. Doug was wasted, and he mentioned a couple of times that he wouldn't be in this mess if you hadn't kicked him out."

Scott couldn't offer anything more, so we chatted about possible scenarios and possible outcomes for Doug for a few minutes, and then he hung up, suggesting I find somewhere else to stay until Doug turned himself in.

The trooper had said the same thing. Now I felt guilty for kicking Doug out, and even wondered if things might have been different if I had let him stay. Did I push him over the edge? Should I have given him more time?

Based on Doug's first arrest, I figured he would get arrested and charged, probably with attempted murder again, but this time they would make sure he didn't get out on bail. I felt sorry for his poor mom, wondering if she would lose her house because he jumped bail.

I sat with my eyes closed and elbows on my knees, feeling deflated. This was far too weighty for early morning precoffee drama, so I rewound my morning, perked a pot of strong coffee, and started my day over. I packed a few bags, and an hour later drove to John and Barb's house to flop for a few days until Doug was picked up. I didn't think he would hurt me, but just in case the surprises hadn't ended, I figured it wasn't entirely a bad idea.

That morning's paper had a short notice about Doug being on the run. The crime report had been my favorite section of the newspaper until that moment, but knowing the article was about my husband changed everything. It was surreal.

Every day, I scoured the news outlets for some word about him, praying police would take him into custody without a fight, and Maria kept me in the loop as much as she could. After several days of worrying, a short blurb let me know that he had turned himself in at the State Police Troop No. 2. He went to jail in lieu of a $500,000 secured bond.

After the excitement came to a screeching halt, there was silence. With no additional information and no articles in the newspaper to keep me informed, I felt more and more estranged from Doug. He was slipping away. Some days were worse than others, days when I felt disloyal, which was something I had never been. There were other days when it all made sense and I thought maybe God protected me from a man I never knew, but the days when I was simply angry with Doug were easier to navigate.

Doug was going to prison, and another divorce was imminent. I wondered if a quick divorce would improve my chances of being hired by one of the police departments, which felt like proof, of course, that I was not only disloyal but completely self-absorbed. There was a great man in there somewhere, and he was lost. I wasn't ready to let go, and that felt sad. The doubt was edging me a bit closer to insanity than I was willing to admit, so I did what I usually do. I refocused on doing things for myself. I filed for divorce in February, almost a month after Doug's second arrest.

My mantra was always *patience is a waste of time*, and I pulled it out when I didn't want to deal with emotional pain or when I was in a hurry to distance myself from an unwanted situation. Sometimes it served me well, but it almost always caused the wound to fester then open up later, making me deal with it. Breaking this pattern of avoiding my feelings only to be slammed with them later has been the longest leg of my journey. Slowing down, feeling the feelings, and analyzing the trauma before moving on might change my response to future circumstances. So often I rushed to an end, any end that would allow me to forget what had happened and move on. I thought it was healthy, sort of a sharp knife cuts cleaner theory, but trying to move on so quickly caused me to repeat my mistakes. Knowing my part and exploring ways to stop repeating bad behavior was progress. If you were to ask me how long it took to change, well, I'd have to say, I'll let you know.

I wondered if the divorce would help the healing process along, and it did, until February 23, 1996, when I received a letter in an envelope marked, "This letter is from an inmate at Gander Hill Prison." It was the first communication I'd had from Doug since our separation in November, and the white business envelope seemed much too formal. I stood immobile for a moment, my heart thumping wildly.

All anger and resentment faded, and my eyes clouded with tears until I could barely see enough to open the envelope. My hands trembled with excitement to hear from him while shame filled my heart for wanting to. I was ashamed not because he stabbed people, used drugs, stole things, or ruined my career path, but because he cheated me out of my life. I was afraid of the finality that might be in those pages, and at the same time, I worried that reading them would open all the gaping wounds that I had painstakingly wrapped in denial and plans for the future.

The envelope lay heavily in my lap while I considered what to do. I tore off the little green card identifying that the letter was from an inmate and ground my teeth, willing myself to get pissed and stay pissed. I gazed at the cool white envelope, turning it over in my hands, looking at the postmark, seeing his face through the familiarity of his handwriting. I worried that I might find myself drawn back in if he said the right things, and it frightened me. I had clawed my way to where I was and I never wanted to fall for his charms again. I couldn't allow his letter, or Doug himself, to have that power over me. But which Doug would I even be getting?

I needed to stop acting like a childish schoolgirl and face reality. I placed the letter on the coffee table and walked into the kitchen, feeling the heaviness of it follow me, wondering if I should open it or throw it away. I was losing my resolve to stay angry. I drew a deep breath, not ready to decide. Feeling helpless and alone in my apartment, I tucked the letter away in my sock drawer, promising to read it when I was ready; it was a good compromise.

I was divorcing my soulmate. The man who had baited my hooks because I was creeped out by slimy worms, who had brought me chocolate-frosted donuts and flowers every week for three years, who had called me sweet pea and caressed my face to show how much he treasured me. I was still in love with him and couldn't reconcile the mix of love and anger I felt, so I strapped on my sneakers and ran for my life. Mile after mile, I recalled our lives together, imagining him running backward in front of me, encouraging me, smiling, and shouting back to me, *Just one more mile, sweet pea. I promise. Just one more mile,* until he faded from sight. I didn't call friends or eat a gallon of mint chocolate chip ice cream. I just sat. I sat staring at the sock drawer, crossing and uncrossing my legs, scratching places that didn't itch, wiping away a few rogue tears, climbing into bed before sunset, knowing that everything I thought was over was probably just beginning.

Much like the end of my first marriage, I refused to acknowledge the pain, and I gave Doug back the only thing he had left me with—his name. I moved on as Mary Sweeney again, replacing pain, sadness, and grief with anger, resentment, and self-righteousness. A sharp knife cut cleaner, but having the right to be angry was a little like having the right to have cancer. Anyone would agree that I should be angry, but it was eating me up inside. Letting go, finding forgiveness, feeling my way through the horror—without judging him—would be true healing.

There is nothing wrong with planning for the future, so that's where I put my focus. I was not healed yet! Maybe later I would find compassion for him, for what he had experienced, and sorrow for being unable to help him, all while acknowledging that he had done his best. But not yet.

I opened the letter many years later when I thought I had moved on. He was kind and apologetic, but it was clear that he had written the letter long before he had had a chance to consider how he felt, or how I might feel. It opened some old wounds, and I cried away the pain, still missing the man who had died long before going to prison. He expressed his love for me and his sorrow at parting forever; he shared the things he loved about me, congratulated me for graduating college, and wished me an early happy birthday.

A year later, Doug pled guilty to first-degree assault and accompanying weapons and conspiracy charges for the first incident and to attempted murder for the second incident. Between the two convictions it appeared that he would spend the rest of his life in prison. From my perspective, we had both received life sentences.

# Chapter Twenty

BY THE END OF JUNE 1997, THE POLICE ACADEMY WAS ALREADY IN its fourth week, but there was a plan to hire three more recruits for this class. Having not been selected in their first round of recruits, I waited painfully for the call that I would be one of those three. Each time the phone rang, adrenaline surged through my body, but every false alarm cost me a bit of enthusiasm. The constant peaks and valleys made it challenging to keep the faith; I called the human resources department every week hoping I might get to talk to someone different, so they wouldn't know how desperate I was. Because of Doug's drama, I knew the odds weren't in my favor, and I felt like an unqualified underdog, too old, too skinny, too female, and way too married to the wrong man to be hired, but I knew I could do this job if they'd just give me a chance. I needed a mulligan.

I hung in suspense until July 2, 1997, when an officer from HR finally called to offer me the position. I wasn't sure how to tell him that I was about to go on vacation, so I stammered something unintelligible, explaining that I was traveling to Niagara Falls, Canada. I offered to cancel my trip, but even though I was a late hire, four weeks into the academy, he agreed to push back my start date. I called everybody I knew, sharing the news just so that I could hear it over and over again.

When the excitement dissipated and I was alone with my thoughts, I wondered what Doug would think of my becoming a police officer. I was sure he supported me when I began my journey, but given how his life had changed course, I wondered what he would think of my choice now. I felt my husband would have been happy for me, but I wasn't sure how the inmate would feel. I knew that Vince would not have supported me in any leg of this journey. He needed me to be passive, an isolated follower. My new position would surely not reflect those qualities.

JoAnna Brogan was one of the recruit officers who had been selected in the first round and was already in the academy. She called to tell me what I needed to have to be ready for my first day.

"Get a few khaki shirts and pants and a belt. The pants usually come with a cloth belt, and that'll be fine. I have a new black baseball hat you can have, and the department will give you a pair of shiny black shoes. You can press the creases in your shirt every day, or I can give you the name and number of a seamstress most of us use. She'll sew the creases in for you. It's easier," she said, laughing. "Unger, you'll meet him, always presses in his creases, but he was in the marines. I say work smarter, not harder, so my creases are sewn in. I'll give you a list of places you can get your clothes, but Goldberg's is probably the cheapest and closest place."

She told me about cutting strings off of shirts and pants and burning the loose threads with a cigarette lighter to avoid leaving any evidence of their presence.

"Strings are the devil," she said. "Anything that makes you look different from any of the other recruits will cost us something, be it push-ups, running, humiliation, standing at attention, or writing a ton of memos. You're one of three late hires. You're five weeks behind the rest of us, and I'll need to catch you up on all the bookwork you've missed."

Poor Brogan was the unfortunate soul assigned to me to ensure I didn't fail. She shared notes and handouts from the classes I had already missed, and I copied them. At the end of the academy, we would be tested on the material, so everything was necessary.

"Thanks for all your help, JoAnna. I'll do my best," I promised.

She chuckled. "Well, that's good, but it won't be enough. Don't let it get to you. You'll be fine."

One of my old martial arts instructors, Sergeant Archer, would be my drill sergeant. Delaware is a small state, and I wasn't sure knowing him socially would be a good thing. It could go either way. I might receive special attention, or I might have to work harder to prove myself. I prepared myself for the latter.

On my first day, I arrived at the academy a half hour early, carrying all my gear in a giant duffle bag, prepared to stand at attention in one of two lines with the forty other recruits, feeling like a dork. A glance in a full-length mirror before I left home had reflected a 106-pound dude, dressed in khaki everything, with no makeup, no jewelry, and a ponytail tucked up under a black baseball cap. As much as I tried to convince myself I looked like all the others, I was sure I stuck out like a sore thumb. Most of the recruits were in their early twenties. They looked like a bunch of kids playing dress-up; at thirty-six years old, I looked out of place, like a senior citizen at a sock hop. I nervously tucked my ponytail deeper into my cap, but nobody seemed to notice because they were busy picking at themselves. Everyone was absorbed in preparing their uniforms.

Forty-one recruits were helping each other get dressed for inspection. All modesty was forgotten as men and women alike stood in lines with their pants dropped almost to their knees, helping one another tuck shirts into their pants in a way that made the shirt look freshly pressed, and using lint rollers to pick up fuzz, loose strings, or pet hair. Grown men slid lint rollers all over female recruit officers' breasts, butts, and everywhere in between, but it was clear that nothing sexual was going on here. I looked around wide-eyed, wondering what I had gotten myself into. The recruits were fear-driven, but knowing I wasn't the only neurotic one helped me relax a little.

Once most of the recruits were prepared for inspection, they converged on the three newbies with cleaning rags in hand.

"Brogan, you take Sweeney," someone yelled, and JoAnna picked up a lint roller. She was all over me, hurriedly removing hair and whatever contraband she saw that might get the whole class into trouble. I thought I looked fine, but the rest of the cadets seemed to be in a panic as Brogan yelled, "Davis, Rogers has a giant freaking rope hanging out the back of his pants."

I smiled nervously, noticing the small white string hanging from the other newbie's trousers.

"Would you get that, please?"

Three recruits feverishly cut strings and polished shoes, cursing in what seemed like a whole different language. I could see myself in the patent leather shoes they provided, but apparently, they weren't shiny enough when they came out of the box, so JoAnna used Windex to remove any latent fingerprints. When she finished, she pointed at a recruit crouching behind me.

"Sweeney, this is Unger. He's going to do your heels. They need edge dressing for shine."

"Hey, Sweeney, welcome aboard," Unger said. "I need you to pull up your pant legs." I indulged, feeling grateful that he was a bit older than the others, and noticed his slight southern drawl, a familiar accent that brought me comfort. He painted my heels, and sounding more like a drill sergeant, said, "Once I get this on here, don't move, or you'll get it on your pants. And just so you know, Sweeney, you look like a soup sandwich."

*Swell*, I thought, feeling offended and unintentionally standing stock still. *What's a soup sandwich?* I conjured up a mental image of tomato soup running out from between two slices of bread and decided he was probably right. I was a mess.

JoAnna and the others clipped on black ties and tie bars, commenting on improperly shaven faces and ill-fitting uniforms in the whirlwind of team dressing. One guy had forgotten his shoes, so he was wearing sneakers, and the other recruits screamed at him about how stupid he was. As if that weren't enough, the sneaker recruit had eaten a sticky bun for breakfast and vomited in the grass, about ten feet from the inspection area. Instead of expressing compassion or concern for his well-being, the scolding continued. I shifted from foot to foot, feeling terrible for him but secretly glad it wasn't me, and quickly took a mental inventory of my clothes. I was painfully aware that I had no idea what to look for. While the others knew the drill, the newbies—me, sneaker boy, and lobster boy (so named because the recruits had decided that his eyes were too close together)—tried to mimic their every move so as not to get yelled at. I could see that the first five weeks had been a learning experience for them.

They were able to get us looking reasonably neat before the academy staff appeared from the building and marched across the parking lot, screwing on their hats as they walked. A dozen hushed "shits" and "fucks" could be heard as recruits tossed rags to the side and hustled to their imaginary footprints on the ground, standing at attention. For about thirty seconds, I thought we were good.

Sergeant Archer marched to the other end of the line and faced the first recruit while another recruit officer with a clipboard trailed behind. It was time for inspection, and I stood at attention, or at least my Gomer Pyle version of attention, waiting for my turn. I tried to see what was happening without looking like I was trying to see. My anxiety heightened as I listened to them moving from recruit to recruit, one at a time down the line, yelling about all sorts of infractions.

*This is insane*, I thought, preoccupied with the sweat trickling down my back, my body trembling as I awaited my turn. It was the longest ten minutes of my life. I had heard stories about recruits falling out in the inspection line, meaning they fainted, and just before inspection, Unger had told me not to lock my knees, or it could happen to me. Damn, now the only thing I could think was, *Don't pass out; don't pass out*, which made me more nervous. *Shit, are my knees locked? What does that even mean—locked?* So I bobbed up and down, trying not to lock my knees and faint. I looked like a piece in the carnival game Whac-A-Mole just waiting to get thumped on the head with a mallet and was sure to be the first thirty-six-year-old, khaki-colored mole to go down in formation. To say doubt crept in would be an understatement, and I prayed silently for this part to end.

My prayers were answered when Sergeant Archer sidestepped in front of me as I tried to ignore him, eyes front. He was shorter than me, so I tried to look straight over his head. I could feel him glaring, his eyes boring into my soul, but then his Smokey the Bear hat nearly brushed against my chin. It struck me as suddenly hilarious. *Oh no!* I stifled a smile as Archer barked, "Is there something funny, Sweeney?"

Blood vessels threatened to burst from his forehead as I looked at him with my best "Bruce, you know me" look on my face.

"Sir, no, sir," I answered, copying the other recruits' response, the smile whisked from my face.

He wore an annoyed look on his now red face. This was not my karate buddy.

"Well, I'm glad you could make it, Sweeney," he barked. "I guess your Fourth of July vacation was more important than being a police officer! Is that it, Sweeney? Are you sure this is where you want to be? Maybe you made a mistake! Is that it, Sweeney? Did you make a mistake?"

I could feel the warmth of his breath as he continued berating me.

"You know, Sweeney, your partners will be counting on you to be there when they need you. You can't just jet off to Canada whenever you want to and take a vacation!"

His voice elevated, and I shifted my weight from one foot to the other, my breathing accelerating.

"And that's another thing: You couldn't find a place in the United States to celebrate the Fourth of July—Independence Day—Sweeney? Are you sure you're an American, Sweeney?"

He was screaming at me, spittle spraying in my face, but I didn't flinch. I was afraid to look at him for fear that I might say the wrong thing. JoAnna had told me that every answer began and ended with "sir," known as a "sir sandwich."

"Sir, yes, sir," I responded as sweat ran down my neck at eight o'clock in the morning. I knew I had screwed up immediately because he started with, "Yes, sir, what, Sweeney?"

I wasn't sure how to answer, so I didn't say anything. I stood frozen, waiting for a brilliant response to come to mind.

"That's just great, Sweeney! You're going to be a winner! Answer me, Sweeney! Yes, sir, what?"

"Sir, yes, I want to be here, sir."

My brain rewarded me with a barrage of f-bombs as I assessed my response, wondering what would come next.

"Sweeney, you'd better straighten up. Just because you started five weeks late, that's no excuse for your lack of preparedness. Do you understand me, Sweeney?" he shouted into my face.

"Sir, yes, sir," I responded.

"Is that all you can say, Sweeney? Dear God, we were scraping the bottom of the barrel with this one," he added disparagingly, pointing out bobby pins sticking out from under my cap, another of many "gigs," or violations, he found with my uniform, and then moved on to the next victim.

Clipboard guy nervously shuffled behind him, recording all the infractions for who knows what reason. I screwed an "I'm so sorry" look on my face as the recruit scribbled notes. He was expressionless, no look of encouragement, which I was sure meant that he hated me.

The process took about thirty minutes, then Sergeant Archer dismissed us to our classroom, and it quickly became apparent that everybody had been yelled at for something. Even so, I was stressed and felt terrible for getting the whole class into trouble.

"We have to do fifty more push-ups because of me and the other new guys," I whined awkwardly to JoAnna. "Jesus, I've never heard my name so many times in a row in my life."

The rest of the class didn't seem the least bit concerned. JoAnna tossed her hat on the desk and, shrugging, said, "Fifty gigs—that's not bad for one day. We used to get more than a hundred. It doesn't matter what the day is like. We're doing push-ups. Get used to it."

JoAnna always had a ready smile, and we were fast friends. She didn't fit the stereotype of the female police officer, having once been the Miller beer girl. She was beautiful and feminine, and even clad in khaki pants and a black tie, she was pretty, like Goldie Hawn in *Private Benjamin*. She was a different kind of tough, unfazed by the constant yelling and criticism, and I was glad she was mentoring me.

The academy building was a fire school designed for far fewer than the forty-one cadets in our class. The plastic chairs around rectangular white tables could be folded up to make room if necessary. It was close quarters. We learned, ate, studied, and took tests in this main classroom, shoulder to shoulder, alphabetically, with our academy mates. The white tile floor was smeared with streaks of black shoe polish from eighty-two shiny, shuffling, marching feet conducting military-facing movements through the hallways. Blackboards and whiteboards made up the entire wall in the front of the room, and the remaining walls were white-painted cinder blocks with no windows to encourage daydreaming. The classroom was the safe zone for cadets, and I immediately felt the energy shift upon entering. Academy staff rarely entered the classroom except when introducing the next instructor, and it was clear that the intention was to ensure that the atmosphere was appropriate for learning.

That first day, I learned about adrenaline and its effect on the body. Even though I was safe, and I knew Sergeant Archer, getting yelled at was stressful and affected my ability to communicate, discern, and respond. I was surprised I couldn't answer basic questions, even though I knew the answers. The whole time he yelled, my mind was pinging from one possible response to another like a pinball machine, with ideas and suggestions coming from all directions, all sounding stupid. Common sense suggested there was nothing to worry about, but it didn't matter. My body responded to feeling threatened with increased blood pressure, shallow breathing, physical trembling, and absolutely no fine motor skills. I dropped stuff, tripped over nonexistent cracks in the floor, and couldn't answer simple questions like "Who dresses you, Sweeney?" with any confidence. I knew it would be essential to control this stress response before hitting the streets. There was a reason for everything we did here.

Since I started the academy late, I had some catching up to do. Thankfully, JoAnna and the others began helping me fill binder after three-inch binder with notes and helped me to prepare for quizzes and tests I had missed. This process helped me form bonds with my academy mates, which wasn't easy given the age difference.

For the next five months, my name became Recruit Officer Sweeney to the academy staff and Mom-Mom to my classmates, as I was one of the oldest female recruit officers at age thirty-six. I didn't feel old, and I was in great shape, so I shrugged it off with a laugh. We ran three days a week, and although I was slower than most of the class, I could run forever. I was thrilled to learn that there would be some martial arts training and knew this would give me an advantage, maybe one of the only ones I'd have over this group of kids.

The academy was a Monday through Friday job from 8:00 a.m. until whenever. We were required to participate in community events, including a 5K race and a formal dance for the elderly. These events taught us the importance of community involvement, volunteerism, and camaraderie, and I enjoyed them.

I came home every night and poured myself into bed. The curriculum was intense. Every day we studied criminal law, constitutional law, traffic law, departmental directives, FOP union rules, domestic violence laws, SPCA procedures, ten codes, radio procedures, civil rights, DUI procedures, and a plethora of other laws and policies. The bookwork was taxing, but I knew how to study, so the written tests came easily. Practical application tests, not so much. My mom raised her kids to mind our own business and keep our hands to ourselves, so that's what came naturally. Police work was different. All we did in practical application was mind everyone else's business and put our hands on people, and it was uncomfortable.

Handcuffing, for example, is more complicated than it looks. To practice, recruits were paired up in lines, facing one another in a large gymnasium, wearing gray sweatpants, a sweatshirt, a black gun belt, a rubber gun, and handcuffs. During one practice my partner, JoAnna, stood facing away from me, hands behind her back, and on command, I withdrew the cuffs from my gun belt and recited the dialogue I had learned.

"Okay, ma'am, I'm going to place these handcuffs on your wrists for my protection and yours. You're not under arrest, but you are being detained until we can figure out what happened tonight. Do you understand?" My voice echoed noisily off the hardwood basket-ball court, along with the voices of the twenty other recruits practic-ing the same mantra. It was loud and distracting, which was probably intended.

"Yes, wait . . . If I'm not under arrest, can you handcuff me?" JoAnna asked.

I learned to continue cuffing while answering the questions we practiced and found it very uncomfortable touching strangers.

"Yes, ma'am. As I said, it's for your protection and mine until we figure out what has happened here."

Talking helped keep the handcuffed person's mind occupied while the officer was completing the task.

I adjusted quickly to academy life, becoming just as bored as the other recruits. By the time staff fitted us for bulletproof vests and uniforms, we were beyond ready to graduate. Five months seemed like an eternity. The issued equipment became mine, and I started to believe my dream would happen. It had been a long-awaited dream that sometimes seemed elusive, but it was here, and I was eager to get on with it.

The twenty-fourth police academy class for New Castle County Police graduated on December 13, 1997. I was among the forty-one officers on that stage, ten women and thirty-one men, a pretty respectable male-to-female ratio for that time. My grandpa, brother, sister, mom, and lots of friends attended the ceremony, where the keynote speaker was a Delaware senator and the future president of the United States, Joe Biden. Graduation was stoic, and I was proud to have my badge pinned on in the company of my biological family and my new police family. I felt like I belonged. I had found my tribe.

# Chapter Twenty-One

With months of classroom training and mock exercises behind me, I received my assignment to B squad. Matt Tower was my field training officer (FTO). There were four squads, and each was broken down into smaller sectors. According to the roster, my assignment was 31 sector, the armpit of the division, an area with numerous high-crime neighborhoods. My shift started at 2300 hours in military time, which was how I would tell time from now on. My first night of rotations began in the locker room, where I stowed all the useless three-ring binders I had brought with me from the academy.

My first field assignment was three months of on-the-job training with Tower as my primary FTO. His nickname was Snippy, so I wondered if I had been stuck with another goose egg along with my sector assignment. I would ride shotgun with him, mirroring his behavior, learning the practical application part of handling complaints, and then in three months, I would be on my own.

My call sign was thirty-one bravo two, but everyone called me Sweeney, just Sweeney. The uniform, call sign, hairstyle, and use of last names removed any feminine qualities from female officers, and as I stared in the locker-room mirror, I looked like a gangly teenage boy or maybe SWAT Barbie, but I wasn't complaining. Nothing could ruin my mood that night.

Tower's primary responsibility was to make sure I didn't get myself killed while learning the ropes. I was a strapping 106 pounds out of the academy, and Tower was a tall, thin guy, so we didn't make a very menacing pair. He was good looking and young, probably ten years my junior. I thought my FTO would be a cranky old guy, wiser with lots of experience and maybe gray hair. I wasn't disappointed but I was maybe a little concerned.

It was a cold December night on the midnight shift. My gun belt with all the accessories like handcuffs, flashlights, baton, gun, and radio barely fit around my twenty-six-inch waist and no hips. Most officers carried two pairs of handcuffs and pouches for rubber gloves on their belts, but there was no room for anything more on mine, so I had to sacrifice them for the critical gear, keeping whatever else I could in my pockets. The bulletproof vest and layers of clothing made it a challenge to get in and out of the car, let alone move. The heavy black radio on my hip had a spiral cord and microphone that clipped to epaulets on my jacket and was my lifeline to the dispatchers who would try to keep me alive for the next twenty years. If that weren't enough, I was assigned a beautiful brown leather car coat with buckles and zippers that created openings to reach all the equipment.

Altogether, I probably weighed in at 146 pounds, and like a kid dressed up to play in the snow, I could barely bend my arms. If there was any advantage to all the extra clothing it was that it made me look bigger, more menacing, and I would need all the help I could get in that area. I couldn't imagine running while wearing so much equipment, and the odds of my catching someone were low; I imagined drawing my weapon, shouting, "Freeze, or I'll fall." The halls at headquarters were filled with activity as I exited the locker room and close to eighty officers entered and exited the building for change of shift. Maria Friswell stopped me in the hallway. "Hey, girl, you ready for this? Who's your FTO?"

"Ha, yeah, I'm ready, all right. Matt Tower's my FTO."

"Oh, awesome. Snippy is squared away, and he's proactive. He'll get you into lots of shit. What sector are you assigned to?"

"Um, I'm 31B2."

"That's great," she said. "31 sector is the busiest area. You'll learn a lot and ten times faster than rookies in other areas. Hey, I don't want to keep you. You should probably get to roll call about fifteen minutes early. In fact, you should be fifteen minutes early for everything for the next twenty years or so. Be safe tonight."

She smiled and one-arm hugged me awkwardly, our uniform pins, buttons, and clasps clattering together.

"Thanks, Maria." I nodded, smiling at her, very aware that she got me to this moment.

My first night began with roll call, only this time I was wearing the brown uniform, and I was one of five new officers sitting in the front row, staring nervously at the lieutenants and sergeants who looked back from the front of the room with poker faces.

"Line up for inspection," Lieutenant Janson commanded.

Six years before, when I sat in roll call with Maria as a civilian, I had butterflies just watching, but I didn't tonight. I was ready for anything. I knew my uniform was in order, and I was the one standing with my shoulders square, staring straight ahead, and this inspection was much different from the academy inspection. The supervisors were looking for the things we had done right. I listened as the lieutenant sidestepped from one rookie to the next, examining hats, slacks, and badges.

"Now that's a spotless gun belt," he said to Schmitt, a new man who was two officers down from me. "You old guys are going to have to step up your game. I think this group is going to give you a run for your money," he said to the seasoned officers.

After inspecting each new officer, he extended his hand, welcoming them. Each one shook his hand and rendered a salute.

My turn came quickly, and I stared straight ahead.

"Welcome aboard, Officer Sweeney. You're on the flagship of the division, and we've been waiting six months for you."

"Thank you, sir," I responded and saluted.

I was surprised to find that the other thirty-six officers were happy that we were there; one at a time, they passed by shaking our hands, welcoming us to B squad. I had assumed that as new, wet-behind-the-ears rookies, we would make their jobs harder, but we were welcomed with open arms as much-needed additional staffing to the squad.

"Okay, Sweeney, the mailboxes are in alphabetical order along that wall." Tower pointed. "You'll need to check it every night. Your subpoenas and any other notifications you get will be there. Go ahead and check your mailbox, and I'll get our vehicle assignment."

I followed his lead immediately.

Officer Tower was quiet and organized, and my first night began much as the ride-along had. He handed me the second set of keys, inspected the vehicle, stowed a shotgun in the trunk, and moment by moment told me what to do.

"We have to let dispatch know we are in-service, so give them our call sign and the number of the car we're driving so they can follow us on GPS."

He fed me the information to relay to dispatch, and I signed us on. I was self-conscious, knowing that everyone on the radio could hear me, and was pretty sure I sounded silly, so I tried not to use my girly voice but also tried not to sound like a dude.

"They've been holding calls, so the shift that's finishing up doesn't get held up on lengthy investigations," Matt explained.

We responded to a few in-progress complaints, which turned out to be insignificant, and I began noticing a pattern. I listened to the officers who worked the area with us and soon recognized which cars and complaints were nearby.

My biggest challenge was knowing my location. I had no idea where we were or how to get from one complaint to the next. Matt handed me a map book, and it occurred to me that I had never used one in my life. Some communities were so congested that an arrow on the map pointed to a cluster of streets with a list of names, suggesting, *It's somewhere in that mess.* The map looked like a jigsaw puzzle with missing pieces, and sometimes it took a few minutes to figure out where I was and where I wanted to go, which often ended up being just a few streets away. I keyed up the mic.

"31B2, 10-69," I said, using police ten code to let dispatch know we were on our way.

As the hours passed, fewer and fewer dispatched calls came.

"Hey," Tower directed nonchalantly, scratching his head. "Since it's quiet, make a right turn here. We're going to an area where there's a lot of drug activity. We'll find something to get into."

I had intentionally avoided this neighborhood all my life up to this point but nodded in agreement.

It was about 3:30 a.m. when an old, beat-up black Toyota with more primer than paint on it appeared out of nowhere, driving toward us with the headlights off. The driver quickly ducked onto a side street, and Tower made a quick turn to follow it. Papers, books, and lunch boxes competing for space in the sardine-can patrol car careened into my lap. I quickly unloaded everything while keeping an eye on what was happening in front of us. We turned the corner, and the Toyota made another turn a few streets ahead of us. I noticed the car was missing a taillight. We followed the car until it turned right, back onto the road where we first saw it. Tower activated the lights and siren, pulling the car over to the side of the busy roadway.

"You approach from the passenger side, and I'll take the driver's side. Watch their hands and stay quiet. I'll do the talking," Matt said.

"Okay, got it," I snapped back, relieved that he would be handling it.

Matt called the stop in to dispatch, telling them our location, the tag number, and the car make and model. The driver was the only one in the car, and he was moving around a lot, bending down like he was looking under the seat.

"Okay, something's up with this guy. Keep your head on a swivel," Matt said.

I got out of the car and turned on my flashlight, shining the beam into the passenger-side rearview mirror, knowing that it prevented occupants from seeing my approach. Instinctive goose bumps raised on my scalp, alerting my mind that my body was approaching DEFCON 1. Matt pressed his fingertips onto the trunk as he walked alongside the car. I knew he did it in case something happened to us during the stop and the driver fled. Detectives would find Matt's fingerprints on the trunk when locating the suspect's vehicle.

I pressed my fingers onto the trunk of the passenger side and warily approached, pacing myself so that I would arrive at the front window at the same time Tower did. My heart thumped out of my chest as my warm breath created smoke signals in the cold night air. I shined my flashlight into the passenger-side window, searching for weapons or anything that appeared out of order. A plaid flannel shirt lay in a bundle on the floorboard, and I leaned in for a closer look, listening to Matt's instructions to the driver.

"Sir, I'm Officer Tower of New Castle County Police. I need to see your driver's license and proof of insurance. Where are you headed?" he asked as the driver fumbled with his wallet searching for his license. Cars swooshed by at high rates of speed, sending icy gusts of wind and funnel clouds of leaves in my direction.

Just then, the shirt moved. I shined the light on the lump and, looking through the fogged-up window, made out a sneaker. "Shit, that's a person under that shirt," I muttered. I tucked my flashlight under my arm and drew my gun, a nine-millimeter Smith & Wesson, with my left hand, supporting its weight with my right, and shouted, "Hey, I have a passenger here on the floor."

Tower drew his weapon and began yelling commands. "Driver, put both hands on the wheel and do not move! Passenger, show me both of your hands. Do it now! Do it now," he shouted, "and move slowly! Driver, don't you move."

The driver, frozen in place, spit out the appropriate responses. "I'm not moving, sir. I'm not moving."

I stayed where I was with my gun aimed at the red plaid bundle as, one at a time, two hands appeared from under the pile, and my heart rate quickened. With my flashlight under my arm, I jerked the door open so I could see better, all the while aiming my gun at the unfolding human, who seemed to be getting bigger and bigger as he righted himself in the seat. Tower continued barking out orders to which the driver and passenger complied. Once the passenger had both hands on the dashboard, Tower removed the driver from the car and handcuffed him. Time stood still for me as Tower asked questions at lightning speed while patting down the driver.

"Who's the guy that's with you? Where are you headed? Why is he hiding on the floor?" His voice faded as he walked the driver back to the waiting patrol car, placing him in the back seat of the vehicle. I was alone with my gun trained on the passenger's head as he leaned forward with his hands on the dashboard.

"Don't you move," I ordered the passenger.

"I'm not, ma'am," the crackling voice responded. My hands shook from adrenaline, the cold, and the weight of the gun.

Once Tower handcuffed the driver, patted him down, and secured him in the patrol car, he returned, took the passenger out of the vehicle, and checked him for weapons.

"Why are you hiding on the floor, dude?" Tower asked as he patted the man's waistband and jacket for anything that might hurt us.

"I have a warrant," the flannel shirt guy said. "I don't have bail money, and I can't spend the weekend in jail. It's not my friend's fault. Don't do nothing to him. He's a good dude."

Matt cuffed the passenger.

"Sit him on the curb, Sweeney, while I check the passenger

compartment for weapons." I holstered my sidearm and walked the man to the side of the car, helping him to a seated position.

"Hey, look, it's cold out here. Can I have my jacket? I'm freezing," flannel shirt guy asked.

I ignored his request and said nothing, nervously watching every move he made, noticing that I wasn't cold anymore. He kept talking. "Why'd you stop us anyway? Hey, you didn't read me my rights. Are you a rookie?"

Slightly stung, I reacted. "Shut your piehole."

It was the first defensive command I had ever made. The next time I would choose better words, but the experience of standing up for myself was empowering. I would never have challenged Vince, but my going along days were over.

I could hear Matt talking to dispatch on the radio, providing names and birth dates for the driver and flannel shirt guy. He returned quickly, and approached the passenger, helping him to his feet. At the same time, another patrol car pulled up to offer help.

"Hey, what do you got?"

"I think he's a 29P," I answered, proud that I remembered the designator for a wanted person, "but I don't know what for yet."

The officer exited his car and walked over to Tower, and together they developed a game plan. The assisting officer returned with flannel guy's jacket, draped it around his shoulders, and escorted him to the back seat of his patrol car.

"I'm taking this guy to JP court. The driver is wanted, too, but has an active warrant, so you guys are taking him to headquarters to be arraigned. Catch you guys later. Be safe."

"Okay, thanks. You too," I said with a nod, walking back to Matt.

"Okay, it's your first arrest, Sweeney. I'll talk you through it. He has a hard warrant, and we have to execute it."

"What's the difference between a hard warrant and a bench warrant?" I asked.

Tower explained the difference and described step-by-step what I needed to do. It was one of the hundreds of questions I would ask over the next few months.

"We'll leave him with the turnkey and do the paperwork, but we have to tow his car first. Can't leave it here. It's all shitted up."

"Should I take notes?" I asked.

"Nope, note-taking days are over. You gotta remember this stuff now. You'll get the hang of it."

I was immediately impressed by Officer Tower and knew I was in good hands. I marveled that he was so calm. His monotone voice didn't waver, and I was pretty sure his hands weren't shaking.

I quickly discovered that "all shitted up" meant the car was not registered and had no insurance, a broken taillight, and a cracked windshield. My job was to call a tow truck and write the tow slip and the tickets, which the driver would receive. It took forever, but I finished, and off we went to headquarters with my first prisoner, who had a warrant for a domestic dispute with his girlfriend.

"I didn't know she signed warrants, man. I love that girl. She's my world."

My first prisoner wasn't what I expected. He seemed like a regular guy. I almost felt bad for him, but then I remembered my experience with Vince, and for a brief moment, he was Vince, a man who had also seemed like an average guy to most people. I strengthened my resolve, drove back to headquarters, and ultimately took the man to jail, feeling just a bit vindicated.

"The turnkey is the guy who takes in the prisoners and collects their property along with their belt so they can't kill themselves. He locks them in a holding cell until the judge is ready to set bail and schedule a court date," Matt explained.

It seemed like a lot to remember, and I couldn't imagine how I would keep it all straight, but Tower assured me it would become second nature. While I worked on my report, he completed the necessary training paperwork, checked off boxes, and added notes that would eventually document that I had learned how to do everything that was required before being released from field training.

We turned in our paperwork as the sun came up and parted company.

"Go home and get some sleep. I'll see you tonight, Sweeney."

"Okay, will do. Thanks, Tower," I said.

As he walked away, it occurred to me that I hadn't even made it through my first night without drawing my weapon. Strangely, I wasn't afraid. The adrenaline spikes were powerful, and when that plaid bundle had moved, my training kicked in and my body responded. Everything that followed was academy training. I don't remember consciously deciding what to do next. My training guided my actions during tense situations, which gave me confidence. I wasn't making potentially life-altering decisions alone but was drawing on the experience of decades of police academy instructors. If I were creating a recipe for police work, it would be one part knowledge, one part common sense, and one part confidence. Situations like the one that night would happen many times throughout my career, and with every extreme situation, I added another dash of experience or pinch of confidence to my recipe.

I changed clothes and drove home in my own car, absorbing the feeling of having completed my first night, but the excitement and the shift in my schedule kept me awake for hours. I cleaned my gear, wrote some notes about a few things I had learned that I didn't want to forget, and ate a light lunch. My phone rang several times, and I excitedly described how my night had gone to my brother and other callers, who checked in to make sure I was all right. I turned off the ringer on my phone and climbed into bed, sleeping for a few hours before springing back awake way too early in anticipation of another exciting night.

This became my routine, and chats with my academy mates

proved that I was not alone. We were making mistakes as fast as we could and were learning on the fly, but we were all excited and the academy ties would bind us together for life. One thing we all agreed on was that we couldn't wait to be out on our own.

# Chapter Twenty-Two

THREE MONTHS WENT BY QUICKLY, AND I WAS BOTH THRILLED AND terrified to be on my own. Matt stopped by to offer support as I prepared to go into service on my first solo night.

"Don't worry. I'll be there whenever you need me, and for a while, I'll stop by your complaints to make sure you're okay. You'll be fine. You got this, and you're not alone. The other guys in our sector will be watching over you, too, until you get your feet wet. Listen, you'll develop a reputation based on how you work your first year, and it'll follow you your whole career, so bust your ass." He nodded in dismissal. "Later, Sweeney. Be safe."

I thanked him and prepared to go into service. I was less nervous than I thought I would be, and knowing that Tower would have my back was comforting. It was March, so I shed the winter clothing, and twenty pounds lighter, I was ready to fly. I was confident in handling most types of complaints. The most difficult thing to adjust to was the rotating shifts. Seven days on daywork and two days off followed by seven evenings and two days off followed by seven of the midnight shifts was brutal, especially if I had to be in court on one of the scheduled days off. My body had no sooner adjusted to one schedule when another began. I was always tired, and not your usual tired but the woozy, Bloody-Mary-in-the-middle-of-the-day kind of tired. But I was a rookie. I was thrilled to be on my own and they couldn't work me too hard.

Not only was B squad prepared for me to be on my own, but the citizens of New Castle County must have gotten word, because it was busy. The streets were jumping, and the radio traffic never stopped as dispatched complaints from 911 calls flooded the airway. One minute I was talking to a lady about her neighbor's barking shih tzu, and the next I was speeding to a shooting in progress, meaning that someone was shooting at something or someone at that very moment. I never knew what was coming, and I loved that fact.

As soon as I cleared from one call, another waited. There were no breaks that first night and no dinner. I finished the paperwork and went to my third domestic complaint of the night, which sounded volatile. Dispatch updated me as I sped to the house, wishing I was more familiar with the area at times like these.

I arrived and saw a car idling in a driveway two houses down from me with its headlights on and someone throwing furniture and clothes out one of the home's second-story windows. I stopped the car, got out, and let the dispatchers know where I was and what I saw. They dispatched additional units, but for the moment, I was alone. There were no streetlights, and it was dark, so I approached the house with a flashlight and lots of caution. The fogged-up car windows suggested someone might be inside. The car was covered with clothes, a lamp, shoes, and lots of broken glass, so I couldn't see. Beads of sweat formed on my face and palms as I approached.

"Dispatch, I have an older black model Ford Taurus, Delaware tag CL293851, parked in the driveway. Lights are on, and it's running. I'll be out checking."

Dispatch came back immediately: "31B2, that vehicle comes back to that address, registration expires January 1999."

I tapped on the window with the butt of my flashlight and got no response. Blood thumped madly in my neck, seemingly keeping tempo with the vehicle's blinking turn signal that was still click-clicking. My mind was laser sharp and focused on the car. Shouting came from inside the house, but it became background noise as I focused on the immediate threat—the vehicle. I quickly jerked the passenger-side door open. The car was empty so I slammed the door shut, starting for the front door of the two-story house. I was still on my own as I ran through the grassy front yard, up the steps, and banged on the front door, shouting, "Police! Open the door!"

A sudden cloak of silence descended over the scene. It was chilling.

"Police! Come on, open the door," I shouted again, resting my hand on my sidearm.

Footsteps drew near the door, and I turned my body sideways, preparing to defend myself. At the same time, my shoulder mic alerted me that another officer had just arrived. The door opened, and I stepped back and out of view so as not to make myself a big target.

"Hello?" came a small voice from inside the house.

I stepped forward to see a doe-eyed little boy, about five years old, peeking shyly through the door in his bare feet, wearing Barney pajamas, his face pale.

*Damn!* I thought, taking a deep breath, immediately glad I hadn't drawn my gun. I softened my voice.

"Well, hello, young man. Is your mom or daddy home?" I asked.

"Yeah, but they can't come to the door right now," he whispered to me as if it were a secret.

I whispered back, "I'm going to need you to go and get one of them for me. Tell mommy that it's the police, and she has to come downstairs and talk to me."

He held up one finger in a "wait-a-minute" manner and turned his back, scurrying off. The door nearly shut, but I reflexively thrust my foot between the door and the jamb before it closed. If things got ugly, I needed to be able to get inside to help.

While I waited for someone to return, another officer arrived. "Hey, Sweeney, what have you got?"

I didn't know the officer. He was wearing a blue uniform from another police agency, but I was happy he was there.

"Domestic. I haven't spoken to anyone yet, but it was going pretty good when I got here. It's a third-party call, probably a neighbor. Little kid answered the door and went to get one of his parents."

"Yeah, saw the front yard. Cue the banjos." He chuckled. "Looks like somebody was pissed."

His joking helped me to relax again. "Yeah, no kidding," I said as the front door opened and a man dressed in gray sweats, a T-shirt, and a hoodie appeared.

"Hello, I'm Officer Sweeney. Do you mind if we come in?"

The man didn't answer.

"It looks like the neighbors have seen enough of your business tonight," I added.

He stepped back, allowing the door to swing wide. The house was dark and the smell of cigarette smoke wafted out the door. I couldn't tell if it was sparsely furnished or if the furniture that should have been in the room was in the yard.

"Would you mind turning on the lights, please?" I asked.

He flipped the switch without comment. Food was strewn all over the kitchen floor. Newspapers, paper plates, and cups littered the living room coffee table. The dishes were clean, so it was apparent that no one had eaten yet. A butcher's knife lay on the floor beside the table. My partner saw it and moved between the man and the table. The large man stood between me and the mess, seemingly hoping I hadn't seen it.

"What's going on here tonight, sir?" I asked.

"My wife and I had an argument." He looked down at the floor, red-faced and drenched in sweat.

He was a big guy with a bald head, probably about thirty years old and over two hundred pounds. He nervously shoved his hands into the pockets of his sweatpants, and I could see the outline of his massive biceps through the sweatshirt.

"Sir, would you mind taking your hands out of your pockets, please?" I asked.

He complied, showing me his palms.

"Where is your wife, sir?" I continued.

He shrugged. "I guess she left."

"What do you mean, you guess she left?"

He shifted from foot to foot, gazing at the floor.

"I could hear you guys from a block away when I got here."

"Look, it's no big deal. We were just arguing. Yeah, I know we shouldn't have thrown the stuff out the windows, but it's our stuff, so that ain't a crime, right?"

I shrugged back at him. "No, it's not a crime, but you know, you guys caused quite a stir, and it looks like things got a little out of control. I think we've all been there, but we need to make sure everybody is okay. That's all. Everyone argues. We just need to see her, chat for a minute, and we will be on our way. What's her name?" I asked.

"You don't need to know her name. Nothing happened, and y'all can just go on and harass somebody else." He placed both of his hands on his hips in a Superman stance. The change in his demeanor and body language affected our approach, and as I glanced at my partner, it was clear that he agreed.

"Okay, sir, I'm going to need you to turn around and put your hands behind your back." I pulled my cuffs from the pouch at the small of my back and moved toward the man slowly, still talking.

"You're not under arrest. I'm going to put these handcuffs on you just until we figure out what happened here tonight. It's for my safety and yours."

My partner was muscular, and he moved forward with cuffs in hand. His size shifted the odds in our favor, and I was grateful he was there.

"What? Why are y'all handcuffing me? I didn't do nothing. I know my rights! I told you, we just had an argument," he shouted.

His body language was adversarial as he puffed up in front of me, attempting to intimidate me, which instantly reminded me of Vince and pissed me off. My partner took over negotiating for a peaceful resolution.

"Dude, this is no big deal. We do it every day, and as soon as we talk to your wife and make sure she's okay, we'll take them back off again, but you have to understand, we can't just take your word for it. We have to make sure she's okay. We don't know you, and what if she turned up dead or something? You know what I mean?"

He said this as he proceeded to handcuff the man, who was still protesting and threatening to get a lawyer and sue.

"Go ahead, Sweeney. You check the house. I'll stay here with this knucklehead," the officer said.

It was a small house, and I made my way from room to room, flipping on lights and checking closets until, by process of elimination, I got to what appeared to be the master bedroom. The door was closed, and it looked like the lights were out.

I knocked on the door with the butt of my flashlight and in a low tone said, "It's okay; you can open the door now."

The door opened slowly, and a petite woman appeared, wearing pajamas, a bathrobe, and slippers. The little boy I'd seen earlier clung to her side.

"Are you okay, ma'am?" I asked.

Her face was puffy and wet with tears, her eyes red and swollen.

"Yeah," she said.

"What happened here tonight?" I asked.

"It was all my fault. I was mad at him, and we were arguing," the woman said.

How many times had I thought that same thing? I knew that whatever she said next would not rise to the level of the carnage we were seeing, and images of my bloody, damaged apartment shuffled through my mind's eye. I took out my notepad and pen and took notes.

"What were you guys arguing about?" I asked.

"He's shady," she said.

"Shady?" I repeated.

"He's running with some woman from West Side. Meantime, I got his kid here, and we half starved while he's wining and dining her! I'm done!"

"I see. How did all the stuff end up on the front lawn, and whose car is that in the driveway?" I prodded.

"It's his car. He was out with her, and I called him on his phone. I knew he was with her and told him I was throwing his shit out. Oh, sorry about my language. I told him I was throwing his stuff out, and he could move in with her. I know I shouldn't have done it, but I was mad. I guess he was close by because he came flying into the driveway."

"What happened next?"

"He came running in mad, and I was throwing his clothes and stuff out the window. That's about when you guys showed up."

"At any point tonight did it ever become physical? I mean, did your husband ever push, punch, slap, or hurt you physically or threaten to?" I asked.

"Well, not really."

"What do you mean, 'not really'?" I asked in an even tone, still staring at my notepad.

"Well, when you guys got here, he said I'd better stay in the bedroom and shut up, or he'd put me through the wall."

"Okay, he said he'd put you through the wall. So, he never put his hands on you?"

"Well, except for he had his hands around my throat when he said that."

The little pajamaed boy burst into tears, shouting, "He was choking Mommy. I tried and I tried to make him stop, and he just wouldn't. I'm sorry, Mommy. I'm so sorry, Mommy. I couldn't stop him."

His gut-wrenching words came out in sobs and hiccups, as

grief-stricken tears and mucus ran down his face. Everything they taught us about controlling our emotional responses to the victim's account of the trauma went out the window. I wanted to grab him and hold him, and hug her, and promise it would never happen again. My ears thumped as my heart pounded, and I noticed the large red marks on her neck.

"You're okay, honey. It's all over," I said to the boy. "Do you need an ambulance, ma'am?"

"No, you guys got here just in time," she said.

The woman held the little boy in her arms with the vacant look of a girl who had been through too much, stroking his hair and telling him it wasn't his fault.

Though my heart broke for them, I excused myself to check on my partner, and let him know that based on his wife's statement and obvious injury, the man would be arrested.

"Okay, I'll take him over to county headquarters for you. Here's his info." He frowned, handing me a piece of notepaper from his pad.

"Okay. Thanks a lot. Hey, what's your name?" I asked.

"Hertzfeld, but everybody calls me Hertz. I'll log him in for you, Sweeney. What's one of the charges?" he asked.

"Strangulation is the felony charge, but there will be a few more," I said.

Hertzfeld looked at the man, who hadn't said a word since I returned, his head down, and Hertz scolded, "Really, dude?"

He had already patted the man down for weapons, so I waited as Hertzfeld explained what was happening to him.

"I'll shut off the car and give you the keys since it's your car, but you're going to have to have somebody else pick it up for you. You will have a no contact order due to this arrest, so you won't be allowed to come back here. It's a felony charge, so you might need bail money. Do you work?"

"No, I'm on disability," the man answered.

"Okay, well, depending on your history, you might need bail money, so when you get to the station, the judge will arraign you on the charges, and you'll be able to make a call to arrange for the bond. You can't call your wife, and if you are released, you can't come back here. Do you understand?"

The man's demeanor had changed entirely. He was compliant and polite. "Hey, thanks, man. I'm sorry about all this. You know, I'm not a bad guy."

Suddenly, I recalled sitting on the commode, watching fingerprint bruises appear on my neck, and his words made me sick. As if a good guy normally choked his wife to keep her quiet while his son watched. People probably liked this man, but they never saw this side of him. For her and her son, and maybe a little bit for me, I would make sure they did tonight.

I returned to the victim and explained what was happening to her husband and what she should expect from a legal standpoint. She didn't say anything. I couldn't leave her in this condition, so I stayed a little longer, asking the little boy, whose name was Charlie, to play in the other bedroom.

"Ms. Walker, I want to talk about a few things the courts won't tell you." She nodded toward a chair, and we both sat.

"As I said earlier, he's going to have a no contact order. Be prepared. At some point, he may violate that order. He might call or come back, and if he does, he will probably tell you that nothing like this will ever happen again, and he'll be convincing. You might want to believe him, which doesn't make you crazy. This isn't your fault. No one deserves to be strangled, pushed, punched, slapped, or mistreated in any way."

She nodded, her eyes filling with tears. Her response suggested that this wasn't the first physical confrontation between them.

"Listen, unless he gets help, this will probably happen again, and the next time, it could be worse," I said.

"How do you know? I mean, you don't know him." She dabbed her eyes and blew her nose.

"Ms. Walker, I don't know you or your family, and no two couples are exactly alike, but there are consistent behaviors we typically see in abusive relationships. Let me describe some domestic situations and how the abusers behave. See if you recognize any of this in your relationship with your husband. You don't have to tell me. I just want you to listen and see if any of it sounds familiar."

She nodded, and I began.

"Lots of abusers come from families with an abusive background, where mom or dad beat on each other, or they hit the kids. The abusers might control their partners by withholding money, dictating who they can hang out with, where they can go, what they are allowed to wear, or who they can talk to on the phone. They might check their partner's phone or grill them about their whereabouts. It often gets worse if the victim threatens to end the relationship. They might threaten to kill them, take the kids, or cut off finances."

She nodded at various points in the conversation, suggesting that she could relate to some of these behaviors, and I continued.

"Abusive relationships start in much the same way as any healthy one. The abuser seems to love his partner, and he's attentive in the beginning, like in any new relationship. The longer the couple is together, the more comfortable they become, and they begin to experience conflict, which is normal, but this is when the dysfunction shows itself. They argue, and things get heated. As it progresses, there may be cursing, name-calling, or threats to hurt or kill, but there's almost always a steady increase in the severity and frequency of the violence."

Ms. Walker was nodding, and tears filled her eyes again as she wrapped her arms tightly around her body.

"Most victims say that after an argument, the abuser is remorseful and makes promises never to let it happen again. Some victims

say they feel closer to their abusers after an argument, and the court-
ship begins all over again. It's been called the honeymoon period.
Eventually, things even out and get back to normal again. This lasts
for a short while, until they start to bicker again, and it continues
until the next explosive brawl. They make up, then the honeymoon,
then normal bickering, and another battle. This becomes the norm
until the arguments become physical."

"This is the first time he ever laid his hands on me," she said. "He's
threatened to kill me if he ever catches me cheating. That's the cra-
ziest shit. He's the one running, not me. I mean, he's pushed me a
few times, but he never punched me or anything. I seen some of my
friends get their eye dotted before, but that ain't me," she said.

"Well, I'm glad to hear that, and I want it to stay that way. Jealousy
is another common thread, but you're not a punching bag, and it's
not okay for him to push you, either."

"What am I supposed to do? I can't afford to live here on my own.
I have to think about Charlie. I have family, but they're just getting
by too."

She was asking practical questions. I hadn't asked them when I
was in the hospital after Vince had attacked me, but she was further
along than I was. Tonight, I was Ms. Walker's Nurse Sarah, and I
couldn't stop sharing my strength with her, like if I didn't save her, I
might die myself. I squeezed her hand.

"You don't have to know all the answers at once. Just take that
first step, and I bet the next step will present itself. You'll see."

I had earned the right to tell her this. I didn't have a plan when I
took that first step, but I got out. I glanced down at my freshly pressed
uniform to convince myself, or maybe to be sure I hadn't dreamed
it all.

Charlie broke the spell when he bounced back into the room,
leaped into her lap, and kissed her cheek, showing off a little for me.
She hugged him back and half smiled at me with a nod of thanks.

"Ms. Walker," I said, "you're asking great questions, and I assure you there are reasonable answers to them. I want to talk to you more, but I've got to go. I'm going to give you the phone number of one of our victim advocates. Call her in the morning, and she'll help you understand the court process. If you're interested, she can explain the process of getting a protection from abuse order (PFA), which could permit you to stay in the house with Charlie and require your husband to continue making payments. I hope I never see you again under these circumstances, but if I do, I promise to tell you this all over again."

She thanked me, and I reminded her not to let him in if he came back but to call 911.

I smiled on the way back to my car, feeling satisfied. I felt like I had helped her, and I liked it. I wanted to make this a habit, and dispatch would ensure I did, as they sent me to another domestic complaint nearby.

I handled five domestic complaints that night, which was discouraging, but at the same time empowering, like I was swooping in to save the day. I was proud of these women for calling the police and proud of myself for taking on the bullies who took advantage of their smaller, weaker partners.

Loosely defined, a domestic dispute was a disagreement among any cohabitating individuals, so it didn't matter whether they were married, dating, straight, gay, parents, siblings, or roommates. If they lived together, it was a domestic. It was shocking how comfortable people became calling the police to referee their arguments. They told me everything across the board, no matter how intimate or embarrassing. Nothing was off-limits. They threw glasses, remotes, spaghetti, and nearly anything else they could get ahold of at one another. They slapped, punched, pushed, stabbed, and threatened murder regularly, and there were no boundaries.

Children were almost always present, and it added another layer of potential victims turned perpetrators to next year's complaint load as the children learned how to manage conflict from their parents. These family brawls didn't even interrupt *The Simpsons*. Children sat cross-legged on the floor watching TV without much disruption as I collected information from their parents, and I wondered how it would affect their future lives.

Older kids sometimes ran away from violent families, and the system required me to bring them back. Eventually, they became old enough to be the aggressors, and the cycle continued.

What I saw on the street reminded me of my own trauma, but at first, I couldn't see it. When I stripped off the uniform, economic differences, race, and specific details, we weren't so different. They fought over money, infidelity, and disrespect. The calls were always volatile, not only for the cocombatants but also for the officers trying to intervene. The things people argued about ranged widely, and the number of times I went back to the same houses was staggering. Drugs or alcohol were involved in almost every case.

In every situation, fear was a factor. Sometimes the fear was about cheating, but more often it was over money or disrespect. They were mean to each other. And they were afraid of losing each other, but that was rarely what happened. They both wanted to be together, but neither believed it.

These calls became my area of expertise, and I went to as many of them as I could, learning from and comparing cases, watching the family dynamics for any sign of something that worked to deter the fighting.

One thing that was guaranteed was the increase in volatility. If they didn't get help, verbal abuse became physical abuse until they finally separated. Like Vince and me, people broke up and got back together over and over. I started asking the victims why they went back. There were a handful of reasons, including money and kids, but most of the time, their reason for staying was hope, my new four-letter word. Just like me, so many women remembered how their relationship had been in the beginning and were sure that they would get back to the way they were when they were happy. When drugs or alcohol were involved, both parties were often drinking or drunk when I got there and their conflict resolution skills went out the window.

I empathized with the victims, but doubted anything would change and was often proven correct. Like me, they moved from crisis to crisis, putting out fires along the way. They licked their wounds, picked themselves up, brushed themselves off, and never analyzed what happened or why. They saw these incidents as things that happened to them and chalked it up to bad luck, circumstances, or the wrong partner, never suspecting they had a choice or a part in what happened. Some of the victims were independent, financially stable, and well-balanced. The well-off weren't immune; they were just better at hiding it. No one would have suspected they were involved in a relationship with someone who was hurting them. The victims I met were all courageous, and I knew the desperation it took to end the relationship.

I didn't feel sorry for the abusers, but I understood them. They wanted to stop. Like an alcoholic after a bender, Vince was remorseful after every fight, and he shed real tears of shame. I knew it, and it was why I always gave him another chance, but knowing he was sorry wasn't enough. Without a plan to correct the problem, another chance always led to more abuse. He had been addicted to control, and frankly, he was a bully. He had the ability to control his anger, because it wasn't like he was picking fights with other men. He chose his wife to fight with, a sure thing. Though he swore he would never become "that guy," he did. It became a cycle and that's what I saw in each of the domestic service calls I handled.

At the end of one of my day shifts, I hurried home, changed into shorts, a T-shirt, and sneakers, and went for a run. The ugliness of the complaints had a way of clinging to a person, the way cigarette smoke lingers long after the smoker has left the area. On nights that I didn't run, I found myself replaying the events of the day, which often led to sleepless nights, so running was therapeutic.

The rotating shifts wreaked havoc on my social life. Most of my friends were off on the weekends and finished their workdays at normal hours, so I saw my old friends less, and made new friends with fellow police officers who understood what I dealt with every day and who I was becoming. It made dating a challenge, which was why so many police officers dated other police officers, nurses, or teachers—people in the helping fields.

Like so many others, I began dating an officer in the department. Brad had been on the job for six years when I was hired, and I was enamored of him. He was funny, attractive, and had the gift of gab. He carried conversations like the class clown and was easy to be around. He was tall, with short, dark hair, and he was fit, like most of the guys on the job. He had been in the air force, which left him with a propensity for neatness, always making his bed, shaving, and keeping his home in order, which appealed to me. He was divorced, with a thirteen-year-old daughter who would grow up to be a heartbreaker. He saw her in the summer months because she lived in Virginia and the custody agreement was like the one Doug shared with his ex-wife.

My sense of independence seemed to appeal to him, and it was a casual relationship, which allowed me to learn my new job without constantly having to apologize for my lack of availability. I could focus on my work. We were on the same squad and worked the same schedule, so I knew what kinds of complaints he was responding to, and vice versa. It made for great banter at the end of our days.

He wasn't great at connecting on an emotional level, which felt safe to me, like he wouldn't be looking for anything too serious. I'd had enough, lost enough, and endured way too much to put myself in a position to be hurt again so soon, and I didn't have the desire to explain myself. I wanted to put my past behind me. I didn't tell my coworkers about any of it. It was a little like having a dirty, little, shameful secret. Keeping it from Brad was easy because he never asked.

# Chapter Twenty-Three

I soon became considered an expert at testifying in cases involving domestic violence, which was a simple honor to attain since the requirement for being considered an expert in Delaware was "having specialized knowledge, more than an average person." I had more knowledge than the average person before I got the job, so my new title didn't affect the size of my head. As time went on, I became proficient in handling domestics, like many of my colleagues.

I worked as a patrol officer for the next three years, focusing on domestic violence and child abuse cases. My victim interviews, evidence collection, warrants, and report writing improved with each case. Details made these incidents come to life for the jury and attorneys. I photographed holes in the walls from prior incidents at scenes to show a pattern of violence. I learned to use statements from children who overheard fights and could articulate hearing hands slapping skin or objects being thrown against walls. Creating a visual image became an art form. It was one thing to say, "The victim's son witnessed the incident." It was quite another to say, "Johnny, the couple's five-year-old son, sobbed as he stated, 'I saw Daddy punch Mommy in the face with his fist.'" These details helped the jury feel what happened in a more visual way.

I knew the Division of Family Services (DFS) caseworkers by name and learned everything I could about family dynamics. I made sure my cases were complete and my reports thorough. Nearly every case reminded me of my own past personal hell in some way. I shared some of the same characteristics with each victim and saw myself in them. I listened to frustrated coworkers make comments just like my friends and family had, because they knew we would be back at the same house next week. I knew they were right, and having been on both sides of that fence, I was conflicted.

I liked talking to people, so investigations became my strong suit. Learning how to interview suspects was different from talking to victims or witnesses, so I made it my business to watch the detectives via closed-circuit TV as they interviewed suspects. Each investigator had a style all their own, and it was fascinating to watch how they talked to all types of people.

Cliff, for example, had a reputation as a fantastic interviewer. As a detective in the Robbery-Homicide Unit, his style lent itself to the people committing street crimes. He typically interviewed witnesses or suspects in homicides, robberies, burglaries, shootings, and other violent felonies. One night at the end of my shift, I walked past the Criminal Investigations Unit (CIU) room and noticed Cliff involved in an interview. I stopped and stood out of the way, watching the live interview as it unfolded. The suspect sat in a chair, with Cliff positioned alongside the desk with his left elbow resting on the corner of it, but he wasn't taking notes.

"Hey, what's he got?" I asked the other detectives.

"It's a robbery suspect," his partner, Gooch, answered, his chin resting in his hand. "He's been at it for a couple hours now. I think we're almost done," he said.

The suspect's black sweatpants were too long, the bottoms draping over his sneakers. His black, hooded sweatshirt had 19720 emblazoned across the chest, the zip code for New Castle, Delaware, in large white block letters, a weird fad that was a source of pride for the perp, but let the police know where he lived. I shook my head, thinking to myself, *You can't make this stuff up.*

I listened to the other detectives, who were also standing around watching.

"See how the guy's shoulders are sagging, and his head is down looking at his sneakers? He's thinking. Cliff should close the space between them here shortly."

I listened to the banter for information about the case and what to expect next. Soon the man began spewing forth details of the crime.

"That was amazing. He's really good at interviewing. What's his secret?"

"It's no secret. It's the Reid School of interview and interrogation," Gooch answered. "If you want to be a detective, you need to know the basics. It's not just what is said but how it's said and what their body language suggests."

Our agency offered the Reid School to potential detectives every year, and the training was coming up. I wanted to go, but having only been on the street for two and a half years, I was unsure about asking. There were 240 officers in the department and I was sure that a lot of them wanted to go. For the first three years I was a rookie, meant to be seen and not heard. We were last in line for vacation and never called out sick. We spent most of our days off in court and worked every holiday, including Christmas. Who was I to make such a request? Would it be arrogant?

I drove home thinking about whether to ask, and if so, how to ask. I had been proactive and even worked a couple of good cases alongside the Detective Unit. If I didn't get the training this time, I would have to wait another whole year, and I didn't want to wait. I was desperate for it. I walked in the door, changed into my running gear, and headed out to clear my head. I showered when I got home, and then met Brad for dinner at a nearby restaurant where we talked about it.

"Go for it," Brad said. "You work your butt off out there. Yes, there will be lots of people putting in memos asking to go, and you should, too, but maybe you should talk to your sergeant. Don't just ask to go;

tell him why you deserve it. It always helps to have your supervisor's support. You'll get it. I know you will, but you won't unless you ask."

When I got home, all of my insecurities melted away. I hadn't gotten this far by cowering. I spent the next hour practicing what I would say, sounding sincere but not cocky. Since I was feeling humble, I knelt in prayer before climbing into bed that night, asking God to guide my words, begging for the opportunity, wishing for the same confidence I felt when I *just knew* I would be a cop.

The next day after roll call, I knocked softly on the doorjamb at the entrance to the lieutenant's office, and my sergeant waved me in.

"Sir, I was wondering . . . the interview and interrogation school is coming up, and I was hoping you might consider sending me this year." The words stuck in my throat, but I continued as my face flushed. "I've been proactive in my investigations, and I've worked with detectives on a few cases. Remember the one with the elderly lady that got robbed four times? We cleared three open cases from that arrest."

He nodded with a look of annoyance at the interruption. "Send me a memo. I'll talk to the lieutenant."

"Will do. Thank you, sir." I stood there beaming just a little too long, and he looked up from his papers.

"Anything else, Sweeney?"

"No, sir. Thank you, sir." I turned and exited, nearly running into the door that had partially swung shut behind me as I bounced out of his office like Tigger. Brad was right. I had asked, and even if they didn't choose me, they knew I was interested. It was out of my hands.

Helping someone, or maybe the feeling of righting a wrong, kept me drawn to the investigations like an addiction. My request for the interview and interrogation school was approved, and I soaked the information in like a sponge. I took on as many felony cases as I could, learning how to interview suspects, victims, and witnesses under as many different circumstances as possible. Officers at the

patrol level didn't write many search warrants because the calls for
service were high priority and lengthy investigations were time-con-
suming, so most felonies were turned over to the Detective Unit. I
wrote as many warrants as time and my sergeant would allow. On
busy nights, frequent 911 calls made it so we couldn't spend all the
time we needed to conduct thorough investigations at the time of the
incident as we had to move quickly from scene to scene. Because of
this, some cases took a while to close.

I drove through a neighborhood one cold midnight shift and
saw my sector partner, Dan Camilli, parked in a church parking lot,
exhaust steaming from the tailpipe of his vehicle, and I pulled up
alongside him. It was quiet, and nobody was afoot in the neighborhood. As my window slowly lowered, I felt the icy breeze invade the
warmth of my car, and we extinguished our headlights to share a cup
of coffee.

"What's up, Sweeney?" he asked.

"Just looking for a spot to sit and work on follow-ups."

"You must have a ton." He shook his head. "What's the attraction?"

"I know, right? Sometimes I could kick myself because I know
it's the end of my shift, and I know I'm going to end up working
overtime, but I can't help myself. I guess I just love it. Brad thinks I'm
crazy too. He said I should just go to the complaints I'm sent to and
let the others go."

Dan shook his head. "I know. I hear you going, and it ticks me off
because I know I have to go too." He raised his coffee and blew, the
cold December air sending clouds of steam billowing from his lips. It
was a clear night and he looked up through his open window at the
nearly full moon and stars and said, "I'm surprised it's not a busy
night with that full moon so bright."

"Don't jinx us. Hey, mind if I ask your opinion about something?"

He shook his head, swallowing a gulp of coffee. And I continued.

"Captain Janson stopped me in the hall and suggested I put in a memo requesting a transfer to the Drug Unit."

"What? You're going into detectives?" Dan squawked, nearly spilling hot coffee all over his uniform.

"No, he didn't say that. He said if I was interested, I should put in a memo."

"Nah, Sweeney, that wasn't a request. You can't refuse. You'll never go anywhere if you refuse. You have to put in your memo." He seemed exasperated.

"Really? I want to go into detectives, but I'm not sure I'm ready. And the Drug Unit? I don't know if that's me. It seems too soon, and given a choice, I would never have requested the Drug Unit." I shuffled through a folder full of sample memos for something that seemed appropriate as we talked.

"Well, maybe you could get in and then later transfer laterally to somewhere you want to go, but you'd best put in your memo. That's awesome, Sweeney. What does Brad think?"

"Yeah, it is awesome, but I'm kind of nervous. I'm not sure I'm ready. Brad thinks I should put in a memo too. He said if I didn't, it would be career suicide."

Dispatch sent out a request for backup for a nearby officer and Camilli waved me off. As he drove away, I drafted my memo and turned it in. When January 2000 came, I jumped onto the computer looking for the list of detectives to be posted like every other officer interested in transferring. When it finally came out, my name wasn't there. I sat scouring the list repeatedly. Camilli had me so convinced that I was going in that it was a kick in the gut. It was like having the rug pulled out from under me, and a rush of disappointment washed over me.

Dan hunted me down immediately. "Damn, Sweeney, I'm sorry. I can't believe you didn't get in. I wonder what happened. Are you okay?"

"I don't know what happened. I haven't even had a chance to digest it. I'm glad I didn't tell anybody but you and Brad. That would have been embarrassing."

"Yeah, that hurts. I'm sorry, but I'm sure you'll get in next time."

"I'm kind of happy I'm not going to the Drug Unit, though. Still, just at the time I got my head around it, bam."

"Yeah, no kidding. No offense, Sweeney, I didn't want to say anything, but you look like Sandra Dee, all innocent and shit. You would have stuck out like a sore thumb."

"Oh, shut up, Camilli."

"Good comeback, Sweeney," he shouted sarcastically as he sped off to a dispatched burglar alarm. I wanted to sit and wallow in self-pity, but instead switched on my headlights and followed him, pushing the doubts from my mind.

Winter came and went, and spring arrived in full bloom. My request for a transfer into the Detective Unit was active for one full year, and when a position came open in March, I found my name on the transfer list. Mary Sweeney—to the Criminal Investigations Unit, domestic violence squad. I sat in my car alone, looking at the computer. The DV squad was sort of a junior detective position, a place to cut your teeth. If you did a good job there, your options opened. I spent a few minutes reading and rereading the memo, making sure I wasn't dreaming, and I thanked God. He had known what was best for me after all.

I felt like I had come full circle. I knew firsthand how hard it was to get out of an abusive relationship. I also understood how it felt to be on the police side. It was discouraging watching so many victims drop the charges or not show up for trial. After seeing so much abuse, putting in so much hard work, and having so many fail to show, it was no wonder everyone quit on the them. Society blamed them. The agencies protecting them got tired of seeing the same faces week in and week out and gave up on them. The worst part was that, little by little, we quit on ourselves. Feeling that loss of hope was a dangerous place to be, a revolving door of shame and frustration. I knew being on the DV squad was an enormously important job. I wouldn't blow it. I would pay forward the gift that Nurse Sarah had given me. I vowed not to let anyone else make the same mistake I did.

Dan startled me out of my daze, tapping on the car window.

"Geez, Dan, you nearly gave me a heart attack."

He chuckled, clearly happy with himself for scaring me. "Well, pay attention, or you're going to get yourself killed! And congratulations, Detective Sweeney. It looks like you have a couple of weeks to wrap up your street cases, huh?"

"Yeah, I guess so. I'm in pretty good shape, I think." I smiled broadly at hearing my new title. "I'm going to miss you, Dan."

"No, you won't, Sweeney. You won't have time to miss anybody. You're going to be so busy with overtime, being on call, and learning the ropes, you won't have time to think about us."

Phone calls, emails, and text messages from other officers on the squad and my academy mates kept me in a euphoric state until I bid my squad a final farewell. My transfer would take place in two weeks, on my thirty-ninth birthday. I would be finished with working seven days straight with only one or two days off between shifts. My new position would come with a new schedule. I would work Monday through Friday either days or evenings, but no more midnight shifts. My weekends were scheduled days off unless I was on call.

A business suit would replace the brown uniform, so I allowed myself the excitement of a justified shopping trip, excited to be dressing and feeling a little more like a woman.

Brad took me out for dinner at a posh restaurant to celebrate not only my birthday but my new position. He was happy for me, and proved his pride with a gift, a brand-new briefcase, usually reserved for lawyers and corporate CEOs. Had we known how this new position would affect our time together, we might have lingered a little longer that night, drank a little less, and made love a little more slowly.

# Chapter Twenty-Four

TWO WEEKS FLEW BY, AND I FOUND MYSELF ASSIGNED TO AN OFFICE off-site from headquarters where detectives investigated child abuse cases. The intimate nature of the interviews and telephone calls required privacy. Our building had been converted from a bank to offices and had two floors—the top story was for police detectives and the bottom floor was for the state Division of Family Services (DFS) caseworkers. I was one of two detectives investigating domestic violence.

The fact that only two detectives worked in DV was not a fair representation of the number of felony cases but rather showed the lack of priority in investigating and prosecuting them. It wasn't that no one cared, but the lack of victim cooperation made it hard for investigators and prosecutors to move forward with court cases, much less stay motivated. Patrol officers handled felony domestic violence cases, too, so the ones assigned to detectives were often complicated.

Six detectives were assigned to investigate allegations of child abuse. Three worked the day shift and three the evening, and they took turns rotating. The formal name for the unit was the Family Services Unit, or FSU, but it was irreverently referred to as "kiddie crimes" by the other detectives.

Detective Claudine Malone managed notifications for Megan's Law—the federal law making information about registered sex offenders public. She was young and friendly, having graduated in the academy class before mine. She greeted me as I arrived on my first day.

"Good morning, Mary. Congratulations and welcome. You're going to like it here. Your office is up here." She helped me carry some office supplies, calendars, and other necessities to the second floor, giving me a guided tour.

"I'm glad you're here. It's nice to finally add a little estrogen to the gene pool," she said, laughing. "It's almost all guys. There's a Brew HaHa! next door if you want coffee, and Cromwell's is a decent lunch spot next to that, but it's expensive. Most of us pack our lunches. We have a fridge and microwave. I'll show you where the kitchen is. Sergeant Sloan, your new boss, is on vacation, so I'll get you settled. If you need anything, let me know. I worked DV cases before I was assigned to Megan's Law, so I'm up on everything. Love your suit, by the way."

I liked her right away. She delivered me to my office, and I began setting up my desk.

My job for the first week was simple. A stack of police reports from the weekend overflowed my inbox, and my job was to read them and follow up with victims. I didn't mind this part of the job and felt like the countless hours I spent on the phone helped people. It was proactive. Every day another stack of domestic violence reports appeared in my inbox, forwarded by patrol officers from the night before. The volume was overwhelming. I had no idea that there were so many calls for service.

Perusing the Saturday morning newspaper on my day off was always an eye-opener, comparing the sensationalized media stories with the facts. My blood pressure spiked every time I read another dramatic exaggeration or blatant misrepresentation. I pored over crime reports in the local paper, catching up on arrests and the nature of the crimes. The names of habitual repeat offenders were already becoming familiar. It was discouraging but a good cardio source first thing in the morning, along with my coffee.

It was early afternoon on one of my first Saturdays off when my pager sounded, and I called Sergeant Sloan back immediately.

"Hi, Mary. Thanks for getting back to me so quickly. I know you're not on call, but I need someone to handle a rape investigation. It's domestic related, but the on-call DV detective is already out on an assist for a robbery case, so he's not available. I know the case's particulars and feel confident that you can handle it. I'll message you the address. Once you have conducted the interviews at the scene, give me a call, and we'll figure out what you need and go from there. Are you okay with that?"

"Sure," I answered excitedly. "I think so, sir. What squad is working, and who's at the scene?"

"It's B squad. In central. It's Officer Provenza, and you don't have to call me 'sir,' and she's expecting you. You need to be there in thirty minutes from the time of the call. Can you make it?"

"Thanks, Sarge," I replied. "I think I'll be okay. I'll call you as soon as I can."

I dressed and rushed out the door to my new-to-me, unmarked, silver Crown Victoria police car, affectionately known by other detectives as the Bondomobile because of its flat gray color. It was the first unmarked car for many detectives before me and was a well-loved hunk of junk. My adrenaline rushed with the excitement of my first case, and with address in hand, along with a notepad, pen, and portable tape recorder, I raced to the scene. I was glad to hear it was Provenza. She was squared away and I knew she would have answers to all my questions and the scene would be preserved.

Last week I was a fellow squad member, but now I gave instructions to my former partners on how to move forward with the case. Feeling a bit like a poser, I expected an eye roll from my coworkers, but Deb and I had been in the academy together, so I knew she would be supportive. I arrived, pulling my spiral notebook from my new black briefcase. Maybe it was the freshly pressed Jones New York suit, but no eye roll came.

"Hey, Deb, what do you have?" I asked.

"The victim is on her way to the hospital for a sexual assault exam. She broke up with her boyfriend three weeks ago. He didn't take it well and wouldn't leave her alone. She showed me her phone, and he's been calling her nonstop. They all show as missed calls, so she hasn't been engaging with him, at least not with this phone. She said that he came to her house two days ago and knocked on the door. He was drunk and crying, so she let him in, she says, to tell him again that it was over. He got mad and accused her of sleeping with somebody. It escalated, and she said he forced her to the floor and raped her vaginally. She has fingerprint bruising on her biceps and a couple more bruises on her legs."

"Okay, has the boyfriend contacted her since, and why didn't she report the incident two days ago when it happened?"

"She was embarrassed and felt like it was her fault for letting him in in the first place, so she didn't report it. He called her right after the incident. She confided in a girlfriend, who talked her into reporting. We didn't interview her. I figured you'd want to do that. He called her that same night, after the incident, and left her a message on her phone. I heard it. He's crying and apologizing for what he did. It's not quite a confession, but it's pretty close."

"Great. Do we have the phone?"

"Yes, we turned it off, collected it, and it's logged in as evidence. I'll shoot an email to the evidence guys letting them know it's there and that you'll want to hear it. The victim just got to the hospital, and I think you missed your window of opportunity to talk to her. The exam already started."

Officer Crowley was at the hospital with the victim, and Officer Provenza ripped a sheet of paper with her cell number from her pocket pad and handed it to me. The evidence team had been notified, but they were already on a robbery complaint so there would be a wait.

"What do you need from us?" Provenza asked, smiling a little.

I returned a knowing glance, acknowledging that we'd both been here before.

"Look, I know you guys are busy, so if you could lock up the apartment and put a car out front, that should be sufficient. Maybe grab someone who has paperwork to complete. No one goes in until the Evidence Detection Unit finishes. Has a neighborhood canvas been done?"

"Yeah. Not many folks are home on a beautiful Saturday afternoon, so I'll have the next shift finish up if we don't get to talk to everyone. Only one person responded so far, and he didn't even know they broke up."

I took the case number knowing Deb would have the report finished by morning. Crowley would collect the assault kit and the victim's clothes. The victim went to the hospital with a change of clothes from her home, but the clothes she had been wearing the night of the assault were in the hamper in the house. The bedding was still on the bed, so it would be tagged and collected. She had showered, so there probably wouldn't be much evidence collected during the SANE exam.

The suspect was unaware of the report, so we had time. We just needed to ensure that the victim had a safe place to stay until he could be picked up.

As Deb walked away, the sound of Saturday mayhem squawked from her shoulder mic, and I felt a little guilty not to be jumping in to help with the complaint load. I knew the squad wouldn't get dinner tonight, and bathroom breaks would be at a premium. Women learned not to drink much during their shifts because of the shortage of opportunities for bathroom breaks and clean, safe places to go.

I would pick up the case Monday morning, allowing the victim to rest and recover from the trauma of the report and exam. I climbed into my car and called Sergeant Sloan with an update and then relayed the plan to Officer Provenza, and with that, my first callout ended.

It was a long weekend, and I barely slept, instead poring over the details of the case, excited to be handling my first callout. I reported to roll call Monday morning, feeling a little more like an actual detective. I hustled into the Criminal Investigation Unit at headquarters, taking a seat at the roll call desk, which was a massive mahogany table about the size of my first apartment. Twelve detectives sat around the table while about fifteen more rolled their chairs up close to create an outer circle. The office was too small for the number of detectives it housed, and the chatter was a bit too loud for a Monday morning.

The differences in appearance among the detectives was amusing. There were guys in plain clothes sporting beards and long hair, looking like drug dealers except for the police badges hanging from chains around their necks. There were SWAT guys, clad in black vests with POLICE displayed in large letters on the front and back. They wore black, knit hats and bandoliers across their chests that carried what looked like hand grenades, but I hoped were flash-bangs or tear gas canisters. There was an array of different colors of cargo pants and T-shirts or polo shirts. Some guys wore suits, and some wore shirts and ties and khaki pants. Cubicles lined both sides of the room, and two formal offices for supervisors stood at the entrance, but the table took up most of the space in the center of the room.

One thing was for sure. It was a tight group. I listened intently to multiple conversations, and it was clear that they were friends in and out of the office. They talked about kids and families and shared weekends, and covered for one another for on-call status, which made it easier to handle the exhausting schedule and caseload. The secretary, Faye, had been there for more than twenty years and acted like a mother coddling her children, constantly checking to see if the detectives had lunch or when they had slept last. No one got to detectives without going through Faye. She was the gatekeeper.

Monday morning roll call was the time for detectives to share their callouts from the weekend and let the rest of us know who or what they were looking for. Some of them were walking encyclopedias of local perp knowledge, and I wondered how I would ever remember everything.

Leo, a fairly new detective, rushed into the roll call room wearing a rumpled raincoat and looking like the old TV cop Columbo but without the swagger. He was late and so was fair game for ridicule, and a barrage of insults and harassing comments rose from the group.

"Glad you could make it." "Yo, you opened the door; shut it." "Don't worry, we'll wait for you." "Stand up straight. You're such a slouch."

Leo trudged to an open chair in the back of the room, his head down, dropping a file folder full of papers, which spread over the floor. He began hurriedly picking them up, dropping his phone, and one of the detectives nearby shoved his chair with his foot and it rolled away. Leo didn't respond and I shook my head, watching him avoid eye contact with everyone. I couldn't imagine why he would let them push him around like he did. He looked to be in the wrong line of work. Even I didn't like him, and I liked everyone, but his lack of a backbone made me want to join in.

The lieutenant stepped out of his office and sat at the head of the table, and the room fell quiet.

"Okay," he started. "It was a busy weekend, so let's get this started so we can get to work." The lieutenant's eyes went around the table and landed on me. "Sweeney, you had a callout, didn't you?"

"Yes, sir, Saturday afternoon."

I sat frozen, intimidated by the detectives I had idolized for the last few years. I knew I was in the presence of a great deal of talent and expertise and was sure at that moment that I didn't belong.

"Well, you care to share it with the rest of us, Sweeney?" the lieutenant prodded sarcastically.

"Yeah, sure. It was a late-reported, domestic-related rape. Ex-boyfriend."

"Can you speak up, Sweeney? We can't hear you," he challenged.

I cleared my throat and began again. I gave the update in a voice louder and higher than I meant to but hit all the main points, ending with the fact that I would be interviewing the victim later that morning.

"Sounds like a decent case, Mary. Let me know if you need any help."

The offer came from one of the child abuse detectives, and she had mad skills. Everybody called her T, or T-Bird, short for Teresa. She was pretty, thin, in her midthirties, and had long blond hair that fell to her waist. She wore a gray suit and low heels. She was well respected, outgoing, funny, and always willing to jump into the fray with the men, who also liked her. The best part—she had my back.

"Thanks, T. That would be great." I smiled at her, and she nodded with an acknowledging smile in return.

Roll call ended, and Teresa followed me to the back of the office.

"Thanks, T," I said again.

"For what?" She shrugged it off, not waiting for a response. "So, who's your first interview today?"

"The victim is coming in an hour, and then the girlfriend that she told. I'm not familiar with the recording equipment here. Can you give me a hand?" I asked.

The computers, printers, and recording equipment were all outdated.

"Sure. I'll set you up and watch through the monitor. The tapes are only thirty minutes on each side, so I'll page you to let you know I'm flipping the tape. Just stop the interview for a second and let me flip it. If at any point during the interview you get stuck on where to go next, come on out, and I'll try to help. Before you finish, excuse yourself and come back in here, and I'll let you know if I think you missed anything."

"Great! Okay. Thanks a lot," I said.

"Don't thank me. It's what we do. It's a normal day. We all need each other, so there will be days when I need you to help me with cases, too, especially in the Child Abuse Unit and DV. Nobody from other units wants to jump in to help with our cases. It takes a special breed of crazies to do our job, so welcome to the nut hut."

She was very matter-of-fact about it.

"The best advice I can give you is to get in the box as often as you can and interview, interview, interview. You'll get better with each one you do. You're going to make mistakes. We all do, and eventually, you'll learn not to take it too hard but to learn from it. Family Services is the most important unit of all, and the reality is that most of the time the interview is the only evidence we have, so there's a lot of pressure on you to get a confession."

Frank, one of the detectives handling robberies, overheard her comment as he walked by and mocked her in a whiny, singsong voice. "Family Services is the most important unit of all! Look at me. I had my suspect handed to me, so all I have to do is the interview."

"Shut up, jerk," she scolded, then turned to me, laughing. "I hate him," she said.

The interviews went smoothly, and I felt there was a strong likelihood that the case would be prosecuted.

The suspect was located and arrested for rape in the first degree for causing injury to the victim. I had been preparing myself for the suspect interview for days, and I had an idea of how I wanted to proceed, so I was ready. The conversation lasted only two minutes; I read him his Miranda rights, and he invoked his right to a lawyer and ended the interview.

I walked back into roll call, where Teresa waited. "That sucks," I complained. "When he sat down, I could see him already sweating, and that mealymouthed shit could barely get the words out."

"That's the way the cookie crumbles," T joked as she shuffled up behind Gus. "Dude, your socks don't match! Who dressed you this morning?"

"I know. It's weird. I have another pair at home just like it." Gus threw his arm around her, and they headed out the door laughing.

I wondered how Teresa could just blow it off like that, but acknowledged that their lightheartedness made my disappointment a little easier to take. I laughed with them, but I knew that without a confession, the case would be harder to prove.

The next day I had three new reports on my desk and I realized there would be a never-ending stack of reports and cases to manage. There was no time to grieve losses.

# Chapter Twenty-Five

WEEKS AND MONTHS SPED BY, AND I GOT USED TO THE PACE—A DEAD run. I volunteered to assist other detectives with investigations whether I was on call or not, and I learned fast. I went out on everything, and I loved the work.

I was happy to finally have a day in the office to catch up on report writing when Teresa hollered across the room letting me know that Pete from the attorney general's office was on the phone. I picked it up and listened intently as Pete robotically droned on about a domestic violence case he was dropping.

"Wait, Pete. Is this the guy that sprinkled Ambien on his wife's pizza so that he could have anal sex with her while she was sleeping?"

"Yep. They're back together and she doesn't want to testify against him."

"But he confessed!"

"I know, but we can't make her be a victim."

My blood pressure rose as he spoke, and I hung up and kicked the trash can across the office, watching as the contents erupted down the hallway. I paced and huffed, recalling the weeks I had spent collecting and analyzing evidence for that case. Her interview was credible, and his confession clinched the case. He admitted that she had refused to engage in anal sex with him, so he took matters into his own hands. The confession came easily because he didn't think that he had done anything wrong. She was his wife. That interview left me enraged because, to him, she was his property and he could do anything he wanted to her. I knew she would live to regret the decision not to move forward with prosecution, but I couldn't change it.

"That doesn't look like it was good news. You okay?" Claudine asked.

I nodded and began picking up the papers, angrily shoving them back into the wastebasket. "They just dropped a slam-dunk DV case. I mean, I get it. Pete had no choice, but it sucks."

"I know. It gets to you, but unfortunately, you'll get used to it. Let's go grab some coffee."

We walked to the coffee shop, and despite the brisk winter chill, I let my unbuttoned coat flap in the breeze as I described the case while Claudine nodded and shook her head appropriately. She allowed me to rant and curse without judgment, until I had gotten it out of my system, paying no attention to passersby. It wasn't in the training manual, but on any given day, one of us performed this ritual for the other.

Over the next few months, I fell into line with my fellow detectives. The weak were eaten alive in the Investigation Unit, so I learned to do what was necessary to get along. I went into the CIU a quiet, pensive, thoughtful girl, and within a few months, my soft edges were sharp. My skin thickened, and I learned to curse like a banshee, using the f-word as a noun, pronoun, adjective, and most certainly an action verb. I adopted the same cynical mindset that most of the others had. Mostly, I learned to take it and dish it out, which was critical to survival in the everybody-is-an-asshole-but-me, male-dominated environment, and I loved it!

The DV cases were discouraging. Months-long investigations were routinely dropped or never indicted due to the lack of a willing victim. I drafted and executed search warrants for property, pictures, people, blood, computers, and anything imaginable, only to receive a call from the prosecutors who had dropped the charges because the couple had gotten back together again.

Prosecutors dismissed cases at an alarming rate. When cases did go through, I would spend time with the victims and educate them along the way, offering support from victim advocates and the prosecutor's office. Watching women return to their abusive partners over and over was familiar to me, but even though I understood why they returned, it never got easier. I knew why my partners were cynical about making arrests in domestic situations and often felt the same way, but I didn't give up.

After six months in the Domestic Violence Unit, Sergeant Sloan asked to see me in his office.

"Sit down, Mary," Sloan said, smiling.

I sat down and opened up a notepad, assuming a case was coming in.

"I want to let you know that we're pleased with your work. You've come a long way in a short time. We're moving you into general assignment."

"Thanks, Sarge," I responded. "What's general assignment?"

He looked at me incredulously. "What?" he nearly shouted.

I shrugged.

"Well, you'll be investigating crimes against children and some DV cases. They're much more involved, and you'll learn a lot from Teresa, Joe, and Gus. They're great with these cases. Watch as many of their interviews as you can. They each have a different style. You'll develop a style of your own, but you'll undoubtedly adopt techniques from each of them. For now, you'll be tagging along. Once you get your feet wet, you'll switch to the other shift and work with Szczerba. This unit is busier, so I'll need you to hit the ground running. Any questions, stop back by."

"Okay," I muttered, walking out of his office.

I smiled at Gus and Joe. "He's not much of a conversationalist, is he?" I shook my head.

"That's because he's a dick," Gus blurted, shutting the office door as the others burst into laughter.

"I'm already on a case, so T-Bird and Joe Bloch will get you up and running. There's only one way to learn, and that's to do it."

Teresa interrupted, "Yeah, the next case I get, I'll be primary, and you can be secondary, which means you'll be my bitch."

They all laughed, and Gus threw his hands up in the air. "Great. I've already been replaced. Hey, so what do we call her?" He stroked his chin. "Did you have a nickname in the academy?"

"Yeah, they called me Mom-Mom, then as a rookie in patrol, some of the guys called me TWS."

"What's that mean?" they asked, tossing around words to fill the acronym until I interrupted.

"Teeny-Weeny Sweeney. I weighed about a hundred pounds."

"Yeah, we'll just call you Sweeney. It's a great bar name," Gus said.

"Bar name? What do you mean?"

"Yeah," Gus said. "If I see you across the bar, it's a great name to yell out. You know—it flows."

He demonstrated by yelling, "Sween-aaaayyy!" enunciating the last part for effect. "Like, you can't scream 'Jones' across the bar—you have to holler 'Jone-say!' Your name's already got that."

A volley of "Sween-aaaayy" went up from the others, ensuring that it worked, deciding that it did. The irreverence had no bounds, and I glanced back and forth as they volleyed insults, laughing along with them.

Joe disrupted the joking with work. "The good thing is, you'll be in our on-call rotation, which means you only go on call every six weeks, instead of every other week like in the DV unit. Don't get too excited though; we get a lot of cases, and we assist the Homicide Unit all the time, so you'll get called out a lot."

I was happy about the transfer but also a little disappointed. I hadn't changed anything about how we handled domestic violence cases. There were just so many of them, and it seemed like the problem originated too far above my pay grade for me to make a significant difference. They weren't replacing my DV position anytime soon, so I would still be working on some of those cases.

Camilli once said we were just worker bees, and at the moment, it seemed an accurate assessment. Maybe he was right. Perhaps I would just be another fresh face that rolled through the DV unit, hoping to make a difference, and not being able to.

The child abuse cases were involved, and there was a matrix for handling them. As different as each investigation was, they all had commonalities. New cases came in every day, but they weren't all urgent. Many of the crimes were reported years after they happened, and any evidence left behind had long since disappeared. Patrol officers took the initial report and passed it on to their supervisors to be assigned to a detective the following day.

A couple of days after my reassignment, Teresa grabbed me by the arm as I passed her desk, a phone in her other hand pressed against her ear. She motioned for me to wait. I watched as she scribbled notes onto a pad in front of her and saw she was collecting an address. We had a case.

"Okay, DFS just called and said they have a rape involving a thirteen-year-old girl. The suspect is her stepfather. We'll meet at the children's hospital where she's undergoing an exam. We'll get the scoop and check in with the doctor to see if there's any physical evidence. Dr. Jang is a forensic specialist, and he handles most of the felony child abuse cases, so I'm sure you've met him by now."

I nodded.

"To make sure nothing gets missed, we take the same steps for each case, *every single time*." She enunciated the words individually, punching the desk for effect. "The kid is safe now, so we can slow down. No need to rush anything."

I nodded, watching, listening, and taking lots of notes. I learned to write without looking down at my notepad—my illegible scribble evidence that I had crossed into new territory. Gus walked by, glancing down at my notes to see what we had, and said, "Good grief. You write like a serial killer."

He was right. I smiled and continued writing feverishly. I had developed a type of shorthand that no one could understand but me.

"We manage child abuse cases differently than DV cases," Teresa said. "While the investigator interviews the victim in most cases, the Children's Advocacy Center (CAC) conducts interviews with child victims. They use a forensic, nonleading, nonsuggestive technique designed to preserve the integrity of the information. At first, I thought it was unnecessary, but the more cases I handled, the more I saw that it worked."

Teresa was a wealth of knowledge and I studied her interviewing style and manner with all types of cases. I was a willing student and I learned fast.

Child abuse was nearly always an evolution of domestic violence, and the two units blended. Weeks of tagging along assisting Joe, Gus, and Teresa with cases proved Sergeant Sloan right. I cherry-picked skills and techniques from each of them—practicing what I heard and saw until I had created a style of my own. Soon I was working solo, handling my own cases and assisting other units as well as helping my coworkers with their cases. The pace was grueling and I loved it. I enjoyed going to work every day, and it was a good thing because I worked all the time. There was no such thing as a shift. The shift ended when it came to a proper stopping point for that day, and most of the time there was overtime. Brad and I were not happy about having less time together, but the money was great, and I loved almost everything else about the job.

One of Teresa's cases was scheduled for trial, and an autopsy was scheduled for the same day. It was an important case and a detective needed to be present for the autopsy to get the cause of death. In cases involving death, the autopsy was critical evidence, and this was no exception.

"Hey, Mare, I have a dead baby case, and I wonder if you could help me out. The autopsy is tomorrow at noon and I'll be in court. Mom and dad were squirrelly. Their stories are vague and don't quite match up, and I'm not buying it. Mom says that she put the baby down on the sofa and walked away for a second to get a diaper and the baby rolled off and fell onto the floor. Hospital doctors report a skull fracture, so we need to know if the mechanism of injury could cause a skull fracture . Can you cover the autopsy for me?"

Had I known that I would be called out that ho-hum evening before and be out all night on a case, I might have asked her to check with a coworker. I worked as much of my case as I could and rushed to the medical examiner's office, arriving fifteen minutes late.

"Just in time," Dr. Jang said as I accepted a visitor's pass and followed him to the secured area. There were no windows in the building, and the gray cinder block walls were barren; it was like walking into nothingness, and the elevator to the basement smelled of decomposition. No color, no pictures on the walls, no music, and no people, except for the two of us, trod the halls. Dr. Jang wore a white Tyvek suit and goggles with booties covering his shoes. My gray suit matched the emptiness. The closer we got to the area where autopsies were performed, the colder it became. The room appeared to be sterile, like an operating room, with white sheets, knives, and other surgical equipment needed for autopsies. The entrance to the room was wide and included a viewing area with a window at chest height to the right of the opening. A red line was painted on the concrete floor at the entrance, and Dr. Jang offered me a barstool outside the room.

"You can put your things down here," he said. "Come inside and watch if you like, but you have to stay at least six feet away from where I'm working. Most detectives want to be present, but it's up to you. I'll be taking pictures, so let me know if you need anything specific and I'll take care of it. Where's Teresa?"

"She's in court so I'm covering for her. I'm not as familiar with the case as she is, but I'll tell you what I know."

"No need. I spoke to her, so I have a pretty good idea of what the parents reported."

The autopsy began with weighing the baby, and Dr. Jang spoke into a microphone that hung above the exam table, in some cases using medical terms I was unfamiliar with. I stood inside the room as he began making incisions, starting at the crown of her head. I wasn't close enough to see what he saw, but his verbal description made clear what I was witnessing.

Missing sleep was a hazard of the job, and one that I could handle, but lack of food took me down, and my stomach rumbled when we hit the second hour. Dr. Jang took a break, turned off the microphone, and asked whether the baby had been clothed when the incident occurred. I checked my notes and answered.

"Doc, do you mind if I eat my lunch? I brought it with me. I was out on another case all night and I haven't eaten since last night's dinner."

He laughed. "You're going to fit in nicely, Detective. Sure, go ahead. Just stay behind the red line."

By the time I finished lunch, Dr. Jang had finished the autopsy and was prepared to answer questions.

"Okay, Doc. So, mom said that she was changing the baby and put her on the sofa, and then walked away for a second. She said the baby rolled off and onto a carpeted floor. Does that seem feasible, given what you saw?"

"Yes, it's feasible, but only if the sofa fell out a seven-story window first." He laughed at his own joke and continued, explaining that the trauma was so severe that it was more likely due to blunt force trauma, stomping, or throwing. He reminded me that an infant only three weeks old would not be able to roll yet. Given the story provided by the parents, it was likely that one of them had killed or knew who killed the infant. This meant that T probably had a homicide.

I rushed back to the office and shared the information from Dr. Jang, knowing that it would mean everyone would drop what they were doing to assist. Detectives would call home and change their evening plans, spouses would be picking up kids from day care, and the expected time of arrival home would be open-ended. I called Brad and let him know I would be late and asked him to call my friend Chrissy, who was coming the next day for a weekend visit, and let her know that everything was up in the air. This unpredictability was becoming a way of life, but not only did I not mind it; I thrived on it.

Chrissy and I had been best friends since grade school. We grew up together, and we had the kind of friendship that transcended the expanse of time and space. It didn't matter how much time passed or how far apart we lived. It was as if no time had passed when we got together, or so I thought, until she came for that rare weekend visit.

We sat poolside, drinking wine coolers as she shared stories of office drama she was experiencing at her job. These were ordinary, mundane stories of bickering and petty competitive behavior.

"She's been a pill. I used to like working with her, but she's always going to the boss, complaining about something. She doesn't want to do her job, and when she's late coming back from lunch or BS-ing with the boss, I'm stuck doing her job. It's not fair. She used to work at another location, but I heard they had problems with her, too, so she got transferred."

I nodded, understanding, feigning interest. "How have you been feeling since your surgery?" I asked, changing the subject. "Last I heard, you were taking some pretty serious pain meds."

A terrible car crash and resulting broken neck had left Chrissy in constant pain. We chatted about how she was recovering and how her husband, Dwayne, cared for her.

"How's work going?" Chrissy asked, raising a Seagram's wine cooler to her lips, taking a sip, and squeezing the bottle koozie with her fingertips. "You're working with kids now, right?"

"Yeah, I'm in the Crimes Against Children Unit. It's going well—busy. No shortage of assholes."

"What are you working on now, or can you tell me?"

She had become accustomed to hearing funny stories about the people I encountered on the street as a road officer, but things were different now. There were no more entertaining stories. "I'm assisting on a dead baby case. I don't know what happened and may never know. It was a callout a couple of days ago. I went to the autopsy yesterday, but the medical examiner is on the fence about the cause of death. Just saying that it wasn't consistent with the story."

"Oh my God," Chrissy whispered. "That must have been horrible. You had to watch?"

Chrissy was right. It should have been horrible, but while Dr. Jang peeled that baby's head open like a grape, I ate my lunch.

"Yeah, I guess," I answered, and measuring my words, I expressed frustration for the broken system that allowed criminals to go on committing crimes. The look on Chrissy's face didn't match the poolside drinks and sunny day. She dangled her feet in the pool water, gazing at the horses grazing in the distant fields.

"Mary, I'm worried about you. You seem hard, and maybe a teensy bit cynical, and, Lordy, you cuss like a sailor. That's not normal for everyday banter." She laughed, but her face registered concern.

"That's bullshit. I'm fine," I joked. "Seriously, I'm fine, Chrissy. I'm sorry. Sometimes I forget where I am. You know I don't mean anything by it. All my coworkers talk like that, and I guess I've gotten used to it, or maybe it's the wine coolers."

Laughter and alcohol kept the demons at bay, but I knew she was right. I suspected it, but hearing the words from a trusted friend who loved me sealed it. I was becoming desensitized to the pain and suffering of others. The problem was that it was a necessary defense. I had to compartmentalize my life to prevent the ugliness from spilling over where it shouldn't. It's one reason that cops marry other cops or nurses and people in other fields with a bird's-eye view of the ugly side of life. It was also why we did nothing but work and why the divorce and suicide rates were so high for us. We understood one another. Chrissy pointed out that it was spilling into my nonpolice life and not in a good way. It was an eye-opener, and the more I experienced, the less I felt. It had happened so gradually that I didn't notice the changes, but I had become jaded. I was one of them. I was a detective. I fit in.

The following year was a blur of cases, the nature of the crimes a mixed bag. Detectives always shared unusual or funny crimes at roll call, but sharing a child abuse case was rare. No one wanted to hear those details. Cases of mothers trading their teenage daughters for sexual favors in return for drugs and infants with broken femurs became the norm. In the beginning, the cases would take an emotional toll on detectives newly assigned to the unit, but eventually, they would get used to them. The names began to run together. The dates, times, and locations changed, but the crimes stopped shocking me. I wasn't alone, but was in good company with fellow detectives, top-notch prosecutors, and probably judges too.

# Chapter Twenty-Six

IT WAS 2005 AND MY ASSIGNED CASES WERE A BLUR OF CONSTANT action. Over the first five years in detectives, I investigated and assisted with the prosecution of rapes, assaults, neglect, suspicious deaths, and many other crimes against children and victims of domestic violence. I fell into a comfortable routine. I was competent and confident.

It had been an ordinary day. I was just finishing up my shift when I passed by Frank Robinson, who was leaning over Faye's desk on the phone.

He looked at me. "Looks like a case coming in. Nobody is in for the second shift tonight. They've been at court all day. Are you up for kiddie crimes?"

Frank had been promoted to detective sergeant, and cases were issued in rotation. It was my turn to take a new urgent case for my squad.

"Yeah, I think so, Frank."

"Okay, stand by and let's wait and see if we're needed."

"Sure, no problem," I said, though not in the mood for a new case as I sat back down, waiting for the decision.

I waited for about fifteen minutes before Frank motioned "come here" with one hand, holding the phone up to his ear with the other. I was still packing my briefcase when he hung up the phone and approached me at the desk, carrying a notepad.

"What do we have?" I asked.

"Domestic assault, male versus female. She's pregnant and on the way to the hospital with vaginal bleeding. I'll give you the info now, but she'll probably get admitted. She's at twenty-one weeks. The male fled and patrol is looking for him. There's an officer with her, so go ahead over. If you get to talk to her, get a brief statement. Try to get enough for an arrest warrant. Best to get him into custody. If we need to, we can always bump up the charges later."

"Okay, will do," I answered.

I grabbed my briefcase and cassette recorder along with a camera. SANE nurses would take pictures of injuries at the hospital, but I took photos myself whenever possible. It was helpful to have a picture to describe injuries when drafting a search warrant.

It looked like it might be a long night, so I stopped at Wawa for a cup of coffee, a quick pick-me-up. I arrived at the hospital and met with Officer Crass.

"Hey, Rhonda, what have you got?" I asked.

"Hey, Mare. Okay, she's an eighteen-year-old female. It's her second pregnancy and she's high risk. She had a miscarriage about a year ago. She said that she and her boyfriend argued tonight, and during the scuffle, he shoved her against the wall. I didn't get to talk to her much. He fled, and she started bleeding and called 911. That's about it. Patrol is looking for him, but they lived together on Carman Drive. No idea where he might be now. She was in a lot of pain and looked like she might deliver tonight. She's in the ICU. You won't be able to see her, so if you want, I'll complete the report and leave you a copy for tomorrow morning."

"Okay, sounds good." I nodded.

I contacted the on-call deputy attorney general and left an overview of the case to be assigned. There was a witness, so I sought him out for an interview. His name was Rodney; he refused to meet at police headquarters but agreed to talk to me at his house.

"They were arguing about an air conditioner. That's all I know because when things got heated, I went outside," Rodney said.

"Tell me what you mean when you say things got heated," I asked.

"They were yelling at each other. It was stupid. Me and Donald were out all day buying a new air conditioner. It was hot, and when we got home, we put it in the window. Nadine was hollering about which window he put it in or something. I ain't sure. It might have been about how much he spent or where he got it; whatever, but she's pregnant, so she's crazy right now. I told Donald to leave her alone because she's hormonal, but he kept arguing with her. They argue all the time, and Donald's my boy, but I don't get in his business."

"Were you there when it became physical?" I asked.

"I left when they started yelling. That's all I know." He shrugged.

Another half hour of questioning yielded no additional information. If he knew more, he wasn't sharing it with me.

Everything changed the following day. Nadine delivered baby girl Johnson eleven hours after arriving at the hospital.

"She lived for fifteen minutes and died," Dr. Lawson said. "She was just over five months pregnant, so it was a premature birth, but the fetus was viable. She breathed on her own for fifteen minutes. We'll do an autopsy for the cause of death, but I could see that the placenta had pulled away from the uterine wall."

"Okay, is that indicative of trauma? Is it likely that the assault brought on labor?" I asked.

"This type of preterm labor and birth could have been brought on by trauma. The SANE nurse took pictures. Nothing on her abdomen, but the mother had a bruise on her right flank and a contusion on her neck. She has a few fresh bruises. The medical examiner will be in a better position to tell you more."

"Okay, thank you. Can I speak to Nadine?" I asked.

"Yes, but only for a few minutes."

I gathered my briefcase, pulled out a cassette recorder, replaced the batteries, snapped in a new tape titled "Nadine Johnson," and proceeded to her room.

It was a long walk down the hallway as I grappled with memories of my own similar experience. Vaguely aware of the white-clad staff marching past me single file with charts in their hands, I made my way to the area reserved for protected assault victims. The halls were quiet compared to the usual visitor chatter and noises associated with hospitals, and the bleach smell was overwhelming. Since her domestic partner had assaulted Nadine, the hospital treated her personal information delicately, and visitors were carefully screened.

Fleeting images of bright-white lights and sheets draped across my thighs sped through my mind's eye. I slowed my pace, allowing my emotional response to the situation to pass. Feeling like a helpless victim who had lost a baby rather than a detective spooked me. My face felt flushed, and I felt weak. *Jesus, get it together, Mary*, I scolded. I searched for a place to collect myself, slowly wandering the halls. Finding a ladies' room, I slipped inside unnoticed and came face-to-face with a full-length mirror. A detective stared back. She wore no eye patch, had no marks on her face, and stood ramrod straight. She stared at me confidently in her navy-blue Dior suit and white collared blouse until the reflection approached the mirror, reapplied lipstick, and brushed her hair. A subtle smile crossed her lips. She wasn't the same girl I imagined in the hallway. She was a completely different person. She took a deep breath, collected herself, and marched out of the restroom, glancing at the room number on the slip of paper she held, knowing both of us would be fine.

Nadine glanced over at me as I entered the room. She was a young, petite eighteen-year-old African American girl with skin the color of honey. Her face was thin with prominent cheekbones; she had the beauty of a model, except for the scowl she wore. The standard white hospital gown hung loosely on her small frame. She looked like a child attached to blinking, beeping machines by a length of tubing.

I cleared my throat and introduced myself. "Hello, Nadine. I'm Detective Sweeney. Can we talk for a few minutes?"

She shrugged. "About what?" Her pencil-thin eyebrows knit together.

"About what happened last night and how you're doing," I said, but Nadine said nothing in reply.

I put my briefcase on the floor, positioned a chair, and sat down so we could see each other. I removed the recorder from my bag and placed it on the table between us.

"Nadine, I'm going to ask you some questions, and this recorder will help me to remember what you said when I write my report. I can't express how sorry I am that you lost your baby. I'm here to help you if I can. I want to figure out what happened and get you the help you need. I'm glad to see you've gotten some rest. Do you mind talking with me so I can understand better what happened?"

"You can't help me," she barked, and then softened. "No, I don't mind."

Her face was expressionless. It was a face I had worn a thousand times when Vince and I were married. Where there was hope, there had also been hopelessness. I had worn it on my face too. I felt like I knew Nadine already. She folded her arms across her chest.

"Nadine, what happened yesterday?"

"I told the police and DFS already. Didn't they tell you?"

"Yes, they did, Nadine." I spoke softly, the same way Sarah had spoken to me so many years ago, asking almost the same questions and getting nearly the same response.

"But I'd like to hear it from you directly. I'm sorry to put you through this again. I know it's hard, but it's essential to get some details while they're fresh in your mind. I'm not going to ask questions so much as I'm going to let you do the talking. I want to understand how this nightmare happened. Can you start by telling me about yesterday morning and what led up to the event that got you here?"

"Yesterday afternoon, Donald and his friend Rodney went to Best Buy to get an air conditioner."

Her tone was sharp—her eyes narrowed in anger.

"It's been blazing hot, and I was pregnant. I couldn't take the heat anymore."

I nodded, noting the usage of the past tense.

"They were gone for a long time, and it was sweltering in the house. When they got home, Donald and Rodney were more concerned with getting some beers than with putting the air conditioner in the window. I yelled at Donald to get the air conditioner in the window, and he snapped back at me."

"Okay," I prodded.

"They wrestled with it for a while until they got it working, and everything was okay for a little bit. We were chilling. Then they started running in and out of the house, letting the cold air out, and I hollered at him to stop running in and out. He got mad because I embarrassed him in front of Rodney, and I laughed. Rodney practically lives with us! He's not a guest. Anyway, he got mad because I laughed at him and grabbed me by my throat. He threw me on the sofa and started choking me. It happened fast."

"Where were his body and yours when he choked you?" I asked.

"I was lying across the couch, and his body was on top of mine. His feet were on the floor. He wasn't sitting on me, but he was holding me down with his body."

I began to perspire. Vince had pinned me down on the bed the same way. Was there a manual that directed men on how to disable their partner?

"Okay, what happened next?" I nudged.

"I twisted underneath him, trying to get up, and scratched him on the neck with my fingernails. He got up and dragged me off the couch by my bathrobe. We wrestled back and forth and ended up in the kitchen. He shoved me, and my backside hit the wall, and I screamed." She stopped. "Have you seen him?" she asked.

I wiped my brow, noticing the similarities between Nadine's

experience and mine, the dragging, overpowering, and screaming, but mainly the need to escape. I loosened the buttons on my blouse, feeling for the fingerprints on my neck.

"What? Um, no, I haven't met him yet," I said.

"Okay, well, he's not tall. He's kind of short and fat, but he's muscular. He's big compared to me. When I screamed, Rodney came in and grabbed Donald and dragged him out the door. I don't know where they went after that."

She spoke slowly now, her voice monotone. "Anyway, all of a sudden, my stomach started cramping, and I felt something running down my leg."

I knew the feeling exactly: the smell of dirty clothes and stabbing cramps invaded my thoughts, threatening to derail my interview, my hand unconsciously resting on my stomach.

She looked down, placing her hand on her abdomen beneath the sheet, clenching her jaw. "I thought my water broke," she said, "but I looked and saw it was blood, so I called 911, and here I am." She frowned, shaking her head.

"I'm sorry, Nadine," I whispered, allowing the moment to linger. "Was this your first pregnancy?"

"No, I was pregnant this time last year, but I lost it, so I was high risk for this one. Everything was going great." She looked at her hands folded in her lap. "Until now."

"Nadine," I asked gently, "was there a moment during the altercation when you felt an impact or felt pain in your abdomen, back, or anywhere else?"

"I told you, when he slammed my back against the kitchen wall. That's when I called 911."

"Yes. Yes, you did. I'm sorry. Nadine, were you and Donald together last year?"

"Yes, we've been together for about three years," she said.

"What happened to cause you to lose the baby last year, Nadine?"

Dr. Lawson poked his head into the room, ending the interview before I could get an answer to that question.

"Nadine, here's my card. Call me if you want to talk or just need to know you're not alone. You'll get through this. I know you will."

She took the card but didn't respond.

I let her know that we'd meet again for a more detailed discussion when she felt better, or maybe when I felt better. I left the hospital reliving the nightmare of fourteen years earlier, images of not only the assault but of bright lights, screaming, blood, and hospital rooms filling my vision, and I was angry. Vince hadn't paid for his crime, but I would make sure Donald did.

Donald Kendricks had been brought back to headquarters for questioning. He was twenty-five years old, and he was a big guy, five feet, eight inches tall and about 280 pounds. He had a prior assault conviction involving Nadine from about a year before. I had my answer, and I wasn't surprised. I'd make him pay this time.

This would be the most critical interview I ever did, and I reviewed my notes as I approached the box. I took a deep breath and pushed open the interview room door.

"Hello, Donald. I'm sorry for the delay. My name is Mary Sweeney. I'm the detective in charge of this investigation, and I need to talk to you about what happened last night."

He nodded, grinning broadly.

*He was smiling! Did he think if he was nice, it would all go away? No way, buddy. Everybody thought Vince was nice too.*

"Hello, Detective. Hey, I'm hungry. Do you think I could get something to eat? I was just about to sit down for dinner when the police—"

"Not just now, Donald," I interrupted. "Sorry." I stifled my inner eye roll and smiled back at him.

"I'm glad I'm gonna get to tell my side of the story because I couldn't help it. It was an accident," he said. "You don't know her.

She's stronger than she looks, and I was just trying to keep her from hurting herself, but she ended up hurting me. It's okay, though. I don't want to press no charges or anything. I love her, you know? She's my everything. Could I get something to drink? Maybe a Coke?"

Kendricks droned on, while *she's my everything* echoed in my ears. It was Vince's favorite defense. He could never have hurt me because I was *his everything*, yet he had, and Kendricks had hurt Nadine, but not only Nadine. He had snuffed out the life of a child with unlimited possibilities in an instant, and he had no remorse, and neither had Vince. I despised both of them.

"Look at my neck," he hollered, pulling his collar down so I could see her fingernail marks. He hadn't even asked about Nadine or their unborn child. The more he talked, the more pathetic he seemed. Kendricks's story supported Nadine's account of him choking her and shoving her into the wall. He chattered for over an hour, nearly unsolicited, admitting he *might have* pushed Nadine against the wall. He wasn't a strong twenty-five-year-old man but a whiny adolescent justifying his actions, suggesting his pregnant girlfriend was a bully and he was the victim. He would have talked for hours if I had let him, but I couldn't bear to hear another word.

Admitting he pushed her against the wall was damning evidence, but it would be up to the prosecution team and medical professionals to prove that Kendricks's push caused the baby to die. He was arrested for assault in the first degree and held without bail until the preliminary hearing.

# Chapter Twenty-Seven

JACK BUTLER WAS THE PROSECUTING ATTORNEY. HE WAS AN EXPER-
ienced, well-respected man of about forty-five. His full, prematurely
graying beard and glasses made him look distinguished. Over
the years, Jack had earned an excellent reputation as a competent,
no-nonsense litigator, and I was happy that he was assigned the case.
I parked in the garage and took the elevator to the seventh floor of
the courthouse to meet with him and discuss the prosecution. We
had spoken over the phone a few times, but this conversation would
result in a charging decision.

I walked into his small, cluttered office and sat in a chair across
the desk from him. Jack acknowledged me with a nod, shuffling
papers and stacks of files so he could see me sitting in the chair across
from him, then he jumped into the case details.

"Mary, yesterday we had a straightforward first-degree assault
case, but now we have a live birth, so it's more of a decision about
whether to indict on a murder charge or manslaughter. According to
the medical reports, the baby was born alive and died. Interestingly,
we have an additional indictment. It's been on the books since 1999
but has never been used. It's Delaware Code 11-606, abuse of a pregnant female."

I remembered hearing about this code a year ago, but it had not
immediately occurred to me that it applied in this case. I nodded,
wondering whether it mattered if he had known she was pregnant.

"It says that if someone commits a felony, and in the process of the
commission of that felony they cause the termination of a pregnancy,

they are guilty of abuse of a pregnant female in the first degree. In the deciding case, the judge defined a human being as someone completely extracted from their mother and showing evidence of life, such as a heartbeat, breathing, or umbilical cord pulsation. This code is a class B felony, and I think it fits the details of this case." It didn't matter if the assailant knew about the pregnancy.

Jack and I discussed the content of the interviews, the remaining work, and the potential problems with the case. He told me that they had scheduled a fives meeting for this case. I knew that a fives meeting was an assembly of the top five prosecutors in the state to discuss the evidence and appropriate charges for high-profile cases. It was my first experience with a fives, and I was eager but apprehensive.

"I'm going to talk with the medical examiner before the fives, so I need to rush off. I'll call you in an hour," he said.

I gathered my files and notes and shoved them back into my briefcase, following him out of the building. He called an hour later. Kendricks would be indicted for second-degree manslaughter, felony assault in the first degree, and abuse of a pregnant female in the second degree. It was a good case. *Good*, I thought. *Then he'll rot in prison.*

Kendricks was arraigned and held over for trial in lieu of a $500,000 secured bond. He would remain in prison until the court date. If convicted, Kendricks could spend the next twenty-eight years in prison, and I was satisfied with that outcome. It felt vindicating.

Most of the hard work needed to ensure a conviction came after the arrest, and forensic evidence would be critical in this case. I authored search warrants for DNA collection from the fetus and both parents, medical records from Nadine's first pregnancy as well as this most recent one, photos of the scene, autopsy records, recorded interviews, and the 911 phone call placed by Nadine. Testimony from the medical examiner and Dr. Lawson would make most of our work unnecessary, but we did it anyway. A couple of weeks went by and Jack called to let me know he couldn't reach Nadine.

"She went home from the hospital after the assault, and I can't get ahold of her. I wonder if she will change her mind about cooperating with the prosecution."

"No, no, no," I said, panicking a little. "The day it happened, she provided facts, but she wasn't warm and friendly when most victims usually are. I hope she's okay, but I hope she cooperates. I want my case to be tight."

"You and me both," Jack said. "I need to visit her, and I want you to go with me."

We coordinated our schedules to visit Nadine at her home and prepare her for the proceedings, but also to gauge her level of commitment. Jack's suspicions were correct. After several cancellations, we met with Nadine at her mom's house. Mrs. Johnson greeted us amicably, and it appeared that she might support prosecution. If Kendricks had caused two miscarriages by assaulting Nadine, it made sense. It was a cold, rainy day and the dreariness aligned with the nature of the visit. The Johnsons lived in a small brick cracker-box house in an old low-income neighborhood. The front yard, a small piece of property, was well groomed and butted up against train tracks. As we stepped inside the home, the darkness followed us. Mrs. Johnson switched on a lamp and motioned toward a small sofa against the wall for us to sit. Nadine sat with her legs crossed on a brown leather recliner situated beside the sofa, and her mother left the room to get water for her guests. Nadine avoided eye contact, picking at her nails, seemingly uninterested in us. Jack made small talk about the weather and how long it had taken to finally get this case to trial. He began by explaining to Nadine that we wanted to review her prior statement and help her to understand the trial process. He had brought the recording of the 911 call with him, but we hoped not to need it. He described the evidence that the state would be using against Kendricks and asked her questions about that night, mostly to jog her memory. Her mother returned with water and nodded her approval, demonstrating that she may have encouraged Nadine to move forward with this meeting.

Jack jumped into his notes, reviewing Nadine's statement from the moment of the call. "Nadine, you said that Donald shoved you against the kitchen wall, and you began bleeding and that this was when you called 911."

"No," she corrected. "I think I said I fell up against the wall. I'm not sure, but I think he might have still been in the living room when that happened."

The changes in her statement would cause problems with the case, and Jack looked at me, knitting his brow. I reminded Nadine that the interview that night had been recorded and looked at my notes, reading the words that I had written.

"Nadine, I have in my notes that you said he dragged you off the couch by your bathrobe into the kitchen and shoved you against the wall."

"Well, if that's what it says, then that's what I said, but I don't think he killed our baby. I was already high risk because I lost a baby a year before this one. I don't think it was his fault."

"Have you been in touch with Donald?" Jack asked gently. "I mean since his incarceration."

"Yes, we've been talking all along. We're going to get back together when he gets released, because he didn't do what you're saying he did, and we've been together a long time. We're going to get married."

My heart dropped. She had been reluctant to provide information from the beginning, but this was worse. I could feel disgust overtaking my emotions as she painted Donald as a victim, and I struggled to control my facial expressions.

"Nadine," Jack said. "I can't pretend to understand what you're going through, but I believe that Donald is responsible for the death of your baby, and you will hear me say this repeatedly at the trial. I don't know how he normally treated you, but I think everyone here knows what happened that day, and he must take responsibility and face the consequences of his actions."

Mrs. Johnson interrupted, talking about Nadine like she wasn't in the room. "I'll make sure she's there for trial, but it's hard to know what she might say. She's too good for him, and I don't know why, but she loves that man."

Jack spoke with compassion and respect, but he didn't pull any punches explaining to her in the kindest way I've ever heard that the case would move forward with or without her cooperation. The walls seemed to be closing in and the air got thicker in the room as Jack continued preparing her for the inevitable.

"You will be required to testify, Nadine. I know it's frightening, but we will help you to prepare, and we won't require much of you because of the recorded statement that Detective Sweeney took from you on the night this happened. We will stay in touch with you and your mom until the trial date. Until then, I'm asking you to refrain from communicating with Donald, and I will have a discussion with his attorney about witness tampering."

Mrs. Johnson nodded in agreement and after a few instructions about logistics, Nadine agreed to take all future calls from the prosecution team. Nadine hadn't refused to testify, but we had to plan for that possibility.

The first step was the preliminary hearing, which the victim was not required to attend. Nadine didn't participate, but Kendricks had to be present. The hearing was a simple laying out of the facts of the case that resulted in the indictment. I would be the only witness presenting testimonial evidence, and Jack would ask the questions. For the most part, it was a formality, but because of the high-profile nature of the case, the press lined the walls. The hearing was held in a large courtroom to accommodate the participants, families, law students, and legal teams.

I spent hours preparing for what I expected to be ten minutes of testimony, but I was nervous on the day of the hearing. I had seen many accomplished prosecutors wringing their hands in court, but Jack showed no signs of nerves. I wore my favorite charcoal-gray power suit and sensible shoes to boost my confidence, but my cotton mouth sold me out.

I had testified at plenty of preliminary hearings but none quite this weighty. This case would be the first ever to try someone for the law against assaulting a pregnant female, so the media turned out in spades.

The court bailiff called the calendar. "State versus Kendricks."

Kendricks, wearing an orange prison jumpsuit, stood up in front of his chair, his court-appointed attorney standing beside him.

Jack walked to the podium. "We're here, Your Honor."

"Proceed with your first witness, Mr. Butler," the judge ordered.

"The state calls Detective Mary Sweeney," Jack said casually.

I walked confidently up the aisle to the witness box to be sworn in, sat down, adjusted the microphone, and crossed my legs, only to have a roll of peppermint Life Savers topple out of my briefcase onto the floor and down the platform, rolling past three rows of seats filled with reporters. The bailiff captured the liberated roll and brought it back to me, chuckling. I knew him, so I smiled, offering him one, which lightened the mood for everyone in the room but me. If anyone's life needed saving that day, it was mine. I felt foolish, but Jack was a professional. He got right back to business, so there was no time for me to berate myself.

"Detective Sweeney, as a detective for New Castle County Police, were you assigned a case on the afternoon of March twenty-third involving the eighteen-year-old victim and the defendant, Donald Kendricks?"

"Yes, that's correct," I answered.

"Do you see the defendant in the courtroom today?"

"Yes." I pointed to Kendricks. "The man in the orange jumpsuit who stands beside Mr. Cross."

The remainder of the hearing went off without a hitch. Kendricks was bound over and held without bail. He would remain in prison until he went to court, and potentially for nearly thirty more years.

# Chapter Twenty-Eight

I was Vince's punching bag for years until the assault and miscarriage. I didn't go back to him, but I had wanted to, and I might have if it hadn't been for Nurse Sarah. I had missed Vince, loved him, and even had regrets about leaving for a while. Nadine's demeanor and actions were typical under the circumstances, and so were mine. So why was I upset with her? Why couldn't I find the compassion for her that she deserved? Because it was my case? Was it because my pride was at stake? Was I judging her, thinking I was somehow better than her now?

I left the courthouse feeling like everybody was staring at me, like they knew I was a fraud, not a detective but a sniveling victim all dressed up in a designer suit. I wrapped my coat tightly around my shoulders, paid the parking attendant, and drove home on autopilot. I had come too far to be dragged back down to the victim's level, and I didn't want to think about where I had been. I knew that being a victim was a choice, yet it still haunted me more than fifteen years later.

Nadine's admission that she would get back together with Donald even after this nightmare shook my confidence just as quickly as the errant roll of Life Savers had. I expected her to leave him and hate him for what he'd done, but then, I didn't leave when I should have.

Because of my job, I understood the cycle of violence that kept women entangled with their abusers, clouding their judgment. I knew how abusers groomed and manipulated their partners, like water wearing down rocks over time. The changes were so gradual that they were almost imperceptible, and the gradual heating up reminded me of the metaphor I once heard about a boiling frog. If you put a frog in a pot of boiling water, it will hop out immediately, but if you put a frog in cold water and heat it slowly, the frog will stay in the water until it dies. The frog can't tell the water is getting hotter. Like the frog, I didn't recognize the danger when I was in it. Because the rise in the volatility of my marriage was gradual, it took on a feeling of normalcy that nearly killed me. It hadn't killed me, but it had killed my baby, and I still struggled with the emotions surrounding that loss years later. At the time, I didn't understand my behavior, but now I know the thoughts that convinced me to stay, to hope things would return to normal, had been irrational.

Was it too late? Could I still reach Nadine? She was intelligent, well-spoken, and articulate. I knew she was strong enough to leave, but could I be there for her if she made a decision I couldn't condone? How could I support her if she reunited with Kendricks? Maybe I hadn't come as far as I thought.

My mind wandered through the dark places of my past all the way home. I needed to be proactive. By the time I pulled into my driveway, I had an idea. I would write a comprehensive but practical list of ways to identify whether a partner was abusive. I would talk to Nadine about it and give her a copy to keep and refer to when she wasn't sure. I remembered those times when I thought I was crazy, and a list would have helped a lot to assure me that I wasn't, or maybe that I was. Maybe it would help her too.

I could offer examples from my own life experience and other behavioral patterns I learned from my training in the Domestic Violence Unit. This seemed urgent, so I stripped off my coat, flopped into a chair with a pen, and started writing. The list flowed out of me, words dropping onto the page like rain.

I knew the list wasn't complete and that other victims in the same situation would add many more notes to it, but it was a good start. I would talk to Nadine and show her the list the next time we met for trial prep.

Months rolled by, and Jack called with a follow-up on the case from time to time. When examined as a whole, medical records and other evidence provided pretty damning evidence against Kendricks. Nadine refused to cooperate, which was a huge hurdle, but her call to 911, screaming and blaming Kendricks at the very moment she was having the miscarriage, was chilling and powerful.

I wanted to meet with Nadine and review the list I had made as soon as possible, and leave it with her, so she'd understand this wasn't her fault. I wanted her to know there was another way and that she deserved to be respected by her partner. But that opportunity never came.

Baby girl Johnson would never get her day in court. Nearly eleven months after the assault that resulted in her death, Donald Kendricks pled guilty to abuse of a pregnant female in the second degree. In return, the prosecution dropped the manslaughter and assault charges. I found out after the fact. It wasn't a surprise that a case like this might plea, but to drop the two most serious charges in return for a conviction for the untested abuse of a pregnant female charge was tragic.

At the sentencing hearing, Nadine testified that the miscarriage was not Kendricks's fault and called the prosecution arrogant in their dealings with her. Hearing her defend Kendricks and criticize the prosecution team broke my heart, but I understood. She wanted him, no matter what. She would go to the ends of the earth for him, and I understood. It was that four-letter word—"hope."

After Nadine's testimony, Jack stood and made his statement.

"Baby girl Johnson would have been eleven months old in three days. She will never grow up, find love, get married, or accomplish important things because of the actions of Donald Kendricks."

Jack outlined the facts of the case, pointing out that Kendricks had only cared about himself and showed no remorse, taking no responsibility for his actions.

"Someone has to speak for the victim since her mother will not."

I blanched at his harsh words, feeling the tug from both sides of the fence, but he was right! We would never know what baby girl Johnson might have accomplished, and we deserved to. She never had a say, and it was my job and Jack's to give voice to her right to survive and thrive. This plea seemed like a lame attempt to shout about her right to live or to punish her attacker, but Jack had done his best without a willing victim. After a few more formalities, it was over.

The judge sentenced Kendricks to eighteen months in prison and six months of work release for the baby's death, or what I considered her murder. After adding in time served to that point, he would serve only seven more months and then he'd report for work release. Nadine and Donald would be together again in a year.

I had seen it before, but it still baffled me. Why didn't the death of an innocent baby carry the same weight as the death of an adult, a doctor, a football star, or even a ten-year-old girl with pigtails in an Easter dress and patent leather shoes? This baby could have donned a graduation gown or wedding dress, or she could have birthed the next leader, scientist, or Mother Teresa. Why? For the abuse of a pregnant female charge, Kendricks could have received a ten-year sentence, but eighteen months? I agreed that a jury trial without the victim's support might not result in a guilty verdict, but only an eighteen-month sentence, when the judge had complete discretion? I didn't get it. Were they related or something? Was Kendricks his paperboy back in the day?

I watched Kendricks leave the courtroom smiling at Nadine, knowing she had freed him, and my stomach lurched. I hadn't been able to reach her. Either I hadn't tried hard enough, or she wasn't ready. I knew about not being ready but couldn't let myself off the hook. It was my job! I was responsible for making this right, for giving baby girl Johnson her justice. Instead, I stood there with a silly list in my briefcase. I folded my arms across my chest like a defiant child crying no fair, and glared at Kendricks as he left the courtroom. He was a loser, but I felt lost.

Nadine left without a word to anyone, her eyes red and her face hollow. I was glad she had the courtesy not to rub our noses in it, but as I looked at her again, I knew it was more than that. Hers wasn't a face of satisfaction or of a victor. She was downtrodden, and it was an expression I recognized. I had worn it a hundred times. It was the marred face of a warrior, an exhausted, battle-worn warrior with a thousand-yard stare, vacant and disengaged. It was the face of a haggard abuse victim, and I knew it well. That was when my heart went out to her, and I bit my lip, finding compassion.

The stuffy, overcrowded courtroom smelled of body odor and mildew. I felt nauseous as the stench invaded my nostrils, and I picked up my things and turned to leave, allowing space between myself and Nadine.

Jack shook hands a few rows ahead of me, and the media waited just beyond the well-wishers for an interview. It was a win for the state, but it didn't feel like a win to me. It was the first successful prosecution of the abuse of a pregnant female law. *Successful.* I made my way past the crowd of reporters to the elevators and down to the main floor unmolested, looking like all the other suits having *just another day.*

# Chapter Twenty-Nine

Justice wasn't served, and I needed fairness and my much-deserved pound of flesh. I knew a lot of cases ended this way, but this felt different. There would be plenty of cases after this one, some with cooperative victims, but this was personal, and I couldn't get it off my mind. I climbed into my car and drove home in a haze as my mind pored over every word said in the courtroom. I hadn't made peace with it by the time I got home, so I shuffled into the house, changed clothes, and slumped into my favorite overstuffed chair with a pint of butter almond ice cream. We had won the case! Why couldn't I be happy like everyone else?

Halfway through the pint, the answer to my question, why do I *care*, started unfolding slowly. The tug at my conscience was the similarity in our experiences. Nadine's abuse scenario reminded me of mine, and from the time I walked out of the hospital ladies' room, I wasn't fighting for Nadine but for my younger self. I wanted Nadine to fight with me, or more likely for me. Kendricks's light sentence was Vince's light sentence. But I didn't report what happened to me. I hadn't faced my abuser, yet I expected Nadine to, because I was ready now.

Thanks to Nurse Sarah, I had started a new life without Vince, but Nadine couldn't do that, and I felt like I hadn't done enough to help her. I had failed her, or rather, we all had. When I decided to become a police officer, I promised that, given the opportunity, I would pay Sarah's gift forward. She saved my life, and it was my turn to save someone else's, but I felt like I hadn't closed the deal. I was free, but I hadn't freed Nadine, and I was beating myself up. Nadine didn't want to leave Kendricks. She didn't want what I offered, and she certainly didn't see it as a gift. Nadine would be ready in her time, and I could do nothing about that. I knew that everyone's enough wasn't the same, but I couldn't condone her decision, and I was stuck.

The problem was somewhere in my wiring. It was an inside job, and it wasn't Nadine that needed freeing. It was me. Perhaps kicking myself into submission wasn't the answer. I was holding myself accountable to pay forward a gift given to an old version of myself that had grown over time. Suppose there was never a victim side of me, but if there was, maybe I could have both sides of myself live together in harmony.

These were questions I wasn't prepared to unpack, so I did what I knew how to do. I grabbed my earbuds, searched my music for anything that would remind me of who I was, laced my sneakers, and I ran. I ran for Nadine. I ran for old Mary. I ran for who I was now and for the Mary I would someday be. Thirty minutes later, I was fiddling with my keys trying to unlock the door when my phone jangled. It was Brad.

"Hey, sweetie. Are you okay?"

I frowned, my eyebrows furrowed, not realizing that he couldn't see my response, and mumbled, "Yeah, I guess."

I hadn't told Brad any details about my first marriage, so he couldn't have imagined how I might be affected by this case more than others.

"How about I pick you up and we go out for a night on the town? It'll get your mind off things."

"I don't really feel like painting the town red, but how about Famous Joe's for burgers?"

"Perfect. I'll pick you up in an hour."

I didn't want to go, and getting dressed to go out was like slogging through tax prep. I did it, and knew I would probably be glad

I did, but the process was agonizing. When I finished, my clothes matched my mood, shades of gray and black and low shoes, with my hair hanging loosely on my shoulders.

We walked into Joe's and Brad shouted to the host that we wanted a table where it was somewhat quieter. She weaved through patrons clumsily slinging beer glasses, nearly dousing her, as she made her way to a back room usually designated for families and ushered us to a table in the corner. The walls were tan and the wooden tables bare—no cardboard triangular menus advertising specialty drinks or fake flowers in dollar-store flasks adorned the table.

The server took our drink orders and disappeared.

Brad, the class clown, wasn't good with sullen. He didn't know if he should try to cheer me up or talk about the weather, but he sure didn't want to bring up the case. As much as I didn't want to talk about it, I also wanted to, so I brought it up so that we could move on from it and enjoy our evening.

"I still can't believe he only got eighteen months for killing a baby."

"Yeah, it's bullshit, but you know how it is. I mean it sucks, but at least he got something."

"I guess so, but I feel like I should have done more. It just doesn't seem fair."

"Of course it's not fair, but you did your best, honey. It's the system."

The drinks arrived, and Brad held up his glass to toast. "To the best detective I know."

I smiled for the first time since that morning, knowing that I really had done all that I could. As I lowered my glass, my pager sounded. I checked it, knowing that I wasn't on call, assuming that it was a group page, but it wasn't. I recognized the number and excused myself to return the call. Brad shook his head.

"Hey, I have a domestic-related homicide. Are you available?" Frank asked.

"Send me the details. I'm on my way." And I knew every day there would be another opportunity for me to pay it forward.

# Afterword

Someone once told me, "You don't look like what you've been through." Thank God that I survived and found happiness and belonging by doing what I loved. This tale didn't mark the end of my life but the beginning of a new and more fulfilling one. I'm passing on my experiences because I'm excited to make my own life choices today.

In the late 1980s and early 1990s when I was a victim of abuse, domestic violence laws were nearly nonexistent. Protection from abuse orders (PFAs) were in their infancy in Pennsylvania and Delaware, and advocates were few and far between. If police responded to a domestic-related assault, an arrest wasn't typical. It wasn't uncommon for police to separate the couple and give the male half a stern talking-to or just tell him to take a walk around the block to cool off.

Today, society's response to abuse is better. Greater awareness of family violence exists and services are available to victims regardless of gender or their relationship with the cohabitating partner. Law enforcement is proactive, and the court system deals with offenders punitively through counseling, anger management, and prevention work. Advocates help victims receive financial support or secure a place to live and follow them through the legal process, but it's still not enough. The system isn't perfect.

Making mistakes and getting back up took moxie and helped me develop a courage muscle. The more I exercised that muscle, the more I proved to myself that I could make healthy decisions, and the less I feared making them.

The bridging of my two lives, one as a domestic violence victim and one as a police detective, was a gift. I learned to acknowledge my fears and control them, but knowing when to fight and when to flee was key. Facing fear was brave, but I had tombstone courage—the kind of courage where you know you should run but choose to stay (in the relationship) and fight—which could have been deadly.

An occasional glance in the rearview mirror helps me to take stock of who I am and see if I'm reflecting an accurate self-image. I see how far I've come, which silences the negative mental chatter. But as my dear friend Gina Degnars-Graves always reminds me, "Be careful not to stare, or you might crash." Indeed, the past is not where I want to live.

After everything, I remarried and started a new life, continuing my police career in the Robbery-Homicide Unit and later as a patrol sergeant. I retired as the Mounted Patrol Commander in 2016. My life continues to surprise me whenever I follow my heart.

# DANGER ASSESSMENT

Jacquelyn C. Campbell, Ph.D., R.N. Copyright, 2003;
update 2019; www.dangerassessment.com

Several risk factors have been associated with increased risk of homicides (murders) of women and men in violent relationships. We cannot predict what will happen in your case, but we would like you to be aware of the danger of homicide in situations of abuse and for you to see how many of the risk factors apply to your situation.

Using the calendar, please mark the approximate dates during the past year when you were abused by your partner or ex-partner. Write on that date how bad the incident was according to the following scale:

1. Slapping, pushing; no injuries and/or lasting pain

2. Punching, kicking; bruises, cuts, and/or continuing pain

3. "Beating up"; severe contusions, burns, broken bones

4. Threat to use weapon; head injury, internal injury, permanent injury, miscarriage or choking* (use a © in the date to indicate choking/strangulation/cut off your breathing- example 4©)

5. Use of weapon; wounds from weapon

*If __any__ of the descriptions for the higher number apply, use the higher number.*

Mark **Yes** or **No** for each of the following. ("He" refers to your husband, partner, ex-husband, ex-partner, or whoever is currently physically hurting you.)

_____ 1. Has the physical violence increased in severity or frequency over the past year?

_____ 2. Does he own a gun?

_____ 3. Have you left him after living together during the past year?

      3a. (If you have *never* lived with him, check here: _____)

_____ 4. Is he unemployed?

_____ 5. Has he ever used a weapon against you or threatened you with a lethal weapon? (If yes, was the weapon a gun? check here: __)

_____ 6. Does he threaten to kill you?

_____ 7. Has he avoided being arrested for domestic violence?

_____ 8. Do you have a child that is not his?

_____ 9. Has he ever forced you to have sex when you did not wish to do so?

_____ 10. Does he ever try to choke/strangle you or cut off your breathing?

      10a. (If yes, has he done it more than once, or did it make you pass out or black out or make you dizzy? check here: _____)

_____ 11. Does he use illegal drugs? By drugs, I mean "uppers" or amphetamines, "meth", speed, angel dust, cocaine, "crack", street drugs or mixtures.

_____ 12. Is he an alcoholic or problem drinker?

_____ 13. Does he control most or all of your daily activities? For instance, does he tell you who you can be friends with, when you can see your family, how much money you can use, or when you can take the car? (If he tries, but you do not let him, check here: _____)

_____ 14. Is he violently and constantly jealous of you? (For instance, does he say: "If I can't have you,   no one can.")

_____ 15. Have you ever been beaten by him while you were pregnant? (If you have never been pregnant by him, check here: __)

_____ 16. Has he ever threatened or tried to commit suicide?

_____ 17. Does he threaten to harm your children?

_____ 18. Do you believe he is capable of killing you?

_____ 19. Does he follow or spy on you, leave threatening notes or messages, destroy your property, or call you when you don't want him to?

_____ 20. Have you ever threatened or tried to commit suicide?

_____ Total "Yes" Answers

Thank you. Please talk to your nurse, advocate, or counselor about what the Danger Assessment means in your situation.

# Resources for Survivors of Domestic Violence

IF YOU ARE IN IMMEDIATE DANGER, CALL 911

**The National Coalition Against Domestic Violence**
NCADV.org

**The National Domestic Violence Hotline**
1-800-799-7233 (SAFE)
www.ndvh.org

**National Dating Abuse Helpline**
1-866-331-9474

**National Child Abuse Hotline/Childhelp**
1-800-4-A-CHILD (1-800-422-4453)
www.rainn.org

**National Suicide Prevention Lifeline**
1-800-273-8255 (TALK)
www.suicidepreventionlifeline.org

**National Center for Victims of Crime**
1-202-467-8700

**National Resource Center on Domestic Violence**
1-800-537-2238
www.nrcdv.org
www.vawnet.org

**Futures Without Violence: The National Health Resource Center on Domestic Violence**

1-888-792-2873

www.futureswithoutviolence.org

**National Center on Domestic Violence, Trauma & Mental Health**

1-312-726-7020 ext. 2011

**National Deaf Domestic Violence Hotline (NDDVH)**

1-855-812-1001

www.thedeafhotline.org

**Abused Deaf Women's Advocacy Services (ADWAS)**

www.adwas.org

hotline@adwas.org

**Domestic Violence Initiative**

1-303-839-5510 / 1-877-839-5510

**One Love Foundation**

www.joinonelove.org

**Love is Respect**

1-866-331-9474

www.loveisrespect.org

**Break the Cycle**

1-202-824-0707

www.breakthecycle.org

**Deaf Abused Women's Network (DAWN)**
1-202-559-5366
www.deafdawn.org

**Women of Color Network**
1-800-537-2238

**Casa de Esperanza Latino/Latina**
1-651-772-1611
www.casadeesperanza.org

**National Latin Network for Healthy Families and Communities**
1-651-646-5553 -
www.nationallatinonetwork.org

**The National Immigrant Women's Advocacy Project**
1-202-274-4457

**The Black Church and Domestic Violence Institute**
1-770-909-0715
www.bcdvi.org

**LAMBDA GLBT Community Services**
1-206-350-4283
www.qrd.org/qrd/www/orgs/avproject/main.htm

**National Gay and Lesbian Task Force**
1-202-393-5177

# Acknowledgments

Since I first embarked on this chapter of my life in 2017, it has been a journey of reflection and collaboration. Completing this book has taken eight years, and I've wrestled with the challenge of including everyone who has played a role. Though I couldn't capture everyone, I start, knowing this effort has never been solitary.

I owe an immense debt of gratitude to Tama Kieves, not only an author and book coach, but a cherished friend who inspired me to write this memoir. Tama understood that writing would be a path to healing and believed that sharing my story could heal others too. Her kindness, guidance, and humor were unwavering throughout this transformative journey. I deeply appreciate her teaching, persistence, and friendship. Without Tama, I would not be here. Thank you, Tama.

Gina Degnars-Graves courageously accepted "the shitty first draft challenge," diligently reading every version until this final copy. It wasn't an easy task, and I'm thankful for her compassionate Sunday chats with me, which were filled with encouragement and invaluable feedback, both personally and professionally. It takes a great friend to tell you you're wrong. Gina, thank you for never letting me give up on myself; this book is stronger because of you. You will have my first copy.

Of all the readers of *Standing Up*, waiting for my best friend Claudine Wiant's feedback was the most daunting. Amidst a demanding schedule at law school and raising three boys, Claudine generously invested her time and insight into a topic close to many women's hearts, about her lifelong friend. She has been my steadfast companion through the chaos, and I know she will always be my voice of reason. Thank you, Claudine.

My mentor and coach Suzanne Eder guided me through the creation of a nonprofit, only to have it fall a few short years later. As I grieved this loss, she encouraged me to journal, meditate, and open my mind to possibility. That change in perspective opened the door to a fledgling new love of writing, and to this book. I said, "Yes," thanks to you.

Colleen Chambers patiently listened over countless glasses of wine, offering thoughtful questions and unwavering support as only a true friend can. Your perspective and presence were invaluable during the ups and downs of this journey. Thank you for your enduring friendship.

Elizabeth Ridley, one of my favorite editors, skillfully molded this book, making minor changes that brought about major improvements while always sharing her heartfelt reactions. Liz, your advice has been priceless.

To Ann Murphy, who tackled the manuscript in its roughest form, initiating the editing process, I am grateful for your patience and for guiding me through my first editorial experience. Marie Phillips, your willingness to help a stranger speaks volumes; your attention to detail was crucial in shaping this book. Jackie Cangro, your kind words fueled my determination, thanks to the groundwork laid by earlier editors. Michelle Lippold, your patience, understanding, and vast experience brought these characters to life alongside me. *Standing Up* is exactly what I hoped it would be.

Bill and Mary Harden, your generosity in opening your home provided the quiet space I needed for editing. Your hospitality made meeting deadlines not just possible but enjoyable. Bill, I appreciate your male perspective and supportive words.

Jack Cunningham, in 1997 you made a decision that changed

my life. You have remained a friend and colleague ever since. Your endorsement and your candid feedback were generous. I am deeply thankful for your support.

Mariann Kenville-Moore, what a pleasure it has been reconnecting with a colleague who is still doing the good work. Thank you for offering your time without hesitation and also for your kind words in praise of *Standing Up*.

And to all my coworkers who contributed to the rich tapestry of stories and experiences that inspired this book, you will always be my extended family. As always, be safe.

Most importantly, I want to express my gratitude to my family. To my mother, Joann Fratantoni, with whom I have shared this writing adventure, thank you for your sacrifice of our time together as I pursued this passion.

To my brother, Russell Sweeney, thank you for being the ideal brother and a true champion to me. You and Patricia mean the world to me.

To my sister, Lakena Hammond, I understand if you cannot read this, but I hope you will. Stay strong sister.

Rita Hensley and Annie Huggard, you have become like sisters to me, and Mary and Tom Cooke, like second parents. Warren and Mary Anne, you are welcome constants in my life, and I love you both.

I am thankful for you all and blessed beyond measure by your love and support.

# About the Author

photo credit: Gina Graves-Degnars

**Mary Sweeney-Devine** graduated from Wilmington University with a bachelor's degree before joining the police force, where she served in the detective unit, was promoted to sergeant, and eventually commanded the mounted patrol until her retirement in 2016. She now serves as an investigator for the State of Delaware while dreaming of her next book. Besides writing, she loves painting, swimming, hiking, and horses. *Standing Up* is Mary's first book. She resides in Middletown, Delaware.

## Looking for your next great read?

We can help!

Visit www.shewritespress.com/next-read
or scan the QR code below for a list
of our recommended titles.

She Writes Press is an award-winning
independent publishing company founded to
serve women writers everywhere.